THE SYNOPTIC PROBLEM IN RABBINIC LITERATURE

Program in Judaic Studies
Brown University
Box 1826
Providence, RI 02912

BROWN JUDAIC STUDIES

Edited by
Shaye J. D. Cohen

Number 326

THE SYNOPTIC PROBLEM IN RABBINIC LITERATURE

Edited by
Shaye J. D. Cohen

THE SYNOPTIC PROBLEM IN RABBINIC LITERATURE

Edited by

Shaye J. D. Cohen

Brown Judaic Studies
Providence, Rhode Island

© 2000 by Brown University. All rights reserved

No part of this work may be reproduced or transmitted in any form or by any means, electronic or mechanical, including photocopying and recording, or by means of any information storage or retrieval system, except as may be expressly permitted by the 1976 Copyright Act or in writing from the publisher. Requests for permission should be addressed in writing to the Rights and Permissions Office, Program in Judaic Studies, Brown University, Box 1826, Providence, RI 02912, USA.

Library of Congress Cataloging-in-Publication Data
The synoptic problem in rabbinic literature / edited by Shaye J. D. Cohen
    p. cm. — (Brown Judaic studies ; no. 326)
    Includes index.
    ISBN 1-930675-02-X (cloth : alk. paper)
    1. Mishnah—Comparative studies. 2. Tosefta—Comparative studies. 3. Talmud—Comparative studies. 4. Talmud Yerushalmi—Comparative studies. 5. Midrash rabbah. Genesis—Comparative studies. I. Cohen, Shaye J. D. II. Series.

BM497.8 .S96 2000
296.1´2066—dc21   00-060801
                                                                CIP

Printed in the United States of America
on acid-free paper

Contents

Introduction   vii

GENERAL

1. Is "The Talmud" a Document?
   Robert Goldenberg   3

MISHNAH AND TOSEFTA, TOSEFTA AND BAVLI

2. Mishnah As a Response to "Tosefta"
   Judith Hauptman   13

3. Uncovering Literary Dependencies in the Talmudic Corpus
   Shamma Friedman   35

BAVLI AND YERUSHALMI, THEMATIC STUDIES

4. *Halakhah le-Moshe mi-Sinai* in Rabbinic Sources:
   A Methodological Case Study
   Christine Hayes   61

5. Rabbinic Portrayals of Biblical and Post-biblical Heroes
   Richard Kalmin   119

YERUSHALMI AND GENESIS RABBAH

6. Texts and History: The Dynamic Relationship between Talmud
   Yerushalmi and Genesis Rabbah
   Hans-Jürgen Becker   145

INDICES

Index of Scholars   161
Index of Rabbinic Texts   163

Introduction

Since the 1780's, Matthew, Mark, and Luke have been referred to as the Synoptic Gospels (from *synoptikos*, "seen together"). The extensive parallels in structure, content, and wording of Matthew, Mark, and Luke make it even possible to arrange them side by side so that corresponding sections can be seen in parallel columns. . . . Such an arrangement is called a "synopsis," . . . and, by careful comparison of their construction, compilation, and actual agreement or disagreement in wording or content, literary- or source-critical relationships can be seen.[1]

Much of ancient rabbinic literature is as synoptic as Matthew, Mark, and Luke; because of their extensive parallels in structure, content, and wording, rabbinic texts should be "seen together." Much of the Mishnah is paralleled by the Tosefta and the tannaitic midrashim, much of the Tosefta is paralleled by the beraitot cited in the two Talmudim, much of the Bavli is paralleled by the Yerushalmi, etc.[2] The first person to apply the term "synoptic" to rabbinic literature may well have been Morton Smith in his doctoral dissertation, published as *Tannaitic Parallels to the Gospels*. By using this term Smith did not mean to suggest that the relationship of the Mishnah to the Tosefta was the same as that of Matthew and Luke to Mark; rather he intended to suggest that the synoptic problem faced by rabbinic scholars was of the same kind as that faced by scholars of the New Testament.[3]

---

[1] *Encyclopaedia Britannica Macropaedia* (1974, 15th ed.), "Biblical Literature," 2.950.

[2] I leave aside the extensive parallels within each document.

[3] Morton Smith, *Tannaitic Parallels to the Gospels* (Journal of Biblical Literature Monograph Series 6; Philadelphia: Society of Biblical Literature, 1951). See also Morton Smith, "The Synoptic Problem in Rabbinic Literature: A Correction [reply to J Neusner, 105:499–507 1986]," *JBL* 107 (1988) 111–112; Smith's position was misinterpreted by Jacob Neusner, "The Synoptic Problem in Rabbinic Literature: The Cases of the Mishna, Tosepta, Sipra, and Leviticus Rabba," *JBL* 105 (1986) 499–507. See Shaye J. D. Cohen, "Are There Tannaitic Parallels to the Gospels?" *JAOS* 116 (1996) 85–89.

Long before Morton Smith introduced the term "synoptic" into the discussion, medieval scribes and scholars of rabbinic texts noted the extensive parallels among these corpora. Scribes would routinely harmonize texts with each other, especially with the Bavli. In his commentary on Mishnah Zeraim R. Shimshon (Samson) b. Abraham of Sens (ca. 1200) cites virtually the entire Tosefta that parallels the Mishnah, and comments on both texts; in his commentary on Mishnah Negaim he cites extensively from the Sifra, and comments on both texts together. R. Shimshon's goal, of course, was not synoptic criticism but the explication of the Mishnah; still, he has the merit of having realized that a complete understanding of the Mishnah requires an understanding of the Tosefta (and Yerushalmi) as well.[4] I think that R. Shimshon would have endorsed the view that "synoptic texts must always be studied synoptically," for this is what he did.[5] With the emergence of historically minded Jewish scholarship in the nineteenth century the synoptic problem in rabbinic literature became a question of source criticism, textual priority, and literary relationship. Is the Tosefta a commentary on the Mishnah, or an early version of the Mishnah from which our Mishnah derives? Are the tannaitic midrashim reactions to the Mishnah, or sources for the Mishnah? Did the Bavli use our Tosefta, or did the two corpora draw on a common source? Did the Bavli know our Yerushalmi? These questions and others like them define the synoptic problem for scholars from the middle of the nineteenth century to the beginnings of the twenty-first.[6]

In an attempt to sort out some these questions and possibilities, I organized a small conference on "The Synoptic Problem in Rabbinic Literature." Here is the call for papers, as sent out to the invitees:

THE SYNOPTIC PROBLEM IN RABBINIC LITERATURE

A CONFERENCE SPONSORED BY
THE PROGRAM IN JUDAIC STUDIES, BROWN UNIVERSITY

March 1–2, 1998

The conference is dedicated to *The Synoptic Problem In Ancient Rabbinic Literature*. By "synoptic problem" I mean the following (I exclude Targumim and the later midrashim from consideration here):

1. The relationship of the Mishnah to the Tosefta

---

[4] On the Mishnah commentaries of R. Shimshon of Sens, see E. Urbach, *The Tosaphists* (4th ed.; Jerusalem: Bialik Institute, 1980) 298–312 (Hebrew).

[5] Shaye J. D. Cohen, "Jacob Neusner, Mishnah, and Counter-Rabbinics: A Review Essay of *Judaism: The Evidence of the Mishnah*," *Conservative Judaism* 37,1 (Fall 1983) 48–63, at 56.

[6] Among recent monographs I mention Alberdina Houtman, *Mishnah and Tosefta: A Synoptic Comparison of the Tractates Berakhot and Shebiit* (TSAJ 59; Tübingen: Mohr-Siebeck, 1996), and Ronen Reichmann, *Mishna und Sifra* (TSAJ 68; Tübingen: Mohr-Siebeck, 1998).

2. The interrelationship of the Mishnah, Tosefta, the tannaitic midrashim and *beraitot*
3. The relationship of the Bavli and the Yerushalmi to the Tosefta and the tannaitic midrashim
4. The relationship of the Bavli to the Yerushalmi
5. The relationship of the Yerushalmi to Genesis Rabbah, Leviticus Rabbah, Lamentations Rabbah, etc.

There is abundant scholarship on all five of these problems, but little scholarly consensus. Because of my own personal interests I would hope that the presenters at the conference would focus on either nos. 1, 2, or 4, but presentations on nos. 3 or 5 are welcome as well. Presentations may deal with either macro or micro issues; they may be large overviews of intertextual relationships or they may be analyses of specific *halakhot* or *sugyot*.

Closely related to the synoptic problem is the documentary hypothesis championed by Prof. Neusner. To what extent do individual rabbinic documents (i.e., Mishnah, Tosefta, Bavli, Yerushalmi) constitute wholes that may/must be studied independently, and to what extent may/must they be studied only in comparison with other documents? What are the advantages and limitations of the non-synoptic study of rabbinic documents? Do rabbinic documents, in fact, constitute integral wholes with editorial or thematic unity?

The conference will be small, consisting of approximately 10 presentations, by specialists for specialists. Each presentation will be given a substantial block of time for discussion; I hope that each presentation will be pre-circulated in advance so that conference time can be devoted exclusively to discussion. Presentations will be published as a volume in *Brown Judaic Studies*.

In actuality the conference consisted of seven presentations, six of which are contained in this volume. Each paper was pre-circulated among the participants; at the conference each author in turn was given ten minutes or so to reflect on his/her work, after which the participants joined in a vigorous discussion for an hour or more. Over the course of a day and a half the participants thoroughly discussed each of the papers. This volume, which contains revised versions of the presentations, does not give any sense of the seriousness and collegiality of the discussions, just as it does not—cannot—survey the problem as a whole. Still, the six essays published here well illustrate various aspects of the synoptic problem in rabbinic literature.

In the opening essay Robert Goldenberg (State University of New York at Stony Brook) poses a serious methodological question, "Is 'The Talmud' a Document?" Goldenberg assesses the documentary premise (or approach or hypothesis) championed by Jacob Neusner and his disciples and finds it wanting. According to the documentary premise the only data that rabbinic texts afford are the texts or "documents" themselves. Each document attests to the worldview, philosophy, and opinions of its editors, nothing

x   *Introduction*

more. Attributions of statements to named individual sages are unreliable and fundamentally can be ignored, because the voice of rabbinic texts is not the voice of individual sages but the voice of the text itself. Similarly, according to this premise rabbinic texts do not preserve "sources," at least not sources that can be identified and recovered. Goldenberg sensibly objects that the documentary premise presumes what it needs to demonstrate; it ascribes to rabbinic documents a self-conscious unity, coherence, and intentionality that they never possessed or claimed to possess. In addition, Goldenberg observes that the boundaries and definitions of these documents are elusive and somewhat arbitrary (for example, is tractate Avot part of the Mishnah or not?). Goldenberg instead proposes that rabbinic texts be regarded as anthologies, whose composition is partly purposeful, partly not. That is, the documents may well contain material that their editors found objectionable, but which was incorporated into the anthology nonetheless. Goldenberg does not develop this suggestion but clearly implies that the anthological character of rabbinic texts, at least of the Mishnah, Tosefta, Bavli, and Yerushalmi, does not preclude synoptic study or source criticism. I shall return to this question below.

Now we turn to two essays on the Tosefta. In her "Mishnah As a Response to 'Tosefta'" Judith Hauptman (Jewish Theological Seminary) offers an alternative to the widely-held view that the Tosefta is a commentary on, and reaction to, the Mishnah. If I read Hauptman correctly, she too concedes that the Tosefta, as it exists today, is indeed secondary to the Mishnah, but she argues that the Tosefta frequently contains, in unedited or lightly edited form, the "stuff" out of which the Mishnah itself was created. The Mishnah, being more coherent, formulaic, and consistent than the Tosefta, revises this material far more than the Tosefta does. Thus, Hauptman concludes, the Mishnah is dependent on an earlier collection of material that is preserved by the Tosefta. She supports this conclusion by observing that in many Mishnah-Tosefta parallels, the Mishnah version is cryptic, almost incomprehensible, while the Tosefta version is fuller and readily comprehensible. We might, of course, argue that the Tosefta is simply explaining the Mishnah, but this argument fails to explain the purpose and method of the Mishnah's redactors: why should they have produced a text that was cryptic, almost incomprehensible? Surely it is easier to explain the Mishnah, argues Hauptman, if we assume that it is a condensed version of the fuller and readily comprehensible text that now finds its home in the Tosefta. The Mishnah could afford to be brief because its source was readily available. Hauptman, I think, would readily concede that this argument is suggestive, not probative, but it strengthens other arguments in support of this position that have been advanced elsewhere.

Shamma Friedman (Jewish Theological Seminary and Bar Ilan University) addresses the problem of the Bavli's citation of beraitot that resemble our Tosefta but are not identical with it. If we leave aside various permutations and implausible possibilities, we have two fundamental possibilities by which to solve the problem: either the Bavli and the Tosefta are independent of each other (that is, each corpus is citing a bona fide version of a tradition that circulated in various forms), or one is dependent on the other (that is, that the Bavli has purposefully reshaped the Tosefta that it cites). In his "Uncovering Literary Dependencies in the Talmudic Corpus" Friedman briefly reviews the history of the research on this problem and concludes that the correct model for understanding the Bavli-Tosefta relationship is not that of "independent parallels" but "the edited parallel"—the later source, in this case the Bavli, has revised and improved the source that it cites. Friedman argues that the Bavli introduced these changes for a variety of motives: to harmonize one source with another, to improve the style, to update the language, etc.

The next section of the volume contains two thematic studies. The first is by Christine Hayes (Yale University), "*Halakhah le-Moshe mi-Sinai* in Rabbinic Sources: A Methodological Case Study." Hayes contrasts the documentary (or synchronic) approach championed by Prof. Neusner with the source critical approach. Some of Hayes' criticisms of the documentary approach echo those of Goldenberg in the first essay of this volume, but her real contribution is the careful attempt to apply both approaches and to balance the limits of the one against the limits of the other. She studies the term *halakhah le-Moshe mi-Sinai* (or HLMM), "a law given to Moses at Sinai." After observing that the Mishnah provides contradictory signals as to the meaning and application of this term, she notes that a diachronic (source critical) reading of the Talmudim shows important development, either ideological (Yerushalmi, where later tradents see HLMM as equivalent to scripture but early ones do not) or terminological (Bavli, where later tradents use the term *halakhah* or *halakhot* as synonymous with HLMM, but early ones do not). A synchronic (documentary) reading of the Bavli and Yerushalmi reveals a whole series of parallels and contrasts between them, suggesting that the presence of sources and layers within each document does not necessarily impugn the presence of a unitary setting or purpose. In particular, Hayes suggests that the Bavli's use of HLMM reveals some anxiety over rabbinic authority and over the justification of that authority, an anxiety that seems to be absent from the Yerushalmi. Thus both the synchronic and the diachronic approaches have utility.

Our second thematic study is by Richard Kalmin (Jewish Theological Seminary), "Rabbinic Portrayals of Biblical and Post-biblical Heroes." Here, in consonance with some of his earlier work, Kalmin questions the utility of the documentary approach by observing that various themes or patterns emerge from rabbinic texts precisely if the documentary origins of the evidence are ignored. If we assume that statements ascribed to tannaim are actually tannaitic, even if they are attested only in amoraic documents; if we assume that statements ascribed to sages of the land of Israel are actually Israelian (Kalmin uses the term "Palestinian"), even if they are attested only in the Bavli; if we assume that statements ascribed to early amoraim are in fact earlier than statements ascribed to later amoraim; in other words, if we assume the fundamental historicity of the ascriptions in rabbinic corpora and ignore the identity of the documents in which they appear—a survey of the evidence can yield meaningful and consistent results. As a specimen of this method Kalmin studies rabbinic self-assessment (thereby treating some of the same texts treated by Hayes), specifically the equation of rabbinic worthies with biblical ones. Such equations are the work of tannaim and early amoraim, not later amoraim; such equations are formulated somewhat differently when attributed to tannaim, Israelian amoraim, or Babylonian amoraim. Rather than assume that we have before us evidence of massive and massively skillful pseudepigraphy, Kalmin concludes that it is far more plausible to assume that the attributions are fundamentally reliable across all these documents and that the documentary origin of each attribution is not significant. This demonstration is highly suggestive, and gains force when set beside other such demonstrations that Kalmin himself has made elsewhere. Kalmin has not disproved the documentary hypothesis, of course; when judged by other criteria or other methods perhaps the individual documents can be shown to be distinctive or to have shaped their materials in distinctive ways. Still, Kalmin clearly has proven that the source critical method can work and can yield meaningful results.

The final paper, "Texts and History: The Dynamic Relationship between Talmud Yerushalmi and Genesis Rabbah," by Hans-Jürgen Becker (University of Göttingen), is perhaps the most radical and brings us back to some of the issues that were discussed by Goldenberg. Becker argues that the documentary approach cannot yield meaningful results because it assumes that rabbinic texts are closed, fixed documents, whereas they are not. Creation, redaction, transmission, inscription—in the case of rabbinic texts these four activities are virtually synonymous. Rabbinic texts seem not to have attained closure and fixity until the age of printing. Becker has elsewhere carried out extensive comparisons between Genesis Rabbah and the Yerushalmi; he concludes that both texts used a series of written sources, but that the redaction of each of the two texts is a protracted process, not a momentary event. These texts constitute primary evidence for their own internal literary histories, but hardly constitute evidence for a documentary view of anything, let alone for rabbinic Judaism in the fourth century. Becker endorses the source critical approach, but only on condition that we do not move too quickly from literary history to social history. Becker himself tries to show what kind of "history" can be extracted from the literary history of the texts—one can talk about the "big picture," nothing more. All in all, this is a very stimulating paper that defends an intellectually consistent, if extreme, position. If Becker is correct, not only does the documentary hypothesis lack any foundation, but so does most of current rabbinic historiography.

It is striking that four of the six presentations reject or question the documentary approach championed by Prof. Neusner. Goldenberg and Becker reject its intellectual foundations outright, Kalmin demonstrates the utility of the source critical method, and Hayes allows the utility of the documentary method only if accompanied by the source critical method, too. Hauptman and Friedman do not address the documentary approach outright, but each provides a fine illustration of the source critical method at work. The clear message emerging from this volume is that the methodological exclusivity claimed for the documentary method by Prof. Neusner is completely unjustified, and that the method itself is based on assumptions and foundations that are not universally accepted. The synoptic problem in rabbinic literature still endures.

Shaye J. D. Cohen
Brown University, Program in Judaic Studies
Providence, RI 02912-1826

P.S.: I would like to thank two graduate students in the Program in Judaic Studies for their assistance: Mr. Nat Levtow for administering the conference and attending to numerous organizational details, and Mr. Abe Hendin for copyediting and formatting this volume.

General

Chapter 1

Is "The Talmud" a Document?

Robert Goldenberg
State University of New York at Stony Brook

The corpus of ancient rabbinic literature has come down to us in the form of several discrete bodies of writing that we habitually treat as separate books. We quote them that way, citing each by title and subdivision, our history books and encyclopedias speak of them that way, discussing the particular origins and character of each, we catalogue them that way in our libraries. In this paper I wish to speak of the most important set of these putative books, those that constitute the so-called Six Orders. The Mishnah, the Tosefta, and the two Talmudim are the central "documents" of ancient rabbinic literature. For efficiency of presentation, and in imitation of another very famous set of purported documents, I shall refer to these by the initials M (Mishnah), T (Tosefta), Y (Yerushalmi), and B (Bavli), and the focus of this paper will amount to the question whether it makes sense to refer to MTYB as documents at all. I propose to explore the implications of such a way of speaking: what is gained, and what is lost? Do the materials themselves really support our understanding them in this way?

I pose these questions in reaction to the recent ascendancy of a particular viewpoint that I shall call the Documentary Premise. This premise, associated with the work of Jacob Neusner and many of his students, can briefly be stated as follows:[1] Our knowledge of ancient rabbinic Judaism

[1] Neusner himself tends to use the more familiar phrase "documentary hypothesis," but that expression conjures up a literary situation that differs from the one under discussion here. Characteristic formulations of the Documentary Premise can be found in *Making the Classics in Judaism* (BJS 180; Atlanta: Scholars Press, 1989), esp. 19–44; *The Documentary Foundation of Rabbinic Culture* (South Florida Studies in the History of Judaism [SFSHJ] 113; Atlanta: Scholars Press, 1995), esp. ix–xv and 1–110; *Are the Talmuds Interchangeable?* (SFSHJ 122; Atlanta: Scholars Press, 1995), ix–xxix.

rests almost entirely on the contents of the literature that ancient rabbis produced. That literature now consists of a number of books: MTYB, the component parts of Midrash Rabbah, and so on. We know nothing, or virtually nothing, about ancient rabbinic Judaism beyond what those books tell us, and that means we know nothing, or virtually nothing, about ancient rabbinic Judaism beyond what the authors or editors of those books wanted us to know. Those Sages quote hundreds of colleagues as having said thousands of things, but we cannot be certain these quotations are accurate with respect to wording, context, or attribution. They tell hundreds of stories about events of their own and previous generations, but for similar reasons we cannot determine whether or how they changed those stories in the re-telling, and whether or how the meaning of those stories has been affected by the contexts in which later tradents have placed them. In general, we can never know for whom (other than themselves) these individuals spoke, and therefore we can never assume their works reflect any views other than their own or the state of anyone's knowledge other than theirs.

The upshot of this approach is that every rabbinic document must be taken as a world unto itself, the product of the particular individuals or groups who produced it and the embodiment of their views alone. Even where various documents appear to cite parallel materials, each document has nevertheless placed those materials in contexts of its own editors' choosing and has formulated those materials according to the judgment of those same editors. We cannot say what anything might have meant in any other setting.

The Documentary Premise thus stands in the way of any continuous, synthetic history of early rabbinic Judaism. We can examine the versions of a concept in each of the documents MTYB, but we cannot explore how these four versions are historically related to one another because we cannot trace the channels or identify the links that would have constituted those relationships. We cannot say that later versions developed out of earlier versions because we cannot reconstruct the course of such development. We cannot correct one citation on the basis of another, or use one citation to shed light on the meaning of another. We can have a photo album of early rabbinic teaching, but any possibility of video or cinema is out of the question.

* * *

At first glance the caution in this approach seems commendable; there is a certain honorable rigor in refusing to go beyond the evidence, and one can readily admire the refusal to claim what cannot be demonstrated. In fact, however, the Documentary Premise is a deeply problematic stance; it claims both more and less than its own principles allow, and it stakes its own position at a midpoint offering no advantage over the alternatives it rejects.

For the Documentary Premise to make any sense at all, a "document" must have an inner integrity giving voice to a coherent point of view; the degree of attention a document receives should correspond to the degree of seriousness supposedly invested in that document as it came into being. It need not be assumed that such a document is entirely consistent, as it may have been assembled from initially unrelated elements, but it must be assumed that this assembly was carried out for an intelligible purpose by people who knew, or thought they knew, what they were doing. Similarly, it need not be supposed that any particular copy of a document is free of errors (with ancient, hand-copied materials this would be most unrealistic), but it must be possible to rely (with appropriate caution) on its testimony about the intentions of its original author(s). In the absence of such an assumption, the modern reader can get nowhere: a piece of writing generated through the accidental combination of two entirely separate items could pass for a document and be treated with completely undeserved seriousness, while a piece of writing so badly miscopied that it was full of incoherence and gibberish would say nothing useful whatever about its purported authors or origin.

This is the sense in which the Documentary Premise claims more than its own principles allow, and it leads to unpredictable violation of those principles by those who invoke the premise. The Documentary Premise rests on the claim that the four putative documents MTYB reflect coherent, intentional viewpoints, but those who employ the Documentary Premise are prone to modify this claim at unpredictable moments and violate the integrity of their own "documents." What does it mean, for example, to invoke the Documentary Premise in a study of the use of the term "Torah" in rabbinic literature, but then to write a chapter on "Torah" in Avot that is separate from the chapter on the Mishnah?[2] It is now widely recognized that Avot was added to an already existing collection of tractates, but the canonical document "M" has included that tractate for over a millennium; does it not violate the integrity of the Documentary Premise when "M" is quietly dismembered?

Once the excision of Avot from "M" is tacitly accepted, moreover, the matter has no end; description of the Judaism of "the Talmud" (Y or B) should now begin by listing the tractates used for that description and the

---

[2] See J. Neusner, *Torah: From Scroll to Symbol in Formative Judaism* (BJS 136; Atlanta: Scholars Press, 1988). Avot is considered separately from the rest of the Mishnah because "its connection to the Mishnah lies only in the names of Sages appearing both in Abot and in other tractates of the Mishnah" (p. 32). The uniformity of those "other tractates" is apparently assumed; see below.

tractates excluded, and should then provide a justification for those sets of choices. In actual practice, however, analyses based on the Documentary Premise almost never provide such justifications. The result is to reduce the documents M, T, Y, and B themselves to the status of untested hypotheses.[3]

Another problematic aspect of the Documentary Premise is its apparent assumption that MTYB are all documents of more or less the same kind. This assumption gives rise to a standard procedure based on the Documentary Premise in which some theme, or idea, is traced through all four of the MTYB documents in turn; if a moving picture remains impossible, this procedure presumably allows for a useful photo album whose individual snapshots can then be synoptically compared.[4] The problem with this method, however, is that the Mishnah is not merely separate from or earlier than the Talmud, it is also an entirely different sort of work; one must allow for its possibly different aims, different inner logic, different audience, different *Sitz im Leben*.[5] If a theme prominent in the gemara (for example, explicit hostility to the Roman Empire) is absent from the Mishnah, one cannot simply interpret this silence to mean that Sages at the time of the Mishnah had not yet developed the ideas underlying that

---

[3] The matter is not hypothetical; see the discussion by J. N. Epstein cited in n. 8, below. A search of the following key locations in Professor Neusner's writings, however, turned up no indication that the contours of the Bavli itself need to be defined:

Judaism: The Classical Statement: The Evidence of the Bavli (Chicago and London: University of Chicago Press, 1986). There, on p. 5, it is indicated that the book rests on analysis of five tractates of the Bavli, representing ten percent of the whole: "the sample at hand suffices because of the rhetorical and redactional uniformity of the Talmud of Babylonia." The key word here is "uniformity": the discovery of common features in talmudic tractates has apparently eclipsed Epstein's previous exploration of equally important differences. *The Oral Torah: The Sacred Books of Judaism: An Introduction* (San Francisco: Harper & Row, 1986), 129–149 similarly proceeds on the basis of a "probe of three tractates" drawn from the slightly larger group just mentioned, and see also *Introduction to Rabbinic Literature* (Anchor Bible Reference Library; New York: Doubleday, 1994), pp. 21–29, 182–188, where the prehistory of the tractates, but not the prehistory of the collection, is considered at length. Finally, see n. 2, above.

In *The Bavli's One Voice* (SFSHJ 24; Atlanta: Scholars Press, 1991), on p. 455, Neusner discusses "anomalies" in the character of particular tractates or chapters, but then remarks that he has disregarded these in his general conclusions.

[4] See Neusner, *Torah*, already cited above, n. 2, or Gary G. Porton, *The Stranger within Your Gates: Converts and Conversion in Rabbinic Literature* (Chicago and London: University of Chicago Press, 1994).

[5] See Goldenberg, *The Nations that Know Thee Not: Ancient Jewish Attitudes towards Other Religions* (New York: New York University Press, 1998), 81–2.

theme;[6] one must first develop some theory of the Mishnah that explains why such ideas would have been expressed if they were already circulating. This cannot always be done: the Mishnah in particular is so terse and spare that the reader should never be surprised when a certain topic somehow fails to appear in its pages.[7] In other words, the Documentary Premise not only reifies "documents" without demonstrating their historical integrity; it then also homogenizes those documents without regard to their own diversity.

Finally, there is little point in insisting that MTYB reflect the mind of their respective redactor(s) and no one else when we cannot really say who those redactors were, or whether the final assembly of tractates was even carried out with the kind of purposeful attention the term "redactor" suggests. The Bavli contains around three dozen tractates: of these, most sound as though they could well have a common origin but a few do not.[8] Which "redactor(s)," then, are reflected in the final "document," the redactor(s) of the respective tractates, or the cut-and-paste operator(s) who included them in a single large collection, quite possibly without any further revision? Recent scholarship has made admirable progress in figuring out how the tractates came to be, but almost none in determining how they were collected into "the Talmud." Speaking of "the Talmud" as a document overlooks the difficulty that we have almost no idea how and why it was assembled, who its redactors were, or how they operated.

* * *

This means the Documentary Premise also claims less than its own principles allow. While the Documentary Premise rightly insists that any such anterior documents must remain hypothetical and shadowy, the ori-

---

[6] Compare Neusner, *Judaism and Christianity in the Age of Constantine* (Chicago and London: University of Chicago Press, 1987), 65–67, also idem, *Judaism in the Matrix of Christianity* (Philadelphia: Fortress, 1986), 73–87.

[7] The question is always the opposite, namely why some discursive digression found its way in. Examples of such digressions might include the midrashim in Sotah 5, or the list of items beginning "there is no difference . . ." in Megillah 1, or the dispute stories in Yadayim 4. In an unclear passage, Neusner apparently labels the Yadayim materials "appendices" attached to the Mishnah "solely" because certain formulary similarities called them to the redactor's mind. While expressing relief that the Mishnah does not engage in such free association more often, he declines to inquire why it did so here. See *A History of the Mishnaic Law of Purities. Part Nineteen: Tebul Yom and Yadayim* (Leiden: E. J. Brill, 1977), 108.

[8] On Nazir and Nedarim, see J. N. Epstein, *Introduction to Amoraic Literature* (in Hebrew; Jerusalem/Tel Aviv: Magnes/Dvir, 1962), 54–83. In fact one can say this about all four of the "documents" M, T, Y, and B; most of the constituent tractates in each case appear to have a common origin, but never the entire canonical set.

gins of MTYB themselves are hardly less so. If the Documentary Premise were a case of *bari* (certain) and *shema* (possible)[9] it would be one thing, but that is hardly the case. The Documentary Premise presents the scholar with grades of *shema*, and the reward for its scruples in confronting such uncertainty is outweighed by the loss incurred. Careful analysis will sometimes permit the identification of pre-existing materials that have been incorporated into the canonical documents M, T, Y, and B: by stripping away extraneous materials, one can sometimes identify proto-documents that do possess the integrity the Documentary Premise requires.[10] Why should those proto-documents not receive attention in their own right? They can no longer be reconstructed with certainty, to be sure, but there is little question of their presence, little question that various pre-existing lists, compilations, and so forth can be found within the current texts. These earlier materials are often more interesting than the final assemblages now found as MTYB: the canonical documents, taken as a whole, show fewer signs of careful shaping and yield less information about the views and goals of their authors. True, it remains significant that the Babylonian Sages saw value in producing the enormous body of material now found in the Bavli, and useful results can emerge from asking what sorts of people would have done this and why; nevertheless, the Bavli as a whole has no overt message or theme, whereas some of its ingredient materials do seem endowed with these.[11] The really creative minds in the early history of rabbinic Judaism were the authors of these ingredients, not the compilers who mechanically assembled them. To ignore these early authors is no virtue; scholars should be doing everything they can to bring these earlier minds to life.

* * *

In short, the integrity of the four elementary documents MTYB is more stipulated than demonstrated, and the Documentary Premise delivers results that are both arbitrary and incomplete. It may be useful to modify that Premise, and the remainder of this paper offers a hesitant step in that direction.

It appears that certain tractates in MTYB (e.g. Nazir or Nedarim in the Bavli)[12] were produced separately from the others and incorporated into

---

[9] These are, respectively, the terms in Talmudic law for a claim asserting fact and a claim acknowledging possibility.

[10] See above, n. 7, for examples of such pre-existing bodies of material in the Mishnah.

[11] Jacob Neusner, the author and pre-eminent exponent of the Documentary Premise, vehemently rejects the line of argument in this paragraph; see, for example, *The Bavli's One Voice* (above, n. 3), xvii–xxix, 1–12, 453–465.

[12] See above, n. 8.

the larger collections only as (more or less) finished products; this suggests that MTYB themselves should be described as anthologies or collections rather than as simple documents in their own right. The actual documents or "tractates" comprising these anthologies will have been composed by one set of hands, or several, but then assembled by others.[13]

Seeing MTYB as anthologies rather than as documents raises new questions. Were the compilers always careful to include only those materials that reflected their own views or ways of thinking? Surely that is not always the case with modern anthologies, nor was the Qumran library (to choose a different sort of case) restricted to texts expressing a single, sharply defined viewpoint. This is not to suggest that MTYB were assembled at random, without any principles of selection at all, but it does raise the question whether the existing collections were assembled in the service of a coherent ideology, viewpoint, or style: beneath a very thin surface, the coherence which the Documentary Premise ascribes to these four sets of material may be entirely imaginary, or stipulated without sufficient cause. In other words, not every assemblage is an anthology at all. Real anthologies are themselves documents of a certain kind: an anthology has an editor or compiler if not an author, and one can ask about the intentions and purposes which guided that person's work. However, documents can be stitched together for quite accidental reasons and with quite misleading results; it is therefore necessary to have an account of the origins of any assemblage before we know whether it is to be considered a meaningful anthology, let alone a "document," at all. In the case of MTYB such accounts have not yet been (convincingly) produced.

Leaving this aside, we know almost nothing about the particular circumstances in which any existing rabbinic texts were created: we cannot name their authors or the places they were assembled, nor can we state the time of their production with any precision at all. Rabbinic tradition occasionally supplies the name of an author or editor, but this information cannot be verified and often seems to conflict with the internal evidence of the texts themselves; it is therefore of little value for purposes of historical reconstruction. It is better, therefore, simply to speak about the texts themselves without attempting to say anything further about the people who produced them: the Bavli tells the story this way while the Yerushalmi tells

---

[13] See Eliezer Segal, "Anthological Dimensions of the Babylonian Talmud," *Prooftexts* 17 (1997), 33–61. Useful comments about the particular nature of anthologies can be found scattered throughout Clifford Siskin, *The Work of Writing* (Baltimore and London: The Johns Hopkins University Press, 1998). While speaking about a very different historical setting (England in the early nineteenth century), Siskin notes (see p. 63) that to assemble an anthology is to make a selection—to include this and exclude that—under specific historical circumstances.

it that way, and so forth.[14] The texts themselves are voluminous and have plenty to say; they offer copious testimony as to the way some ancient rabbinic Sages thought about many different topics. We must simply accept that we cannot always name those Sages or say why they held these views. One way around this difficulty is to read everything synchronically, to approach the entire corpus, and not just each constituent "document," as a single large repertoire of teaching available to later generations seeking to carry the rabbinic tradition into unfamiliar times and places; this is the ultimate extension of synoptic/synchronic method. The other way around (where this is possible) is to dissolve MTYB themselves into their ingredients, and to say what can be said about the origins and character of each.

These texts have incorporated abundant earlier materials which can often be identified as such, and these earlier materials often display as much textual integrity as the existing collections MTYB themselves. With respect to questions of origin and transmission-history, one can often say just as much about these incorporated materials as about MTYB themselves (that is, very little); in many cases MTYB themselves are interesting primarily on account of the manipulations of these predecessor texts which they can be shown to have carried out. The lost texts are lost only in the sense that no separate copies of them remain available; in fact, however, careful analysis of the existing texts of MTYB often yields a pretty clear picture of what they said. A true documentary approach to rabbinic literature, therefore, amounts to identifying as many different rabbinic documents as possible, including documents that no longer exist independently of others; this procedure increases the number of shadowy rabbinic authors and editors to the greatest possible degree, and gives as much flesh-and-blood reality to the founders of rabbinic Judaism as is ever likely to be available. If the Documentary Premise is to serve the craft of history, surely this is what we need, and what we should want.

---

[14] Neusner deals with this problem by speaking of the respective "authorships" of MTYB without trying to identify them.

Mishnah and Tosefta, Tosefta and Bavli

Chapter 2
Mishnah As a Response to "Tosefta"

Judith Hauptman
Jewish Theological Seminary

The Tosefta has attracted much attention in the last decade. Probably because Lieberman's critical edition made it so much more accessible than it used to be, parallel examination of Tosefta and Mishnah has become standard scholarly practice. It is somewhat ironic, therefore, that studies have begun to emerge that question the assumption that lies at the base of Lieberman's work, namely, that the Tosefta is a commentary on the Mishnah.[1] A number of scholars, myself included, have suggested that the Tosefta is not exclusively a response to the Mishnah but that much material in the Tosefta seems to be the very "stuff" from which the Mishnah was fashioned.[2] Having seen this reverse relationship to be the case in tractate Gittin, where

---

[1] Saul Lieberman assumes that whenever the Tosefta quotes a mishnah, it does so for the purpose of then explaining it. He understands the Tosefta as a running commentary on the Mishnah. As Shamma Friedman notes (*Tosefta Atiqta*, forthcoming), this is a direct outcome of Lieberman's acceptance of Rabbenu Tam's principle, "It is the practice of the Tosefta, in a thousand places, to cite a little from the Mishnah for reference (*zikhron devarim*)" (Saul Lieberman, *Tashlum Tosefta* [Jerusalem: Wahrmann, 1970], 21). See Friedman's discussion of Lieberman's theories, in *Tosefta Atiqta*. Abraham Goldberg also steadfastly asserts that the Tosefta is a commentary on the Mishnah ("The Tosefta—Companion to the Mishnah," in *Literature of the Sages*, part 1 [Philadelphia: Fortress, 1987], 283–302, at 283ff.). See n. 7, below.

[2] See my articles "Pesiqah Lehumra Bemishnat Gittin," in *Proceedings of the Tenth World Congress of Jewish Studies: Division C, Jewish Thought and Literature* (Jerusalem: World Union of Jewish Studies, 1990), 1:23–30; and "Qiyum Merazon Shel Mitzvot Aseh Shehazeman Geraman Al Yedei Nashim," in *Proceedings of the Eleventh World Congress of Jewish Studies: Division C, Thought and Literature* (Jerusalem: World Union of Jewish Studies, 1994), 1:161–168. See Friedman, *Tosefta Atiqta*, bibliography. See, in particular, Peter Schäfer, "Research into Rabbinic Literature: An Attempt to Define the Status Quaestionis," *JJS* 37 (1986): 139–152.

there appears to be a deliberate move on the part of the redactor of the Mishnah to rewrite paragraphs of the Tosefta in a more stringent manner, I now ask myself, whenever I compare two parallel, similarly worded passages of Mishnah and Tosefta, Which is based on which? The answer I most often arrive at is that the Mishnah appears in these cases to be based on the Tosefta. I believe, however, that the evidence warrants an even stronger, more encompassing conclusion. It seems to me that the redactor of the Mishnah had at his disposal not merely individual passages of tannaitic provenance that he then reworked and edited into a collection, but rather an extensive, ordered collection of tannaitic materials, much of which is embedded in the extant Tosefta.[3]

What leads to this conclusion? We know that the beginning of the amoraic period is the *terminus ad quem* for the publication of the Mishnah, most likely in oral form, because the comments of the amoraim in both Talmudim form a running commentary on the Mishnah. In like manner, if we examine the two Talmudim closely, we will find that the skeleton of many *sugyot* (units of discussion; singular *sugya*), i.e., the collection of sources that served as the basis for later commentary, is composed not of *memrot* (statements ascribed to individual amoraim; singular *memra*) but of beraitot. If, in an effort to trace the chronological development of the sugya, we drop the memrot and the *stama*[4] from the sugya, what is left is a mishnah and associated beraitot. It is thus clear that the first step in studying a mishnah in antiquity was to read it in conjunction with related beraitot.[5]

I will now go just one step further and claim that these clusters of related beraitot coalesced into a collection even before the publication of the Mishnah. Since much recent scholarly work has shown that the editor of

---

[3] This study attempts to establish the relationship between these two works in the long course of their evolution. The importance of establishing this relationship lies in the fact that if the Tosefta is a response to the Mishnah, and if the Tosefta is shown to be more liberal and the Mishnah more conservative, then we can say that Jewish law evolved from the more conservative to the more liberal. If the Mishnah is based on earlier passages in the Tosefta, however, then we can say that Jewish law evolved from the more liberal to the more conservative.

[4] By *stama* I mean the anonymous materials themselves (*stama degemara*) as well as any tannaitic or amoraic texts inserted by the editors of the stama to support their arguments.

[5] See my *Development of the Talmudic Sugya: Relationship Between Tannaitic and Amoraic Sources* (Lanham, Md.: University Press of America, 1988), chapters 2 and 5. See also my article "Development of the Talmudic Sugya by Amoraic and Post-Amoraic Amplification of a Tannaitic Proto-Sugya," *HUCA* 58 (1987): 227–250. See also Yaakov Elman, *Authority and Tradition: Toseftan Baraitot in Talmudic Babylonia* (Hoboken, N.J.: Ktav and Yeshiva University Press, 1994) 275–281, who claims that a compiled, redacted Tosefta was *not* available to the redactors of the Bavli. I disagree, as I will explain below.

the Mishnah rewrote one beraita after another, in this way turning them into mishnahs, I think it reasonable to conclude that he did not stumble upon each one of these "source" beraitot in a different place but rather that there already existed a collection of formally and thematically related passages. In a more or less systematic way he edited it, paragraph after paragraph, to make it reflect his own point of view. Once his mishnah was "published," it made excellent sense for the ancient masters to study it in conjunction with the collection of beraitot that had given rise to it. Stated in general terms, I am claiming that the Mishnah is not the earliest edited tannaitic work but a response to an even earlier collection.

I have recently found new support for these ideas. In the course of reading through Mishnah and Tosefta Moed, I began to notice that the Mishnah, on many occasions, could not be understood on its own. It would make halakhic statements or refer to some quasi-historical incident but not provide enough information for the reader to understand fully what it was saying. To make sense of these statements, he or she had to turn to a commentary on the page, such as that of Hanokh Albeck, who often cites a beraita to explain the mishnah. Or else, and far preferable, the reader had to consult the associated passages in the Tosefta, because they spelled out the matter in full.[6]

This recurring, perplexing phenomenon can be explained in several ways. One possibility is that the redactor of the Mishnah did produce—intentionally—a partially incomprehensible document, either orally or in writing. It was therefore necessary for a supplementary document to come into being, one that would give the background of the laws or fabricate stories or adapt folklore motifs to flesh out the obscure references of the primary document. According to this explanation, the Mishnah is older than the parallel passages in the Tosefta, and the toseftan material was created to explain the Mishnah.[7]

A second possibility, which is a variation of the first, is that a cryptic or shorthand reference in the Mishnah was sufficient for the reader (or "hearer") because much ancient material circulated in independent units,

---

[6] At the SBL Convention in San Francisco, November 1997, I reported on this same phenomenon regarding cryptic references to minor historical events. The instances I dealt with, in addition to M. Suk 5.2 below, are M. Suk 5.8, M. Yoma 3.9, and M. Taan 3.5–8.

[7] Goldberg ("The Tosefta," 283–4) says that the Tosefta is a supplement and companion to the Mishnah. He goes on to say that it is also a continuation of the Mishnah in that it records the teachings of the last generation of tannaim. Together with the Mishnah, it is the basis of the teachings of the following generations, and these teachings resulted in the Bavli and Yerushalmi. The Mishnah and the Tosefta are, in his opinion, one interwoven literary work. For this reason it is irrational to search out differences between the two.

orally or in writing, and even if the Mishnah gave no more than a hint, the reader, who had access to that broad assemblage of materials, could figure out to which halakhic practice or historical event the redactor was referring. If so, it was only some time after the Mishnah was published that it became necessary to produce a supplementary document, to collect and order the bits and pieces that preceded the Mishnah and served as its basis. According to this view, the Tosefta came into being in response to the Mishnah, although its constituent elements were older.

A third possibility, which is a variation of the second, is that the clear dependence of the Mishnah on earlier tannaitic materials, as noted above, may imply that the Mishnah is *not* older than the Tosefta (in its early form), but that, on the contrary, there existed a tannaitic collection, or at the very least clusters of material, that preceded the Mishnah and that were self-sufficient, i.e., that presented a full explanation of the halakhot that then found their way into the Mishnah. These tannaitic materials served as the raw material of the Mishnah. For reasons not entirely clear, parsimony of language being one possibility, when the redactor of the Mishnah reshaped these early tannaitic materials he chose merely to make mention of certain halakhic practices or events but not to report them in full. He knew, it seems, that the reader had access to the older, associated tannaitic collection and could and (probably) would pursue the matter further himself. If so, the Mishnah as it was produced in the third century was *not* an incomprehensible document—as it is today when it is read on its own—but was in fact fully comprehensible when read together with the older tannaitic collection.

A fourth possibility is that the Mishnah is simply one extraction of material from all the "stuff" that was circulating at the time and the Tosefta is another extraction from the same pool of "stuff." It therefore makes no sense to compare the two collections to each other and analyze in detail which preceded which or which is based on which. I reject this line of thinking because the similarities between the Mishnah and the Tosefta are so great that even if both derive from a third source—which is no longer extant (if it ever was)—much can be learned about the evolution of rabbinic legal thinking by comparing these two end products. Painstaking comparison of mishnaic and toseftan sources leads to the conclusion that what lies before us is evidence of ingenious editorial activity: we find sources that were made to look as if little change had been introduced when in reality they had been totally transformed. Little of this would come to light if we dismissed the value of comparative studies.

I favor the third explanation of the relationship between the Mishnah and the early Tosefta. The literary coherence of many parts of the Tosefta and the fact that the passages of the Tosefta that explain the cryptic references of the Mishnah are embedded in elaborate, independent literary structures, lead me to doubt that the Tosefta came into being as a paragraph-by-paragraph commentary on the Mishnah, as suggested by the first and even second explanations. For something to be a commentary, it needs to be written in response to the source document. In addition, the relationship between the commentary and the source text should be clear at most points. It also goes without saying that the material should appear in roughly the same order in both the source and the commentary. But the Tosefta reads in many places like a document with its own literary integrity, with a beginning, middle, and end to its sections and with its own halakhic and aggadic points. It does not appear to be a response to some other document in these instances, despite its great similarity in form and content to that other document. Most telling, and often noted in the past, is that the passages of the Tosefta in many places do not follow the same order as those of the Mishnah.[8]

It therefore seems to me that the Tosefta of old, much of which is embedded in the Tosefta of today, was an independent collection of tannaitic materials. It came into being gradually, as individual sources and clusters of sources coalesced into a collection. It further seems that the Mishnah, with all of its cryptic references, may be an "edited down" version of this older tannaitic collection,[9] reworked by the redactor for the purpose of making a statement of his own legal and even political philosophy. He appears to have condensed a considerable number of the Tosefta's halakhot and anecdotes, presenting them only as brief notes whenever this served his purposes. He did not feel impelled to record them in full since a brief note would apparently be sufficient to enable the reader to seek out the full account elsewhere.

The most important benefit of positing that the beraitot in the Tosefta that are associated with a given mishnah are older than that mishnah and are the very materials from which that mishnah is created, is that this assumption makes it possible to read the Mishnah with greater depth and precision. By seeing what materials were accessible to the redactor and how he reshaped them, we can arrive at a far more nuanced interpretation

---

[8] Goldberg (ibid., 284–5) claims that the Tosefta diverges from the order of the Mishnah for pedagogical reasons. Y. N. Epstein (*Mevo'ot Lesifrut Hatannaim* [Jerusalem: Magnes, 1957], 257–9) claims that the Tosefta has its own independent order. See S. Friedman's discussion of Epstein in *Tosefta Atiqta*.

[9] This is not the same thing as saying that the Mishnah of the Bavli is an extraction of the Tosefta by the Babylonian amoraim. According to M. S. Zuckermandel, the amoraim took the Tosefta, which was Rebbe's Mishnah, shortened it, and then arranged it according to their own customs. See Goldberg, "The Tosefta," 294 n. 20. According to my theory, the redactor of the Mishnah was rejecting (in part) the Tosefta's teachings, not accepting them, as suggested by Zuckermandel. See Epstein, *Mevo'ot*, 250; Hanokh Albeck, *Mavo Latalmudim* (Tel Aviv: Devir, 1969), 76.

of his words, at *mishnah kifeshutah*. This interpretation will often differ significantly from the traditional one, which assumes the Tosefta to be a commentary on the Mishnah.

I will now illustrate this proposition with two examples of the many that I have found. The first mishnah to be examined is generally clear, but contains one totally opaque statement. I will show that this statement can be understood only if read together with the Tosefta, although the Tosefta passage seems to have had an independent and early existence of its own.

I. The Women's Gallery and *Simhat Bet Hashoevah*

M. Sukkah 5.1–2

... אמרו: כל מי שלא ראה שמחת בית השואבה לא ראה שמחה מימיו.
במוצאי יום טוב הראשון שלחג ירדו לעזרת נשים
ומתקנין שם תקון גדול
ומנורות שלזהב היו שם ...

> ... They said: Anyone who has not seen Simhat Bet Hashoevah has not seen rejoicing his entire life.
> At the end of the first day of Sukkot they would go down to the Women's Gallery *umetaqnin sham tiqqun gadol*.
> There were golden candelabra there ...

In the midst of a detailed description of Simhat Bet Hashoevah, a once-a-year, grand celebration, apparently the first stage of the water libation ceremony,[10] we find one phrase that makes almost no sense—*umetaqnin sham tiqqun gadol*. In general, the verb *letaqen* means "to correct," "fix," "prepare," or "enact," and the noun *tiqqun* means "a correction," "an improvement," "setting things straight." But there is no situation in need of repair mentioned in this mishnah. Moreover, the grammatical form of *metaqnin* (present plural) suggests a repetitive action, which means that a *tiqqun gadol* was made year after year. If we take these factors into consideration, the phrase may mean that "they" (apparently the priests) made some kind

---

[10] M. Suk 5.2 implies either that Simhat Bet Hashoevah took place only once a year or else that only the first of a series of celebrations was grand. T. Suk 4.5 makes reference to the fact that there were repeated celebrations, one on each night of Sukkot. Simhat Bet Hashoevah is most likely the first stage of the water libation ceremony (M. Suk 4.9). During the night, men and women made merry in the Temple and then, at dawn, formed a procession to go down to the Shiloah, a pool near Jerusalem, to draw water (hence Shoevah, or "drawing of water") for the libation ritual which followed. Neither the Mishnah nor the Tosefta states explicitly that the ceremonies connect in this way, but most commentators suggest such a sequence. Maimonides (Hilkhot Lulav 8:12ff.) does not connect the two rituals. The difficulty is that in both the Mishnah and the Tosefta the description of the water libation ceremony precedes that of Simhat Bet Hashoevah.

of preparation every year for the celebration in the Women's Gallery. It is not clear, however, what kind of preparation they made, or who made it, or for what reason it was necessary to make it.[11] The next phrase of the mishnah sheds no light on this one—it goes on to describe the golden candelabra that would illuminate the nighttime festivities.

M. Middot 2.5, which also mentions the Women's Gallery, makes a cryptic reference to a change in its architecture:

עזרת הנשים היתה ארך מאה שלשים וחמש על רחב מאה שלשים וחמש . . .
וחלקה היתה בראשונה והקיפוה כצוצרה שהנשים רואות מלמעלן והאנשים מלמטן
כדי שלא יהו מערבין.

The Women's Gallery was 135 [cubits] long and 135 [cubits] wide . . . It was smooth at first. They then surrounded it with a balcony so that women could see from above and men from below so that they would not mingle.

The expression "it was smooth" means, according to the commentaries, that at first there were no structures jutting out from the walls. They, either priests or rabbis (see discussion of this point below, n. 14), then surrounded it with a balcony so that women could see from above and men from below, so that they would not mingle. But what did women and men need to see? For what reason should they not mix? Did they not regularly mingle in the Women's Gallery, an area that men had to pass through on their way to the Israelite Gallery to offer a sacrifice? This mishnah in Middot is almost as opaque as the one phrase of M. Sukkah 5.2.

If we now turn to T. Sukkah 4.1, we find answers to all of these queries. This passage follows a lengthy description of the water libation ceremony in 3.14–18 (‖ M. Sukkah 4.9, 10), and introduces a long discussion of the Simhat Bet Hashoevah celebration (T. 4.1–5 ‖ M. Sukkah 5.1–4).

T. Sukkah 4.1

בראשונה כשהיו רואין שמחת בית השואבה
היו אנשים רואין מבפנים ונשים רואות מבחוץ
וכשראו בית דין שהן באין לידי קלות ראש
עשו שלש גזוזטראות בעזרה כנגד שלש שלש רוחות
ששם נשים יושבות ורואות בשמחת בית השואבה
ולא היו מעורבין.

At first, when they used to watch Simhat Bet Hashoevah, the men would watch on the inside and the women on the outside. And when the court

---

[11] Maimonides says, in his commentary on M. Suk 5.2, that *tiqqun gadol* means "of great benefit" (*gedol hatoelet*), i.e., that they prepared a place for women and for men, with the women higher up so that the men do not look at them. In his commentary on M. Mid 2.5 he says that women looked out at men from a protected chamber. I do not see any basis for these remarks about men and women looking at each other in the rabbinic materials. See n. 12.

saw that this led to [excessive] levity, they made three balconies on the three sides[12] so that women could sit there and watch Simhat Bet Hashoevah and not mingle [with men].

If we read T. Sukkah together with M. Middot, we see that both are referring to some incident that made separation of men and women necessary. If, according to the Tosefta, men used to be on the inside and women on the outside, then, even to begin with, they were separated. If so, how did this lead to excessive levity? Since most women could not see over men's heads, and since seeing the Simhat Bet Hashoevah celebration was what everyone wanted to do, as the various texts note, some women may have infiltrated the ranks of the men, maybe even asking men to pick them up. This physical nearness, as well as the general atmosphere of celebration, might have led to sexually inappropriate behavior.[13] By placing the women's vantage point higher than the men's, the rabbinic court solved the problem.[14]

Thus, M. Middot, when read with T. Sukkah, makes sense. The Women's Gallery acquired a superstructure in order to ward off possible promiscuous behavior at the yearly celebration. If we now return to the statement in M. Sukkah, *umetaqnin sham tiqqun gadol*, we see that although it probably means that they engage each and every year in elaborate preparations for the celebration—in this case the construction of balconies or bleachers—the mishnah's phrase might serve as a double entendre. The redactor is telling us that these extensive preparations were necessary year

---

[12] The three sides are the north, south, and east, because the "show" took place in part on the steps leading down from the Israelite Gallery. See M. Suk 5.4. Lieberman (*Tosefta Ki-fshuta,* Sukkah [New York, N.Y.: Jewish Theological Seminary of America, 1962], 886) says that the *tiqqun* was performed each year, that even if there were some parts of the structure that were left in place, other parts had to be set up again and again. This explanation resolves the seeming contradiction between M. Sukkah, which says that they would make a *tiqqun gadol,* presumably each time they celebrated, and M. Middot, which says that the gallery used to be smooth but they then erected balconies, presumably ones that remained permanently in place. Lieberman notes that the verb *metaqnin* forced Rashi (B. Suk 51b, s.v. *hiqifuha gezoztra*) to say that they made protrusions from the walls (to support planks) which remained in place permanently, but that the planks were laid down each year anew. Albeck (commentary on M. Middot, 322) says that "it was smooth" means that at first there were no protrusions from the walls. It is rather clear that he, too, follows Rashi.

[13] See B. Suk 52a (‖ Y. Suk 5.2 55b), ". . . if, during a eulogy for the dead, when the evil inclination does not control them, the Torah says that men and women should be separate, here, at a celebration, when the evil inclination does control them, how much the more so should men and women be separate!"

[14] Note that it is the rabbis who impose standards of moral behavior in this telling of the story, even in the Temple, the precinct of the priests! The other two texts are silent about who it was who imposed moral standards.

after year for their own sake and also to correct, or rather prevent, a "social" wrong. His choice of the verb תקן, *which does not appear in either M. Middot or T. Sukkah*, allows for and even hints at both. By "both" I mean elaborate preparations for the celebration and also, at the same time, prevention of social wrong. It appears that the redactor deliberately introduced a verb and a noun, in very close proximity to each other, that are resonant of the terms associated with repairing the social order.[15] That is, the redactor deliberately made an enigmatic statement, virtually forcing the reader either to understand it in the most general way possible—as preparations for the celebration—or else to search out the meaning of this phrase in some other collection and connect it with a specific event of the past. M. Sukkah 5.1–2, much more than M. Middot 2.5, is dependent on T. Sukkah 4.1 for explanation.[16]

We thus see that T. Sukkah 4.1 is the only comprehensive and comprehensible text of the three. Since this passage serves the Tosefta's purposes well, in that it introduces the topic of Simhat Bet Hashoevah at the beginning of Chapter 4, and since it has no linguistic link at all with M. Sukkah—there is no mention of the root תקן anywhere in the Tosefta's version of the story—it seems that T. Sukkah is the oldest text of the three. At the very least, it is not a commentary on the Mishnah or a response to it. The redactor of M. Middot knew the story of T. Sukkah but cited only the element he needed to explain the architecture of the Temple: he tells the reader that a change was made in the Women's Gallery, that balconies were added on three sides for women's "viewing" so that men and women would not mingle. He mentions no time of year and no past event of excessive levity because they do not serve his purposes. The difficulty with M. Middot, as noted above, is that it creates the impression that the balconies were permanent additions to the Women's Gallery, contrary to the statement in M. Sukkah that they were erected each year.[17]

The redactor of M. Sukkah also took only what he needed from the Tosefta story. Since his focus is the preparation for and celebration of Simhat Bet Hashoevah, he needed to say that each year they erected special structures—*tiqqun gadol*—for women's viewing. He did not need to relate why this practice was instituted. Perhaps he did not wish to divulge its less-than-praiseworthy origins and for that reason chose a very vague expression—"they prepared a grand preparation." As for the apparent

---

[15] See M. Gittin, chapters 4 and 5, and elsewhere.

[16] Albeck (Qodashim, 313 [introduction to M. Middot]) states that the goal of M. Middot is to preserve details of Temple architecture so that future generations could rebuild it and replicate it exactly. Josephus's descriptions are, for the most part, similar to those of the Mishnah. Epstein (*Mevo'ot*, 31, 37) claims that M. Middot and chapters 4 and 5 of M. Sukkah are very early.

[17] See n. 12.

contradiction between the two mishnahs—did they erect balconies every year (M. Sukkah) or only once (M. Middot)—there is no easy resolution.[18]

In this way it is possible and also easy to chart the path from T. Sukkah to M. Middot and M. Sukkah. One would have a hard time explaining how to go from M. Sukkah's inscrutable *tiqqun gadol* to T. Sukkah's story.

That M. Sukkah can only be understood by reading it in conjunction with M. Middot and T. Sukkah is already suggested by the amoraim of the Bavli.

B. Sukkah 51b

מאי תַּיקוּן גדול?
אמר רבי אלעזר: כאותה ששנינו חלקה היתה בראשונה והקיפוה גזוזטרא
וְהִתְקִינוּ שיהו נשים יושבות מלמעלה ואנשים מלמטה.
ת״ר בראשונה היו נשים מבפנים ואנשים מבחוץ
והיו באים לידי קלות ראש
הִתְקִינוּ שיהו נשים יושבות[19] מבחוץ ואנשים מבפנים
ועדיין היו באין לידי קלות ראש
הִתְקִינוּ שיהו נשים יושבות מלמעלה ואנשים מלמטה.

What does *tiqqun gadol* mean?[20]
Said R. Elazar, "Like that which we learned about in the mishnah [Middot]: it was smooth at first and then they surrounded it with a balcony and enacted (*vehitqinu*) that women sit above and men below."
Our sages have taught [an editorial introduction to a beraita]: At first women were inside and men outside, and they came to [excessive] levity. They then enacted (*hitqinu*) that women sit outside and men inside, and they still came to [excessive] levity. They then enacted (*hitqinu*) that women sit above and men below.[21]

---

[18] Ibid.

[19] The word *yoshvot*, "sit," makes no sense. It is absent from the Munich ms. Why would women sit in the gallery if they are outside of, or behind, the men and the point is to see the celebration? This word must have changed because of the similar verb in both the preceding memra and the following clause of the beraita. It should have been *ro'ot*, "they see," or else no verb at all, as in the first clause of the beraita. See the variants in R. Rabbinovicz, *Diqduqei Soferim* (1959 reprint of Munich: Huber, 1867–97), note *heh*.

[20] See n. 12.

[21] See Chaim Lapin, "Palm Fronds and Citrons: Notes on two Letters from Bar Kosiba's Administration," *HUCA* 64 (1993) 111–135, at 129 and n. 59. The rabbinic sources describe the Sukkot celebrations in Dionysian terms—carrying and waving of branches, decoration of the altar with branches, water libations, etc. Since these practices do not have a biblical basis, Lapin notes, they are likely to be descriptions of the actual Temple cult. Note also that at the end of M. Suk 5.2 there is a statement that in this place people used to worship the sun, a possible Apollonian influence.

The word *hitqinu* appears three times in this passage—once in the mouth of an amora citing a mishnah (Middot 2.5) and twice in a beraita (a parallel to T. Sukkah 4.1)—but not at all in either M. Middot or T. Sukkah.[22] It is rather clear that either the amora or the redactor or the transmitter added this word to M. Middot as quoted here in the Bavli to make a connection between the *tiqqun gadol* of M. Sukkah and the action reported in M. Middot, i.e., to suggest an intertextual reading.[23] Even without the addition of *vehitqinu*, however, R. Elazar is still equating the *tiqqun gadol* of this mishnah with the erection of the balconies described in M. Middot to prevent men and women from mingling.[24] Similarly, the stama or redactor or transmitter of this beraita added *hitqinu* twice to the text, again to establish links with the *tiqqun gadol* of the mishnah. It is of special note that the meaning of *vehitqinu* in the last line of the beraita is not only "enacted" but also "erected (a gallery)" so that women could sit and watch the event with an unobstructed view. This meaning approaches the meaning of *vehitqinu* in M. Sukkah 5.2. What I am saying is that the amoraim themselves interpret M. Sukkah by reading it together with M. Middot and T. Sukkah, thereby suggesting that all three sources refer to the same incident: the one described in T. Sukkah. This might mean that in the eyes of the amoraim both mishnahs, Sukkah and Middot, are based on the Tosefta, and not vice versa.[25]

---

[22] Note that the phrase "so that they would not mingle," key in both M. Mid 2.5 and T. Suk 4.1, does not appear here.

[23] It is common for tannaitic sources in the Bavli that are brought to explain a mishnah to adjust themselves linguistically to that mishnah. That is, the words of a beraita are changed so that they match the mishnah and thus look like a direct commentary on it. See e.g. B. Eruv 45a and B. Ket 110a. Here, in B. Suk 51b, a mishnah from elsewhere is altered.

[24] It also seems that the Bavli lengthened the beraita to make the point more effectively—the necessity to separate men and women to prevent promiscuous behavior. However, it makes little sense to say that at first women were inside. This lengthening is probably due to the variant readings of this clause in the mss. See *Diqduqei Soferim*, note *dalet*. That is, by repeating the impossibility of letting men and women stay on the same level and avoiding levity, the Bavli concludes that the only solution is different levels. The outcome of adding *vehitqinu* to the beraita is that no explicit reference is made to the erection of a balcony, only that women sat higher than men. The preceding source, M. Middot, already mentions the balconies. We thus see how the Bavli alters its sources to make its points more clearly.

[25] Note that the term *bet din* (rabbinical court), to which the Tosefta ascribes the erection of the balconies, has been replaced in the Bavli's version of the Tosefta by the vague *vehitqinu*. The Mishnah too is vague, but implies priests. If, as I suggest, the Tosefta predates the Mishnah, then the Tosefta is making a political point which the Mishnah and the Bavli play down.

Although Y. Sukkah 5.2 55b, in commenting on this mishnah, does not cite the beraita from T. Sukkah, it does say in reference to the Mishnah's phrase *tiqqun gadol* that they would put men by themselves and women by themselves,[26] and it then quotes M. Middot. The Yerushalmi sugya continues, as does the Bavli sugya, with a discussion of the evil inclination. It is thus making the same point as the Bavli, that the Mishnah's phrase, as neutral as it sounds, is a reference to promiscuous behavior and the rabbinic response to it at some time in the past.

A possible translation of the mishnah, in line with the view of both the Bavli and Yerushalmi, is: they went down to the Women's Gallery and there they would enact a grand corrective enactment, i.e., build balconies. However, since even the Tosefta, which tells the whole story, does not use the word *vehitqinu*—in either the sense of "build" or "correct" (it says, instead, *asu*, "they made")—it seems to me that the phrase *tiqqun gadol* of the mishnah is more likely to mean "a great preparation" or "a great construction." But the Mishnah's choice of words—its repeated use of the verb תקן—may carry with it the remembrance of things past.

In short, the Mishnah's opaque phrase, *umetaqnin sham tiqqun gadol*, is an ingenious and subtle way for the redactor to summarize two events from the time of the Temple: the specific instance of levity and the elaborate, yearly preparations for the "show." Although one can still argue that the Mishnah's opaque statement is the oldest of the three related texts, I think I have made a more compelling case for the opposite claim—that this was a phrase coined in response to an event of the past with the twin goals of mentioning it and also not mentioning it. M. Sukkah and M. Middot each made use of the Tosefta's independent story for their own purposes. Neither told it in full but both made just enough of a reference for someone to be able to go and find the complete narrative elsewhere.

II. *Hashaqah* and *Hatbalah*

The second mishnah we will examine, M. Betzah 2.3a, is very hard to understand on its own. We will again see how reading it together with the toseftan parallel will allow us to make sense of it.

Chapter 2 of Betzah opens with a discussion of cooking food on a Friday festival to be consumed the next day, on the Sabbath (*Shabbat*). The second mishnah of the chapter does not connect thematically but formally. It, too, talks about a festival falling adjacent to Shabbat, in this instance on Sunday, and the problems that such a circumstance creates.

---

[26] Cf. B. Suk 52a, משפחות משפחות לבד.

M. Betzah 2.2

חל להיות אחר השבת, בית שמאי אומרים מטבילין את הכל מלפני השבת ובית הלל אומרים כלים מלפני השבת ואדם בשבת.

If [the festival] fell on a Sunday, the House of Shammai says that one must immerse all [things] before Shabbat. But the House of Hillel says that one must immerse utensils *before* Shabbat, but persons [may immerse] *on* Shabbat.

Since people were in the habit of making themselves and their utensils ritually pure for a festival (*Yom Tov*), the question that arose was, When Yom Tov fell on a Sunday, could a person immerse himself and his utensils on Shabbat for the sake of Yom Tov? The House of Shammai says no, that all immersion of utensils and persons must be performed before Shabbat. The House of Hillel says that utensils must be immersed before Shabbat but persons may immerse on Shabbat for the sake of Yom Tov.

M. Betzah 2.3a continues the discussion of the immersion of utensils:

ושוין שמשיקין את המים בכלי אבן לטהרן אבל לא מטבילין.

But they agree that one may submerge water in a stone vessel to purify it (the water) but one may not immerse.

The opening words of this mishnah, "But[27] they agree that," imply that despite their disagreements in the previous mishnah, here the two Houses agree. The reader, therefore, reasonably expects that the area of agreement will be stated with regard to the area of disagreement: that with respect to the immersion of persons, about which they disagree, there is still some aspect about which they agree.[28] But this is not so. Neither side concedes to the other on a particular case of immersing persons either on Shabbat or before Shabbat. Rather, 2.3a says that both Houses agree that if a person wishes to purify water, then he can do so by pouring it into a stone vessel, which by definition is always pure, and then lowering the vessel into a ritual bath (*miqveh*) until the surface of the *miqveh*-water and the surface of the water in the stone vessel are level with each other, and they "touch" (*mashiqin*). The water in the stone vessel thereby becomes pure. I have used the word "submerge" to describe this procedure. The mishnah does not say when such an activity is permitted—on Shabbat or only before Shabbat. It also follows that ושוין need not refer to the Houses (see below).

---

[27] *Vav* prefixed to the beginning of a word can be translated either as a conjunction or a disjunction. Since "they agree" follows a disagreement, the most reasonable translation seems to be "but."

[28] Cf. the first mishnah of this chapter where they disagree about the number of cooked foods required for an *eruv*, the House of Shammai holding two and the House of Hillel only one, but agree that a fish with an egg coating is acceptable as an *eruv*, even though it is technically only one cooked dish.

The mishnah continues and says "but one may not immerse" (*aval lo matbilin*). But the mishnah does not specify *what* it is that one may not immerse. The entire line seems to be saying that submerging water in order to purify it is fine but immersing it is not. This cannot be the correct interpretation, however, because simple, physical considerations do not allow one to "immerse" water in other water in order to purify it. The object of the verb "immerse" has to be, therefore, the vessel itself (with its contents). But that cannot be the correct interpretation either, because a stone vessel never needs immersion because it cannot become ritually impure. This second part of the statement, therefore, must be referring to some other kind of vessel. We already know from the previous mishnah that both Houses agree that no immersion of vessels for purification is allowed on Shabbat. Therefore, "but one may not immerse" in 2.3a must refer to purifying a non-stone vessel in conjunction with, and incidental to, purifying the water inside it. Since one might think it acceptable to purify an impure non-stone vessel incidental to purifying the water inside it, the mishnah comes to tell us that this is not so. Note, once more, that the mishnah does not state when this prohibition applies, whether on Shabbat or Yom Tov or both.

It should now be evident that this mishnah is virtually impossible to understand without assistance. First, the three words *aval lo matbilin* make little sense because they have no direct object. Second, although it is true that the mishnah presents a rule about submerging and immersion of utensils about which the Houses agree, the subject of their agreement should have been people, because it is about people that they disagree. Third, we do not know if the agreement is in reference to submerging and immersion on Shabbat, Yom Tov, or both. In short, this mishnah is cryptic when read on its own and can only be understood with the aid of later commentary. However, if we instead read the mishnah in conjunction with the associated passage in the Tosefta we will understand the mishnah fully. Most of the above difficulties will be resolved.

T. Betzah 2.9 is relatively straightforward. Note that it explicitly deals with two distinct, although related subjects: the purification of water and the purification of vessels.

T. Betzah 2.9[29]

אין מטבילין את כלי על גב מימיו ביום טוב
ואין משיקין את המים בכלי אבן לטהרן בשבת, דברי רבי.
וחכמים אומ׳ מטבילין את כלי על גב מימיו ביום טוב
ומשיקין את המים בכלי אבן לטהרן אבל לא להטבילן.[30]

---

[29] This halakhah also appears in T. Shab 16.11, with slight changes.
[30] Erfurt ms., להטביל. See n. 42.

One may not immerse a vessel [to purify it] incidental to [purifying] its waters on Yom Tov [and it follows that one may certainly not do so on Shabbat].
And one may also not submerge waters in a stone vessel in order to render them pure, on Shabbat. The opinion of Rebbe.
But the Sages say that one may immerse [and thereby purify] a vessel by immersing [it together with] the waters inside it on Yom Tov, and one may submerge waters in a stone vessel in order to render them pure [on Shabbat or on Yom Tov],[31] but one may not immerse them (the waters) [to render them pure by immersion inside an impure vessel].

Before explaining how the Tosefta's passage resolves the difficulties we found in the Mishnah, we should note that it is not the Houses of Shammai and Hillel who are engaged in this dispute, but Rebbe and the Sages.[32] This is quite astonishing. We see here an instance in which the words of the Mishnah (*veshavin*, "but they agree") lead us to believe that it was the Houses who agreed on these rules and yet the Tosefta reveals that it was later rabbis (not mentioned in this mishnah) who engaged in this dispute.

The first thing to notice about the toseftan passage is that it is fully comprehensible on its own. By first mentioning the matter of immersing a vessel, it is clear that *any* kind of impure vessel is spoken of, except for a stone one which cannot become impure. Second, the words *Yom Tov* and *Shabbat* appear in reference to three out of the four rules so that it is clear when *hatbalah* (immersion of utensils) and *hashaqah* (submerging of water) are permitted and when they are forbidden. In addition, the verb *matbilin* in the first and third sections has a direct object: the vessel itself (which may or may not become pure incidental to purifying the waters inside it). This is in contrast to the verb *mashiqin* in the second and fourth sections, which refers to the purification of the water in a stone vessel, not the vessel itself. Last, there are areas of agreement, not just areas of disagreement. We can deduce that all, i.e., Rebbe and the Sages, agree that the submerging of water is allowed on Yom Tov and that purifying a vessel together with purifying the water inside it is forbidden on Shabbat. It is evident that the disputes between Rebbe and the Sages are not about purification rites in

---

[31] Lieberman (*Tosefta Ki-fshuta*, Shabbat, 273) notes that it is clear that the reference is to Shabbat.

[32] We also see elsewhere in the chapter that the redactor takes liberties with names. Although it is the House of Rabban Gamliel in the Tosefta that used to grind pepper on Yom Tov in [special] pepper mills, M. Betz 2.8 says that it was R. Elazar b. Azariah who permitted the grinding of pepper with [special] pepper mills. This seems to be an example of the redactor of the Mishnah taking a phrase from the Tosefta, של בית רבן גמליאל היו שוחקין הפלפלין ברחים שלהן, and inserting it unmodified into the Mishnah *with a different attribution*. See Lieberman's comments in *Tosefta Ki-fshuta*, Yom Tov, 961. See also M. Betz 2.7 and its parallel, T. Betz 2.15, and Lieberman's comments on this name change in *Tosefta Ki-fshuta*, Yom Tov, 960.

preparation for a Sunday Yom Tov but purification rites, in general, *on* Shabbat and *on* Yom Tov.

We thus see that had M. Betzah 2.3a been referring to Rebbe and the Sages (and *not* the Houses, as is strongly implied), and to permitted *hashaqah* of water in stone vessels on Yom Tov and prohibited *hatbalah* of vessels by indirect purification on Shabbat, and had it mentioned *hatbalah* first with a direct object, as does the Tosefta halakhah, then the mishnah would have made perfect sense and would tally rule for rule with the Tosefta. Since it did not do so, and since it is in many ways incomprehensible on its own, and since the Tosefta is clearly not formulated as a commentary on this mishnah but as an independent statement of disagreement, not agreement (as is the mishnah), it is reasonable to conclude that M. Betzah 2.3a is a reworking or reformulation of this older tannaitic source. As similar as it may be to the beraita, it presents a set of rules that differs somewhat. If we can assume that the reader of the mishnah had access to this beraita and studied the mishnah together with it, then the mishnah's cryptic statements become much more clear.

The mishnah can now be understood in several ways. One interpretation is that *hashaqah* is allowed, even on Shabbat, as the Sages rule in the Tosefta, and *hatbalah* prohibited, even on Yom Tov, as Rebbe rules in the Tosefta (Albeck).[33] It follows that the words "but they agree" mean that the Houses agree with the views of later(!) tannaim, with Rebbe and with the Sages. Another possible interpretation, as suggested by the Yerushalmi, is that the mishnah rules like the Sages, allowing submerging and prohibiting immersion, and refers only to Shabbat. Again, "but they agree" implies that the Houses agree with later tannaim, i.e., the Sages. A third possibility is that the mishnah is in accord with Rebbe, that submerging is permitted on Yom Tov but immersion is not. A fourth interpretation is that the mishnah is saying that Rebbe and the Sages agree that submerging is allowed on Yom Tov and immersing is forbidden on Shabbat, as deduced from the views presented in the Tosefta. According to this interpretation, it is not necessary to suggest that the Houses agree with tannaim who lived much later, because the phrase "but they agree" refers to Rebbe and the Sages themselves. A fifth possibility is that the mishnah is saying that Rebbe's views about Yom Tov, permitting submerging but prohibiting immersion, are equivalent to the Sages' views about Shabbat (Lieberman).[34] Even if we cannot choose from among these options, we now know much more of what the mishnah means than we knew before.

---

[33] Commentary on M. Betz 2.3a (Moed, 291).

[34] *Tosefta Ki-fshuta,* Shabbat, 273. The problem with this interpretation is that it is not likely that a mishnah would say that two tannaim "agree" but mean that they

Were we to make the opposite assumption, that the mishnah came first and that the beraita was written in order to explain the mishnah, we would have to say that the redactor knowingly included impossible-to-understand passages in his collection. It is hard to figure out why he would do so. As noted above, should the response be that there were older materials circulating as independent units that would explain the opaque mishnah, this is no different from what I am saying, except that I am going further and suggesting that these older units were circulating not as bits and pieces but as part of a collection.

We thus see that only by reading the mishnah together with the associated passage in the Tosefta can the mishnah be understood. Is the mishnah's lack of clarity intentional? I cannot answer except to say that if the redactor could rely upon an already-extant tannaitic collection, then his Mishnah "notes" could serve the purpose of presenting his halakhic opinions on these matters without burdening the tanna-as-memorizer with excessive and perhaps unnecessary information. It is precisely because the traditional assumption has been that the Mishnah is the first redacted tannaitic work and the Tosefta a response to the Mishnah that we have not allowed ourselves to consider the possibility that the earlier collection spells things out in detail and later collections need only refer to the earlier rule as a backdrop for the new points they make and for their divergences.

We will now turn to the Bavli's and Yerushalmi's commentary on this mishnah.

B. Betzah 18b

מאי "אבל לא מטבילין"?
אמר שמואל אין מטבילין את הכלי על גב מימיו לטהרו ביום טוב
מני מתניתין, לא רבי ולא רבנן
דתניא: אין מטבילין את הכלי אגב מימיו לטהרו
ואין משיקין את המים בכלי אבן לטהרן, דברי רבי;
וחכמים אומרים מטבילין כלי על גב מימיו לטהרו
ומשיקין את המים בכלי אבן לטהרן.
מני? אי רבי קשיא השקה, אי רבנן קשיא הטבלה
איבעית אימא רבי איבעית אימא רבנן ...

What do the words "but one may not immerse" mean?

Said Samuel: one may not immerse a utensil [to purify it] incidental to [purifying] its waters on Yom Tov.

Who authored this mishnah? Not Rebbe and not the Sages.

For it was taught in a beraita: One may not immerse a vessel [to purify it] incidental to [purifying] its waters,

---

agree in approach only, not in the specifics of the halakhah. The strength of this interpretation, however, is that it elegantly solves the problem of which time period is under discussion.

And one may not submerge water in a stone vessel in order to render them pure, the opinion of Rebbe;
But the Sages say, one may immerse a vessel to purify it incidental to [purifying] its waters,
And one may submerge waters in a stone vessel to render them pure.
Whose [mishnah] is it? If it is Rebbe's [mishnah], the law of submerging poses a difficulty [for he holds that submerging is not allowed whereas the mishnah holds that it is allowed]; if it is the Sages' [mishnah], the law of immersion poses a difficulty [for they hold that immersing is allowed whereas the mishnah holds that it is not allowed].
If you like, I will say it is Rebbe's [mishnah]; if you like, I will say it is the Sages' [mishnah] . . .

Samuel senses the opacity of the mishnah, particularly its last three words, and issues a statement that clarifies[35] two critical points: the goal of the immersion is to purify the vessel, incidental to its water, and the time period when the activity is forbidden is on Yom Tov, which means it is also forbidden on Shabbat. It is no coincidence that the beraita that follows repeats his statement nearly verbatim. Only the words *Yom Tov* are omitted. It is clear that Samuel did not formulate a statement on his own but rather lifted a line from a beraita that was already associated with the mishnah and then specified, it seems, that the prohibition applies on Yom Tov. There are questions about the exact reading of the text of the beraita, however, as Rashi indicates.[36]

If we now compare Samuel's statement to the first line of the toseftan halakhah, we see that he has also added the word *letaharo*. He needed to do so because the Tosefta is clear but the Mishnah is not. The toseftan passage states explicitly in its opening statement that one does not immerse a vessel incidental to purifying its water on Yom Tov. But, as already noted above, M. Betzah 2.3a says that "they" agree that one may purify water in a stone vessel *but one may not immerse,* and it is not clear what it is that one may not immerse. Since the words could mean that a person may not immerse water, Samuel informs the reader that the mishnah is saying that one may not immerse a vessel incidental to water. He is thus interpreting this part of the mishnah in keeping with the ruling of Rebbe in the Tosefta.

As this short Bavli sugya indicates, the toseftan beraita was studied along with the mishnah even before the time of Samuel, an early amora. The amora inserts himself as a mediator between the mishnah and the beraita in order to state clearly and succinctly what the last three words of the mishnah mean.[37] That is, the amora interprets the mishnah according to

---

[35] Lieberman (*Tosefta Ki-fshuta*, Shabbat, 272) says that Samuel's purpose is not to correct the reading of the mishnah but to explain it.

[36] See Rashi ad loc., s.v. *hakhi garsinan detanya*.

[37] It is hard to understand why the stama, following Samuel's statement, then asks מני מתניתין, given that the mishnah is the point of agreement between the House

the beraita, a standard phenomenon in the *gemara*.[38] Since Samuel's statement and the beraita are nearly identical, it seems that with the passage of time the beraita—in its Bavli context—assimilated a word from Samuel's statement (*letaharo*) but also lost some key words, *Yom Tov* and *Shabbat*. Since the beraita makes no sense without these words, it seems that they dropped out in the Bavli under the influence of M. Betzah 2.3a, which also lacks these words.[39] That is, the beraita became similar in wording not just to the preceding statement but also to the preceding mishnah.[40] Because the reading of the beraita in the Bavli is uncertain, however, as indicated by Rashi,[41] these conclusions are provisional.

What was the attitude of the amoraim to the beraitot associated with the Mishnah? Can we determine if they thought that the Mishnah was derived from or based on those beraitot? At this point, all I can say is that it is clear that the amoraim felt it appropriate to interpret the Mishnah in light of the beraitot. In this instance, we see that Samuel recognized that M. Betzah 2.3a was not understandable and that the related beraita was. Is he suggesting that this mishnah is based on the beraita? I don't know.

We see similar developments in the Yerushalmi (Betzah 2.3 61b):

מתניתין דלא כרבי
דתני אין מטבילין כלי אגב מימיו ביום טוב
ואין משיקין את המים בכלי אבן לטהרן בשבת, דברי רבי.
וחכמים אומרים מטבילים כלי על גב מימיו ביו' טוב
ומשיקין את המים בכלי אבן בטהרה.[42]

Our mishnah is not in accordance with [the views of] Rebbe.

For it was taught in a baraita: One may not immerse a vessel [to purify it] incidental [to purifying] its waters on Yom Tov,

---

of Shammai and the House of Hillel. The stama's answer, after the difficulties are resolved, is that the mishnah represents the view of either Rebbe or Sages. How can this be reconciled with the fact that the word ושוין refers to the Houses of Shammai and Hillel? Or does the stama understand ושוין as a discontinuity and the referents must be sought elsewhere, if necessary? Or, is the question מני מתניתין formulated on the basis of the following beraita?

[38] See my *Development of the Talmudic Sugya*, chapter 3, pp. 75ff.

[39] The beraita is thus saying that Rebbe prohibits *hashaqah* and *hatbalah* on Yom Tov as well as on Shabbat, a position more stringent than the toseftan beraita. The Sages allow *hatbalah* even on Shabbat and *hashaqah* both on Shabbat and Yom Tov. The Sages are more lenient than they are in the Tosefta and Rebbe is more strict. This is not likely.

[40] That parts of memrot, in the course of time, are assimilated into beraitot, I have demonstrated in my study of the phrase *tanya nami hakhi*. See *Development*, chapter 4. That beraitot change their wording in accordance with the related mishnah, see above, n. 23.

[41] See n. 36.

[42] Vienna ms., לטהרן אבל לא להטבילן.

> And one may not submerge water in a stone vessel to purify them on Shabbat. The opinion of Rebbe.
>
> But the Sages say: One may immerse a utensil [to purify it] incidental to [purifying] its waters on Yom Tov,
>
> And one may submerge water in a stone vessel for purity.

The passage opens by saying that M. Betzah 2.3a does *not* follow the ruling of Rebbe (contrast Samuel's interpretation of this mishnah in the Bavli—that it *does* follow the view of Rebbe). It then quotes the associated beraita, in a version very similar to the Tosefta,[43] with the introductory term *detani*, "as is taught in a beraita," to provide the basis for the opening statement. This means that according to the Yerushalmi the mishnah speaks of Shabbat and not Yom Tov, and accords with the ruling of the Sages in the beraita who allow *hashaqah* on Shabbat but not *hatbalah*, although they do allow *hatbalah* on Yom Tov. If so, what does "but they agree" mean? Who agrees about what? According to Qorban Edah (*ad locum*), "they agree" refers to the Houses. The commentator is apparently saying that both Houses would subscribe to the view of later sages that submerging water is allowed on Shabbat but purification of a vessel incidental to purifying the water inside it is not—a view consistent with the stands the Houses took in M. Betzah 2.2.[44] That is, "but they agree" refers *not* to Rebbe and the Sages but to the Houses. The point to note, for our purposes, is that the Yerushalmi, like the Bavli, interprets the mishnah in conjunction with the parallel Tosefta passage.

In short: even when we read this mishnah with the Tosefta, some degree of ambiguity remains. It is for this reason that both Talmudim, which studied the mishnah with the beraita, still needed to take a stand on whether the mishnah represents the view of the Sages (Yerushalmi) or the view of Rebbe (Samuel in the Bavli) or the view of either Rebbe or the Sages (stama in the Bavli). Why did the redactor leave that open? I do not know.[45]

If the mishnah is the primary source, then it presents a law that is very difficult to understand. Another text had to be composed to explain all of its ambiguities. If the toseftan halakhah is the primary source, and the mishnah is a condensation and reworking of that halakhah, the mishnah is not that difficult to understand. The remaining problem with this mishnah is that since it does not explicitly mention either Shabbat or Yom Tov, a

---

[43] Some mss. add בשבת in the last line of the Tosefta. See Lieberman (ed.), *Tosefta Yom Tov* (Betzah), 288 and *Shabbat*, 77–78.

[44] This implies that the Houses *allow* immersion of a vessel incidental to the water inside it on Yom Tov. This view, too, is consistent with the Houses' positions in M. Betz 2.2.

[45] The Talmudim do not acknowledge the possibility of a mixed view, as does Albeck (mishnah commentary, p. 291). Maimonides in his Mishnah commentary interprets this entire passage as referring to Shabbat alone, as does the Yerushalmi.

number of interpretations are possible. According to most of them, the phrase "but they agree" is difficult to interpret. If the reader has access to the beraita, almost everything becomes clear. The bottom line is that this mishnah cannot stand alone. Medieval commentators like Rashi, and even modern ones such as Albeck, need to add much explanation to make the mishnah clear. It is tempting to speculate, therefore, that in those cases in which a commentator needs to cite a beraita to explain the Mishnah, the Mishnah is a reworking of that beraita.

Conclusions

The phenomenon of a mishnah making an incomprehensible statement and "relying" on the full report of the anecdote or halakhah elsewhere in order for the reader to understand it is, to my mind, strong evidence of the fact that the Mishnah was not a brand-new formulation of Jewish law, as so many have claimed for so long. Rather, the Mishnah was written in response to tannaitic passages that were already circulating in some kind of ordered collection. The chapters, tractates, and orders did not originate with the redactor of the Mishnah. He produced a new collection in the sense that it was his take on Jewish law but it was not a creation *ex nihilo*. Like Dead Sea scroll texts that present a restatement of the Torah and are original only in the sense that their authors modify the transmitted traditions in order to express views of their own, the Mishnah, too, is a reprise of an already circulating collection.

The importance of showing that a long, clear, understandable passage found in the Tosefta was condensed and made opaque by the redactor of the Mishnah is that this raises a serious challenge to the traditional wisdom that the fuller and more clear source is the later one which came into being to explain the earlier, more difficult and sketchy one. These close readings lead to the opposite conclusion: the clear, full source is the older one and the hard-to-understand source is the later one. But why would someone convert a clear source into an opaque one? The answer is that the clear source is still "there," available to the reader. The opaque source functions like an addendum to the clear source for the purpose of presenting a different view of the halakhah.[46] The ancient reader would read the two together, just as the early layer of the gemara would read a mishnah together with related beraitot. I would turn the challenge around and ask: If the Mishnah is the oldest, edited tannaitic work, why would a redactor produce an incomprehensible work, one that could not possibly be understood on its own?

---

[46] These conclusions put me in Y. N. Epstein's camp, that the Mishnah is a book of halakhah, and not in H. Albeck's camp, that the Mishnah is a compendium.

There is no denying that many paragraphs of mishnah have no parallel source in the Tosefta or anywhere else. But that does not disprove the theory that the Mishnah is, at its core, a reworking of an older collection. The redactor clearly added other statements of law that he found elsewhere or else produced new statements of his own. Similarly, there are many paragraphs in the Tosefta that have no parallel text in the Mishnah, although they do appear in one or both Talmudim, sometimes in association with a closely related mishnah and sometimes with some other mishnah. It is even true that some toseftan halakhot never appear anywhere else. This too does not disprove my assertion that the Mishnah is a reworking of an early Tosefta, since the Tosefta evolved over time and many paragraphs were added. I am simply saying that at the core of the extant Tosefta lies an ancient tannaitic collection that predates the Mishnah and that served as its basis. Since I can show that this is true in passage after passage and chapter after chapter (I have chosen but two representative texts for this study), I think it reasonable to generalize and say that the redactor of the Mishnah did not have just bits and pieces available to him, but an ordered tannaitic collection.

Finally, and most important, the unique advantage of engaging in a sustained analysis of the Mishnah together with related tannaitic texts is that seeing the origins of the Mishnah in a new light gives rise to a much more nuanced, more precise, and deeper understanding of the Mishnah itself.

Chapter 3

Uncovering Literary Dependencies in the Talmudic Corpus

Shamma Friedman
Jewish Theological Seminary and Bar Ilan University

In studying the talmudic-midrashic corpus we often compare similar texts, whether on the lower-critical level, namely, several textual witnesses to one passage, or on the higher-critical level—synoptic investigation of parallel passages. I would like to preface this discussion with two quotations which can serve as paradigms for two contrasting ways of viewing these relationships. The first deals with the textual discrepancies between the two versions of the Ten Commandments found in the Torah (Exodus 20:7 ‖ Deuteronomy 5:11):

זכור את יום השבת לקדשו ‖ שמור את יום השבת לקדשו

This discrepancy is explained in the well-known Mekhilta passage:

"זכור" ו"שמור". שניהן בדיבור אחד נאמרו.[1]

According to the Mekhilta, the relationship of these variants is not one of primary versus secondary, original versus edited. Rather, the two texts are

---

This paper was delivered as a lecture at the conference of the Association for Jewish Studies, 1998 (I acknowledge participants' questions). Many of the examples presented below rely upon fuller analyses of the passages in question, which are available in Hebrew studies cited. I am grateful to Prof. Shaye J. D. Cohen for suggesting this form of presentation. My submission at the synoptic conference was a Hebrew study on Babylonian beraitot (see note 11, below).

[1] *Mechilta d'Rabbi Ismael*, ed. Horovitz-Rabin (Jerusalem, 1960), Hahodesh, parashah 7, p. 229, and parallels; text according to Ma'agarim, The Hebrew Language Historical Dictionary Project.

Other rabbinic texts are cited from the following editions: Tosefta, Berakhot–Bava Batra: *Tosefta*, ed. S. Lieberman (New York, 1955–1988); Sifrei Numbers: *Siphre d'be Rab*, ed. H. S. Horovitz (Jerusalem, 1966); Sifrei Deuteronomy: *Sifrei al Sefer*

accorded equal status. Both of them were pronounced by the divine voice in miraculous simultaneity,² an impossible task for mortals, as remarked by both the Yerushalmi (Nedarim 3.2 37d) and the Bavli (Rosh ha-Shanah 27a):

מה שאי אפשר לפה לומר ולא לאוזן לשמוע ‖ מה שאין הפה יכול לדבר ואין האוזן יכולה לשמוע.

A feat that the human mouth cannot accomplish and the human ear cannot perceive.

We will use this paradigm to symbolize the approach espoused by many scholars, according to which parallel rabbinic texts represent two different traditions of which neither can be proven to be the source of the other.

The second quotation also refers to laws laid down in two separate passages in the Torah, passages which are partly similar and partly different:

זו מדה בתורה, כל פרשה שנאמרה במקום אחד וחיסר בה דבר אחד וחזר ושנאה במקום אחר, לא שנאה אלא על שחיסר בה דבר אחד.³

As worded in the Bavli,

תנא דבי רבי ישמעאל: כל פרשה שנאמרה ונישנית, לא נישנית אלא בשביל דבר שנתחדש בה.⁴

The non-corresponding element of the two passages is an innovation, *innovated* in the second version to supply a necessary clarification or addition to the first version. This paradigm represents the model of *active* editorial change.

The *zakhor ve-shamor* paradigm, which I call the model of independent parallels, has prevailed among scholars during most of the twentieth century. It appears under a variety of names, all signifying independent parallel sources: "different traditions," "separate yeshivot," "different tannaim,"

Devarim, ed. E. Finkelstein (Berlin, 1940); Genesis Rabbah: *Midrash Bereshit Rabbah*, ed. Theodor-Albeck, 2nd printing with additional corrections by Ch. Albeck (Jerusalem, 1965); Deuteronomy Rabbah: *Midrash Devarim Rabbah*, ed. S. Lieberman (Jerusalem, 1940). Page numbers following citations refer to these editions.

² See Horovitz, *Mechilta*, p. 229. ibid.; E. Z. Melamed, *Essays in Talmudic Literature* (Jerusalem, 1986), p. 150; M. Benovitz, "A Critical Commentary on Chapter III of Tractate Shevuot in the Babylonian Talmud" (doctoral dissertation, Jewish Theological Seminary of America, 1993), pp. 140–141, 640 nn. 89–90; B. Schwartz, "'I Am the Lord' and 'You Shall Have No Other Gods' Were Heard from the Mouth of the Almighty: On the Evolution of an Interpretation," in *The Bible in the Light of Its Interpreters*, ed. S. Japhet (Sarah Kamin memorial volume; Jerusalem, 1994), pp. 178–180.

³ Sifrei Numbers 2 (p. 5). The rule is ascribed to the school of R. Yishmael. See W. Bacher, *Die älteste Terminologie der jüdischen Schriftauslegung* (Leipzig, 1899), pp. 100–103, 193; idem, *Die Agada der Tannaiten* (Strassburg, 1903), vol. 1, p. 242; A. J. Heschel, *Theology of Ancient Judaism* (London & New York, 1962), vol. 1, pp. 3–4. See J. Harris, *How Do We Know This?* (Albany, 1995), and specifically p. 261 there.

⁴ B. BQ 64b, B. Shevu 19a, B. Men 10a, B. Bekh 46a.

etc. Ultimately, in my opinion, this is an incomplete concept—in the extreme almost a mystical one—which came into being under the assumption that tradents would not change or alter the received text. Scholars believed that parallel texts which diverged from one another had been transmitted independently from early times, with each representing an equally "original" text.

This theory fails, however, to provide a full, rational explanation for the overall *similarity* which marks these parallels, and for the fact that the differences between them are highly localized.[5] At the same time it closes the door on any detailed investigation of the nature of the differences, differences which, when categorized, often point to qualitatively different types of texts before us—namely, an earlier, more original version, and a later, more edited and reworked one.[6]

The "independent parallels" paradigm corresponds to certain traditional patterns of presentation found in talmudic literature,[7] and can easily be related to specific talmudic concepts indicating independent and parallel transmission, such as בסורא מתנו הכי, בפומבדיתא מתנו הכי.[8] Another is איכא דאמרי. Suffice it to be said here that recent research now points in the

---

[5] See S. Friedman, *Talmud Arukh, B. Bava Metzi'a VI: Critical Edition with Comprehensive Commentary*, Text and Introduction Volume (Hebrew; Jerusalem, 1996), pp. 12–13.

[6] When discussing lower criticism of the Mishnah, J. N. Epstein tries to maintain the historical inviolability of the text of the Mishnah as much as possible. What may appear as alternate forms of the Mishnah's text are perceived as deriving from independent, parallel works. Creative editorial change is largely viewed by him as a negative development of the post-classical period. When mentioned (שינויים של עריכה, הגהות של עריכה) this concept tends to be applied in the sense of the infusion of one text by another (דעה חולקת), which is code for Epstein's concept of these texts being independent parallels. Also on the higher-critical level Epstein tends as much as possible to view different forms as being of equal weight, to such a degree that linguistic development in word pairs contained in the parallels is eclipsed in his analysis. See his *Mavo le-Nosah ha-Mishnah*, 2nd ed. (Jerusalem, 1964), pp. 1–7 (cf. idem, *Introduction to Tannaitic Literature* [Jerusalem, 1962], p. 239), 164–165, 349–353. On the above-mentioned editorial changes, see pp. 218, 250. On Epstein and tannaitic sources cf. A. Rosenthal, "Le-Masoret Girsat ha-Mishnah," in *Saul Lieberman Memorial Volume*, ed. S. Friedman (New York and Jerusalem, 1993), p. 32. On Epstein and parallel traditions: S. Friedman, "Mishnah and Tosefta Parallels (2)—Rabban Gamliel and the Sages (Shabbat 13, 14)" (Hebrew), Bar-Ilan 26–27 (1995) (=*Y. D. Gilat Festschrift*, ed. Z. A. Steinfeld), pp. 277–288, specifically p. 287 n. 49. On Albeck: idem, *Tosefta Atiqta*, Pesah Rishon (in press), introduction and n. 155.

[7] The phenomenon deserves a full historical study in itself. In the meantime, see *Tosefta Atiqta* (as in previous note).

[8] See I. Lewy, *Introduction and Commentary to Talmud Yerushalmi (Bava Qamma I–VI)* (Hebrew; Jerusalem, 1970), pp. 4–12; some other terms are mentioned on p. 13: איכא דרמו להו מירמא, איכא דמתני, איכא דאמרי, ואמרי לה, ואיתימא, and לישנא אחרינא.

direction of non-equality of two statements joined by איכא דאמרי. One of the two can often be identified as the original, and the other as an editorial reworking, motivated by harmonizing purposes or mandated by a specific halakhic agenda.⁹ Parallel accounts of historical events, when developed editorially, can produce conflicting details between the two passages, leading some to the conclusion that two separate events are being referred to: תרי עובדי הוו.¹⁰

The second paradigm which we have presented—*parashah she-nithadesh bah davar*—corresponds much better to the basic and pervasive relationship which we find in synoptic parallels. Similar but differing texts do not spring into existence in primeval twinship. Changes come about developmentally and usually editorially, and their effects can be recognized in terms of a wide range of well-known literary and stylistic categories which are far from unique to our corpus.¹¹ This paradigm, which can be called the "edited parallel," strikes a responsive cord among the *rishonim* who pioneered the perception of the Bavli as reworking its sources. I refer to the words of Rabbenu Tam (Jacob ben Meir of Ramerupt): ועוד תמצא משניות דטהרות וזרעים כשמביאין אותה בתלמוד, מחסרים ומקצרים אותה,¹² and especially as they were interpreted by R. Shimshon of Sens: וכך דרך הש״ס להאריך ולקצר כשמביא משניות מטהרות ומזרעים, ומשנה הלשון כפי הצורך.¹³

Editorial activity as the force which creates alternate forms of the same text can be traced in both lower-critical and higher-critical settings. Regarding lower criticism, the question can be phrased: "Do the variants preserved in the textual witnesses to the Bavli result from the fluidity and free transmission of the Talmud in its primordial stage?" This perception fits

---

⁹ See Friedman, *Talmud Arukh, BT Bava Metzi'a VI: Critical Edition with Comprehensive Commentary*, Commentary Volume (Hebrew; Jerusalem, 1990), p. 60 and n. 26; M. Kahana, "Intimation of Intention and Compulsion of Divorce—Towards the Transmission of Contradictory Traditions in Late Talmudic Passages" (Hebrew), *Tarbiz* 62 (1993), pp. 225–264, English Summary p. vii–viii. Halakhic differences between parallels are commonly set aside in the Talmudim with equalizing terminology; Yerushalmi: היא הדא היא הדא; cf. Bavli: היא היא (Abbaye).

¹⁰ Regarding M. Yoma 2.2 and T. Yoma 1.12 (p. 224), see *Tosefta Atiqta*, introduction and n. 124; and S. Friedman, "Historical Aggadah in the Babylonian Talmud," in *Saul Lieberman Memorial Volume* (n. 6, above), passim.

¹¹ See S. Friedman, "Historical Aggadah," p. 162; idem, "The Beraitot in the Babylonian Talmud and their Parallels in the Tosefta" (Hebrew), in *Atara L'Haim: Studies in the Talmud and Medieval Rabbinic Literature in Honor of Professor Haim Zalman Dimitrovsky* (Jerusalem, 2000), pp. 163–201, at n. 7.

¹² *Sepher Hayashar by Rabbenu Tam*, ed. S. Schlesinger (Jerusalem, 1959), p. 10.

¹³ Tosafot on B. Bekh 27b, s.v. וכי. Cf. Z. Frankel, *Darkhei ha-Mishnah* (Tel Aviv, 1959), p. 232; Epstein, *Mavo le-Nosah*, p. 782. On the creative nature of the Babylonian transmission cf. A. Geiger, *Urschrift* (Frankfurt a. M., 1928), pp. 157–158 (Hebrew translation, pp. 101–102).

the model of independent parallels. Two voices emerge from the early, fluid Talmud, each presenting an independently formulated version. This indeed has been the regnant position, as articulated, for example, by Eliezer Shimshon Rosenthal.[14] I have attempted to argue for a different model, in which the two voices can often be identified as one close to the original text on one hand, and a more reworked, edited version on the other. This approach adds visibility to the editorial categories (e.g. harmonization, updating of vocabulary, etc.), and the regular reappearance of these categories lends further weight to their pervasive role.[15]

Even talmudic terminology, sometimes considered a basic and unchangeable stratum of the Talmud, actually evolved editorially. An example: והתניא presented by one branch of witnesses should be taken as original, and ורמינהו presented by the other is often an editorial change—fine-tuning the language for the purpose of greater clarity, to indicate that the beraita now being quoted contradicts the previous one.[16]

On the higher-critical level and in the synoptic comparison of parallel passages, I have elsewhere dealt with the Mishnah as a corpus which edits its sources. This becomes apparent when parallels to the Mishnah, such as those preserved in the Tosefta or in the tannaitic midrashim, are available for comparison.[17] This analysis provides general insight into the Mishnah's own style and agenda, and particular insight into the evolution of laws or concepts, where the Mishnah can sometimes be construed as containing the latest tannaitic stand. Consequently, passages in the Mishnah should not be assigned to the earliest generations without rigorous proof. The tendency to view many passages in the Mishnah as extremely early was presented by D. Hoffmann in his *Die erste Mischna,* and was often followed by Epstein and other scholars.[18]

*   *   *

One of the most fruitful areas of application of the editorial model is in the relationship between the Tosefta and parallel beraitot in the Bavli. Contemporary scholarship still sees much independence on the two sides of this relationship, and consequently often assumes that the Babylonian version of a beraita represents an actual tannaitic statement.

---

[14] E. S. Rosenthal, "The History of the Text and Problems of Redaction in the Study of the Babylonian Talmud" (Hebrew), *Tarbiz* 57 (1987), pp. 1–36.

[15] See S. Friedman, "On the Origin of Textual Variants in the Babylonian Talmud" (Hebrew, English Summary), *Sidra* 7 (1991), pp. 67–102.

[16] Ibid., pp. 88–89; *Talmud Arukh,* Text Volume (n. 5, above), pp. 25–55.

[17] S. Friedman, "Mishnah and Tosefta Parallels (1)—Shabbat 16:1" (Hebrew), *Tarbiz* 62 (1993), pp. 313–338; "Mishnah and Tosefta Parallels (2)" (n. 6, above), pp. 277–288.

[18] See *Tosefta Atiqta,* Pesah Rishon (in press), introduction.

The "independent parallels" theory regarding the relationship of Tosefta-Bavli parallels was impressed upon our consciousness in J. N. Epstein's famous diagram on page 246 of his *Introduction to Tannaitic Literature*, and in the explanation of this diagram as provided by the author, where he says, "Two descendants sprang forth from the primordial Tosefta—the beraitot of the Bavli and our Tosefta."[19] According to this imagery, common ancestry is a prehistoric issue. In terms of the seeable and the scrutinizable, the two corpora have separate and independent stemmatic identities issuing forth on parallel lines which never intersect: *zakhor ve-shamor*. Epstein's statement and accompanying diagram have exerted enormous influence on contemporary scholarship regarding the relationship of passages paralleled in the Tosefta and Bavli.[20] Since the Babylonian beraitot are described here as being an independent witness to the original Tosefta, it would follow that their readings may sometimes be superior to those of our Tosefta, and may be adopted by scholars when the situation warrants.

According to E. S. Rosenthal in his study "Ha-Moreh" on the work of Saul Lieberman, the precise nature of the relationship between the Tosefta and the beraitot of the Bavli, although an essential question for the proper interpretation of the passages involved, still remains an unsolved enigma. In his words, "The big question, which lies at the heart of source criticism and which affects most of all the commentator on the Tosefta, is: the relationship between our Tosefta and the two Talmudim. This is a complicated question that has occupied many scholars."[21] It is quite true, of course, that the *original* forms of the Tosefta and other talmudic works are not available to us, and cannot be assumed to have been identical with their representations currently in our hands. However, recourse to this truism is not necessary in order to unravel this relationship (Bavli beraitot and Tosefta parallels). In my opinion the primacy of Tosefta passages to their parallels in Babylonian beraitot is a demonstrable fact rooted in the creative reworking that the Bavli brings to bear upon *all* its sources. The approach proposed herein is capable of providing us with one of the strongest keys available to unlock, and often rewrite, the history and evolution of tannaitic laws and concepts.[22]

---

[19] "תוס׳ [פתא] קדומה—שני ילדיה: הברייתא שבבבלי והתוס׳ [פתא] שלנו."

[20] See E. S. Rosenthal, "Hamoreh," *American Academy for Jewish Research* 31 (1963), p. 52 (Hebrew section). As to the fascinating question of the original source of the diagram and the degree that it integrates within Epstein's overall framework, see Friedman, "The Beraitot" (n. 11, above).

[21] "השאלה הגדולה, שכולה עניין לבקורת המקורות, ונוגעת ביותר לפרשן התוספתא: היחס שבין התוספתא שלנו ובין שני התלמודים. בעיה סבוכה, שהעסיקה את החוקרים הרבה" (ibid.).

[22] See "The Beraitot."

Harmonization is often the purpose and the vehicle of the editorial changes found in the Bavli's version of Tosefta parallels. The Mishnah is often the source of the harmonizing element. In other words, many Bavli beraitot are in reality a Tosefta passage with an addition from the Mishnah.

B. Avodah Zarah 42b; B. Hullin 40a	T. Hullin 2.18 (p. 503)
השוחט לשום הרים, לשום גבעות, לשום ימים, לשום נהרו׳, לשום מדברות, לשום חמה לשום לבנה, לשום כוכבים לשום מזלות, לשום מיכאל השר הגדול, לשום שילשול קטן, הרי אלו זבחי מתים.	השוחט לשום חמה לשום לבנה לשום כוכבים לשם מזלות לשום מיכאל שר צבא הגדול ולשום שילשול קטן הרי זה בשר זבחי מתים.

M. Hullin 2.8

השוחט לשם הרים לשם גבעות לשם ימים לשם נהרות לשם מדברות שחיטתו פסולה.

T. Hullin 2.18 presents a list of heavenly bodies: sun, moon, etc. Anyone who slaughters an animal dedicated to these has invalidated the meat for consumption. The Mishnah presents an earthly list: mountains and seas, rivers and deserts. The Babylonian beraita, which is essentially parallel to the Tosefta passage, presents both lists, the celestial and the mundane, by inserting the Mishnah's list into the language of the Tosefta! Thus it seems clear that this beraita was formed by adding part of the Mishnah to the original language of the Tosefta. Since we posit that the Babylonian beraita tradents introduced elements from our Mishnah into their version of Tosefta beraitot, agreement of Mishnah with a beraita can no longer serve as a proof that the beraita is more authentic than its Tosefta parallel. The opposite is true. The beraita is similar to that Mishnah because it was harmonized editorially under the Mishnah's influence.

Other editorializing techniques are observable in these beraitot, such as updating of style, vocabulary, and even names. Converting a less common place-name to a more well-known one, or to the name of a greater center of activity, is a pervasive literary reality.[23] Even when beraitot in the two Talmudim agree on a place-name as against the Tosefta, if their agreement is upon a more popular name, the primacy of the Tosefta version must be seriously considered. Although it is true that the Bavli editorializes much more than the Yerushalmi, the Yerushalmi's conservative approach should not be construed as a rejection in principle of introducing editorial changes, but rather as a tendency to do so less often.[24]

Let us look briefly at the editorial change of place-names. In a passage describing *haroset* and the Passover seder, an episode involving merchants

---

[23] See Friedman, "Historical Aggadah" (n. 11, above), p. 132 n. 57.

[24] For a lower-critical model of conservative editing, see *Talmud Arukh*, Text Volume (n. 5, above), pp. 39–41.

is mentioned. In the Yerushalmi (Pesahim 10.3 47d) and in the Bavli (Pesahim 116a), they are merchants of *Jerusalem*, hawking ingredients for the seder, or specifically for *haroset*. However, in the Tosefta (Pesahim 10.10) they are the high-standing merchants of *Lydda*, appearing in a particular historic setting with R. Elazar b. Zadok shortly after the destruction of the Temple, when the introduction of *haroset* as a new Passover obligation was being discussed. In effect, R. Elazar b. Zadok is saying to them, "Come, merchants of Lydda, and partake of the *haroset* ritual." Scholarly preference for the reading "merchants of Jerusalem" as found in both the Yerushalmi and the Bavli over that of "merchants of Lydda" in the Tosefta[25] places the event in the pre-destruction period. This completely alters our understanding of the history of the seder and of the ritual evolution that took place after the destruction. Furthermore, in a separate Tosefta passage (Pesahim 3.11 [p. 154]) we have independent corroboration of R. Elazar b. Zadok spending Passover in Lydda (despite the fact that the Bavli [Pesahim 49a] also retold *that* account as taking place in Yavneh).[26]

We have seen that even place-names are updated in the process of creative transmission. The appearance of a more prestigious name in the talmudic parallels cited above is not an argument for their originality. The Bavli also shows its hand in reshaping the language of this beraita in the phrase תגרי חרך שבירושלים, which is the specific wording of the above-mentioned beraita (Pesahim 116a). The word חרך, meaning "spices," is a hapax. This meaning is available only in Syriac, and thus demonstrates that this text is being reworked by the Bavli under the influence of Babylonian Aramaic.[27]

Usually the Babylonian reworking is a matter of localized style editing—not free stylistic exchange for its own sake, but part of an overall tendency to refine harsh language and replace it with a more respectable substitute (or other stylistic agendas). For example, it is not לאחר מיתתו של רבי אליעזר, as in Tosefta, Sifrei Deuteronomy and Yerushalmi, but more respectfully לאחר פטירתו של רבי אליעזר, in the Bavli parallel alone.[28] We find the very same stylistic change between T. Niddah 1.5 (p. 641) and B. Nid-

---

[25] See S. Lieberman, *Tosefta Ki-fshuta*, vol. 6 (New York, 1952), p. 654; J. Tabory, *The Passover Ritual Throughout the Generations* (Hebrew; Tel Aviv, 1996), p. 259 n. 32.

[26] See *Tosefta Atiqta*, Pesah Rishon, ch. 21. Regarding the switch from Rabbi Eliezer to Rabbi Joshua in the Bavli passage, see below.

[27] See *Tosefta Atiqta*, ibid.

[28] T. Git 7.1 (p. 272); Sifrei Deuteronomy Piska 269 (p. 289); Y. Git 9.1 50a; B. Git 83a. The extended text paralleled in these four sources provides an excellent opportunity to observe the Bavli's tendency for localized editorial change in short segments of beraitot, which remain otherwise intact. See my forthcoming commentary on B. Gittin chapter 9, sugya three (83a).

dah 7b. Another example of refining language can be found in a passage that recounts an incident in which a husband imposes an impossible condition for the divorce he grants his wife. In the Tosefta and in the Yerushalmi parallel he does it crassly and insultingly: "on condition that you fly in the air."[29] In the Bavli the husband's language is refined and spiritualized: "on condition that you ascend to the firmament."[30] The Bavli imposes this type of style editing upon its sources on a regular basis.[31]

It is true that the Bavli's version of a beraita may be smoother and more focused, and may spell out the halakhic content that the reader is looking for. It is therefore not surprising that scholars have often given preference to the Babylonian version in the course of their research, frequently with no specific proof.[32] In light of the examples given above, we suggest that more caution should be exercised before concluding that the beraitot of the Bavli represent earlier and more original texts.

*　　*　　*

The creative reworking that we find in beraitot of the Bavli when compared with their parallels in tannaitic corpora leads us to a further conclusion. Once we have uncovered significant editorial activity in the Bavli, there is much room for suspecting[33] that some of the Babylonian beraitot with no independent tannaitic parallels may contain post-tannaitic material, especially when they present features which correspond to known editorial tendencies or deal with early tannaim whose statements on basic issues would normally be represented also in Palestinian traditions.[34] This

---

[29] T. Git 5.12 (p. 268); Y. Naz 2.4 52a. For another example of the insulting use of this expression, see M. Ket 13.7; cf. Gen. Rab. 22.8 (p. 213).

[30] B. Git 54a. On the spiritual nature of עלה לרקיע cf. Gen. Rab. 19.8 (p. 176), Deut. Rab. 11.1 (p. 38), and passim.

[31] See *Talmud Arukh*, Text Volume (n. 5, above), pp. 14–15; *Tosefta Atiqta*, index, passim.

[32] Many such preferences can be documented.

[33] And then corroborating or rejecting, through specific investigation.

[34] The question of the Babylonian beraitot in general and their problems has been discussed in the past, sometimes heatedly. See I. H. Weiss, *Dor Dor v'Dorshav* (Vienna, 1876), vol. 2, pp. 215–216; H. Malter, "A Talmudic Problem and Proposed Solutions," *JQR* n. s. 2 (1911), p. 89 n. 15; A. Weiss, *The Talmud in Its Development* (New York, 1954), pp. 37–47; L. Jacobs, "Are There Fictitious Baraitot in the Babylonian Talmud?" *HUCA* 42 (1971), pp. 185–196. Jacobs' examples belong to various categories, and should be commented upon separately; see below, n. 56. Regarding B. Rosh ha-Shanah 24a–b (=Avodah Zarah 43a–b), see my upcoming commentary on B. Avodah Zarah chapter 3. Recent writers have touched on the question *en passant*, usually not conclusively, listing bibliographic references. See D. Goodblatt,

suggestion is not intended as a blanket generalization. Our claim is that alongside the many unparalleled Babylonian beraitot which appear to represent authentic historical tannaitic statements, there are others which present a series of features that, after detailed analysis, lead us to the conclusion that they may be, at least in part, Babylonian creations.

Proliferation of tradents has long been connected with the problem of inaccurate transmission of tannaitic opinions.[35] The many collections of beraitot which already existed shortly after the Mishnah was compiled give testimony to the creative forces operating within these circles.[36] The talmudic authorities required special credentials for a beraita to be accepted as authoritative: "Any tannaitic dictum which did not enter the college is not trustworthy"; "Any tannaitic dictum which was not taught in the college of R. Hiyya or R. Hoshaia is faulty."[37]

"The Story of the Plot against R. Simeon B. Gamaliel II," *Zion* 49 (1984), p. 358 n. 28; C. Milikowsky, "Which Gehenna?" *NTS* 34 (1988), p. 247 n. 17; E. B. Diamond, "A Model for a Scientific Edition and Commentary for Bavli Ta'anit," (doctoral dissertation, Jewish Theological Seminary of America, 1990), p. 320 n. 97; S. Friedman. "Baraiyta," in *The Oxford Dictionary of the Jewish Religion,* ed. R. J. Z. Werblowsky and G. Wigoder (New York and Oxford, 1997), p. 98. Concerning B. Sanh 51b (בה ובת אני דורש), see my comment as quoted in Harris (n. 3, above), p. 279 n. 41; I hope to present the detailed analysis elsewhere. Epstein apparently took this passage as an authentic historical beraita; see his *Introduction to Tannaitic Literature,* p. 521 (cf. p. 659), and his *Mavo le-Nosah,* p. 82.

[35] As already observed in the Tosefta: משרבו תלמידי שמיי והלל שלא שימשו כל צרכן הרבו מחלוקות בישראל ונעשו שתי תורות (T. Hag 2.9 [p. 384] and parallels).

[36] Such collections are mentioned in, e.g., the following passages: אמר ר' יודן ובתורת ה' אין כתיב כאן, אלא ובתורתו, שאם יגעת בה נקראת על שמך, כגון משנתו של ר' חייא, ומשנתו של ר' הושעיא, ושל בר קפרא, וכיוצא בהן, ולמה נקראת על שמן, לפי שיגעו בה (Midrash Tehillim 1.16; cf. Eccl. Rab. 2.1, ed. Hirshman, p. 163 = Song Rab. 8.1); ואינינו חסר לנפשו מכל אשר יתאוה אלו משניות גדולות כגון משנתו של רבי עקיבא ומשנתו של רבי חייא ושל רבי הושעיה ושל בר קפרא (Eccl. Rab. 6.1).

[37] אמר רבי שמעון בן לקיש כל משנה שלא נכנסה לחבורה אין סומכין עליה (Y. Eruv 1.6 19b), and cf. below. See S. Lieberman, *Hellenism in Jewish Palestine* (New York, 1962), p. 90; J. N. Epstein, *Introduction to Tannaitic Literature,* p. 647 n. 33. I have translated "tannaitic dictum" rather than "Mishnah" as used by Lieberman in order to emphasize that no distinction between mishnah and beraita is meant here. These dicta would usually fit our category of beraita. Regarding שיילינהו לתנאי דבי רבי חייא ודבי רבי אושעיא, ואמרי: גבי הדדי תנינן in B. BM 34a, Lieberman wrote, "In case of doubt he [=the college-tanna—SF] was consulted as to the sequence or the arrangement of several clauses in the *Mishnah*" (*Hellenism,* p. 89), even though the reference is to beraitot paralleling our Tosefta; see *Tosefta Ki-fshuta,* Nezikin (New York, 1988), p. 170; and Epstein, *Mavo le-Nosah,* p. 675 (similarly, the terminology of "beraita" is apt regarding B. Nid 43b, mentioned in *Hellenism,* where the genre of halakhic midrash is referred to; see Epstein, *Introduction to Tannaitic Literature,* p. 243 n. 12).

Amoraim cited in the Bavli voice concern that the later collections may contain beraitot which do not represent genuine tannaitic opinions. B. Hullin 141a–b:[38]

מתני׳. הנוטל אם על הבנים, ר׳ יהודה אומר: לוקה ואינו משלח, וחכמים אומרים: משלח ואינו לוקה, זה הכלל: כל מצות לא תעשה שיש בה קום עשה — אין לוקין עליה:

גמ׳. בעי רבי אבא בר ממל: טעמא דרבי יהודה משום דסבר דלאו שניתק לעשה לוקין עליו, או דלמא: בעלמא סבר לאו שניתק לעשה אין לוקין עליו, והכא היינו טעמא, משום דקסבר שלח מעיקרא משמע? תא שמע: <u>גנב וגזלן ישנן בכלל מלקות —
דברי רבי יהודה</u> והא הכא, דלאו שניתק לעשה הוא, דרחמנא אמר לא תגזול והשיב את הגזלה, שמע מינה: טעמא דר׳ יהודה משום דקסבר לאו שניתק לעשה לוקין עליו! <u>אמר ליה ר׳ זירא: לאו אמינא לכו כל מתניתא דלא תניא בי רבי חייא ובי רבי אושעיא משבשתא היא, ולא תותבו מינה בי מדרשא</u>, דלמא אינה בכלל מלקות ארבעים תניא; ת״ש, דתני... לא תשוב ושב, לא תבלה וכלה, ישנן בכלל מלקות ארבעים דברי רבי יהודה, שמע מינה: טעמיה דרבי יהודה משום דקסבר לאו שניתק לעשה — לוקין עליו! דלמא: התם היינו טעם דקסבר תעזוב — מעיקרא משמע? א״ל רבינא לרב אשי, ת״ש: לא תותירו ממנו עד בקר וגו׳ באש תשרופו — בא הכתוב ליתן עשה אחר לא תעשה, לומר לך שאין לוקין עליו — דברי ר׳ יהודה, ש״מ: טעמא דר׳ יהודה משום דקסבר שלח — מעיקרא משמע ש״מ.

The beraita quoted in this sugya in the name of R. Yehudah is, according to the Talmud, not historical and incorrectly extrapolated from the mishnah. The position of the sages in this Mishnah is that one who took the mother bird together with her young (Deuteronomy 22:6) does not receive lashes for violating the negative commandment, for this prohibition contains a positive method of rectifying the transgression: "let the mother go" (verse 7). Since R. Yehudah holds that he is liable to lashes, it was assumed that he does not subscribe to the rule that a positive method of rectifying the transgression precludes lashes. Based upon this assumption, a beraita was formulated in his name stating that thieves and robbers receive lashes, despite the existence of the positive commandment to return what they took illegally.[39] The beraita is eventually rejected[40] in favor of another beraita which explicitly quotes this rule in R. Yehudah's name. That the latter

---

[38] Cf. R. Rabbinovicz, *Variae Lectiones (Diqduqei Soferim)*, 205a nn. 4, 5. The ellipsis represents ר׳ אושעיא ור׳ חייא in the printed editions. The absence or major variations of this phrase in the manuscripts indicate that it is probably a later addition that cannot be used (as by Epstein, *Mavo le-Nosah*, p. 41) to demonstrate the existence of common beraitot taught by these two sages. On R. Abba b. Memel and R. Zera as colleagues, see *Mavo le-Nosah*, p. 1300.

[39] יש תנאים הרבה שמוסיפים על משנתם בדדמי כי הכא משום דשמעינן לרבי יהודה הכא דמחייב סברי טעמא משום דלאו שניתק לעשה לוקין עליו והוסיפו לומר גנב וגזלן וטעו בזה) (Rashi on B. Hullin 141b, s.v. רבי חייא); (Ch. Albeck, *Studies in Beraita and Tosefta* [Hebrew; Jerusalem, 1969], p. 28 n. 3).

[40] And explained through emendation.

beraita is the authentic one, representing the historical position ascribed to
R. Yehudah in the tannaitic period, can now be demonstrated by the fact
that this beraita has been preserved in the manuscript text of Mekhilta de-
Rashbi:

ולא הותירו ממנו עד בקר יכול אם הותיר ממנו עד בקר יהא לוקה את הארבעים
תל׳לו׳ והנותר ממנו עד בקר באש תשרפו. בא כת׳ ליתן עשה על לא תעשה. דב׳ ר׳
יהודה.[41]

Even though we have presented this talmudic precedent, the issue, as
usual, must be decided on the basis of investigation. The regnant position
in talmudic research has been to give full historical credence to Babylonian
beraitot, without requiring confirmation from Palestinian sources or attempting to identify features which could lead to a late dating. This position is often taken by Epstein, as we will cite below. However, it is
significant that Epstein provides an important catalogue of tannaitic statements which appear in changed, evolved or corrupt forms,[42] culminating
in several categories of non-historical beraitot, newly created in Babylonia.
Among these he mentions:

> Sometimes they intentionally reversed the dispute in the mishnah and
> taught a type of "talmudic" beraita in order to have the law they preferred
> stated in the name of that tanna or that house whose opinion is considered
> authoritative. . . . In Babylonia a unique type of mishnah-beraita came into
> existence, beraitot which *summarize* the mishnah, epitomize it, eliminate
> the dispute while adopting the position of one of the disputants according
> to the regnant halakhic rules. . . .
>
> [In the category of] explanatory "talmudic" beraitot . . . belong certain Bab-
> ylonian beraitot introduced by תניא נמי הכי following חסורי מחסרא when their
> language is exactly like the חסורי מחסרא statement . . .[43]

The problem is compounded by the very skill of Bavli creativity, and the
explicit and developed nature of these passages. The scholar can thereby
be led to enticing pieces of information about the tannaim, which he or she

---

[41] Ed. Epstein-Melamed, *Mekhilta de-Rabbi Shimon ben Yohai* (Jerusalem, 1955),
p. 14.

[42] Epstein, *Mavo le-Nosah*, pp. 677–681.

[43] Ibid., pp. 680–681. At this point Epstein refers to preceding passages by page
numbers, but the location of some of the passages is questionable. As to the import
of the statement here, he certainly appears to be suggesting that the beraitot introduced by תניא נמי הכי in these passages were formulated according to the (anonymous) חסורי מחסרא emendations. In the body of his work, however, I have found
only the opposite position. Regarding B. Hag 2b Epstein states: "[Thus,] based
upon this Babylonian beraita the Mishnah was 'expanded' [=חסורי מחסרא] with a
strong hand" (p. 633); regarding B. Hag 7b: "[Thus] the Mishnah has been 'explained' [=חסורי מחסרא] according to the Babylonian beraita" (p. 634); and regarding
B. BQ 16a: "The חסורי מחסרא was certainly formulated here according to the beraita"

would prefer not to discount. As a result, some of scholarship's essential historical conclusions are based upon such beraitot in the Bavli.⁴⁴

This possibility of non-historical opinions ascribed to tannaim in Babylonian beraitot could have major methodological implications for the study of the tannaim. For example: authoritative histories of tannaitic literature assign passages to great antiquity because they are already quoted by early tannaim. Quite often, however, these quotations are found only in Babylonian beraitot. So regarding M. Pesahim 3.1:

אלו עוברין בפסח, כותח הבבלי, ושכר המדי, וחומץ האדומי, וזיתום המצרי, וזומן של צבעים, ועמילן של טבחים, וקולן של סופרים. רבי אליעזר אומר, אף תכשיטי נשים. זה הכלל, כל שהוא ממין דגן, הרי זה עובר בפסח. הרי אלו באזהרה, ואין בהן משום כרת.

The final clause of this Mishnah is assigned to pre-destruction times by Epstein because it is referred to and actually quoted by R. Yehoshua (B. Pesahim 43a):

תניא, אמר רבי יהושע: וכי <u>מאחר ששנינו</u> כל שהוא מין דגן הרי זה עובר בפסח למה מנו חכמים את אלו? כדי שיהא רגיל בהן ובשמותיהן.

The above-mentioned mishnah is, as it were, quoted in this beraita with the introductory formula וכי מאחר ששנינו. Hence Epstein's conclusion: "This mishnah in Pesahim is an ancient one, already mentioned by R. Yehoshua."⁴⁵ R. Yehoshua, who lived through the destruction of the Temple, is perceived here as quoting the text of a mishnah which appears in the very same form in our tractate Pesahim. Therefore it is claimed that this passage should be assigned to the earliest stratum of our Mishnah. However, the style in this beraita is too dialectic to be accepted as a genuine tannaitic statement, and even Epstein himself cast doubt regarding the quotation formula ששנינו, which is found in tannaitic statements only in Babylonian beraitot.⁴⁶ But it is not sufficient to limit the Babylonian reworking to the quotation term alone. The entire beraita, not corroborated by any tannaitic parallel, cannot serve as a proof that R. Yehoshua quotes our Mishnah and provides a dialectic explanation for its language.⁴⁷

(p. 639). Regarding the last example, Jacobs ("Fictitious Baraitot" [n. 34, above], p. 190), takes the opposite stand, that the beraita was composed according to the חסורי מחסרא, as Epstein appears to be saying on p. 681. Jacobs (ibid., n. 12) takes the same stand regarding B. Ber 13b–14a; Epstein (p. 626) follows the manuscripts which do not include the תניא נמי הכי beraita there at all.

⁴⁴ Regarding the historical credibility of the account of Yehudah ben Dortai (B. Pes 70b), see *Tosefta Atiqta,* introduction n. 273.

⁴⁵ Epstein, *Introduction to Tannaitic Literature,* pp. 24, 62, 324, 334.

⁴⁶ Idem, *Mavo le-Nosah*, p. 807: 'שנינו' מצוי כבר בברייתות — אבל ברייתות בבליות בלבד! שהן מציינות בזה ציטאט של משנה (במקום 'אמרו' הקדום): פסחים מג א: תניא א"ר יהושע וכי מאחר ששנינו (ריש פ"ג) כל שהוא מין דגן וכו' למה מנו חכמים את אלו וכו'.

⁴⁷ M. Higger questioned the authenticity of this beraita specifically because R.

Epstein uses this method regarding other passages as well. In a beraita at B. Pesahim 38b R. Ilai queries both R. Eliezer and R. Yehoshua regarding the obligation of eating matzah:

תניא: אמר רבי אילעאי, שאלתי את רבי אליעזר: מהו שיצא אדם בחלות תודה ורקיקי נזיר? אמר לי: לא שמעתי. באתי ושאלתי לפני רבי יהושע, אמר לי: <u>הרי אמרו</u> חלות תודה ורקיקי נזיר שעשאן לעצמו—אין אדם יוצא בהן, למכור בשוק—יוצא בהן. כשבאתי והרציתי דברים לפני רבי אליעזר, אמר לי: ברית, הן הן הדברים שנאמרו לו למשה בסיני.

Since the language which comes after הרי אמרו corresponds almost exactly with our Mishnah at Pesahim 2.5, Epstein concluded that this must be a Mishnah of ancient formulation, already known and quoted by R. Yehoshua. In his words: "There are mishnayot which R. Yehoshua already quoted ... This mishnah is certainly from the time of the Temple, and R. Yehoshua already referred to it (in a beraita, 38b): *they have said* 'loaves of the thank offering' (הרי אמרו חלות תודה)."[48] However, the beraita containing this quotation by R. Yehoshua is not an independent, tannaitic beraita, but a reworking of a Tosefta passage (T. Hallah 1.6, p. 276) that deals with a similar issue in a different context. There it is *first* R. Yehoshua and then R. Eliezer who are asked a question regarding the laws of *hallah* by R. Ilai:

אמ' ר' אלעאי שאלתי את ר' יהושע חלות תודה ורקיקי נזיר מה הן בחלה אמ' לי פטורות <u>וכשבאתי ושאלתי את ר' ליעזר</u> אמ' לי עשאן לעצמו פטור למכור בשוק חייב וכשבאתי והרצתי דברים לפני ר' לעזר בן עזריה אמ' לי הברית אילו דברים נאמרו מהר חורב.

It was R Eliezer's answer in T. Hallah which was used to create M. Pesahim 2.5.[49] The Babylonian beraita recast the entire encounter, introducing several changes,[50] one of which is that R. Eliezer and R. Yehoshua are switched. R. Yehoshua is now the hero of the story who knows the correct answer and gains ascendancy over R. Eliezer. Another change is that R. Yehoshua is described as quoting this law from our Mishnah, with the formula הרי אמרו.

Consequently, this beraita cannot be used as proof that the historical R. Yehoshua knew this Mishnah. A more likely reconstruction would be: 1. The law was an original composition by R. Eliezer, as the Tosefta language indicates. 2. The formulation of M. Pesahim 2.5 rests upon R. Eliezer's statement. 3. R. Yehoshua is portrayed by the Babylonian beraita as quoting this Mishnah. The availability of a Tosefta parallel in this case strengthens the line of reasoning we took in the previous example, for

---

Yehoshua appears to be quoting our Mishnah in it (*Otsar ha-Baraitot*, vol. 8 [New York, 1945], p. 14).

[48] Epstein, *Introduction to Tannaitic Literature*, pp. 24 (cf. p. 62), 334.

[49] חלות תודה ורקיקי נזיר עשאן לעצמו אין יוצאין בהן עשאן למכור בשוק יוצאין בהן.

[50] See *Tosefta Atiqta*, ch. 8.

which no parallel was available. It corroborates our position that we must be equally prepared for late editorial features in Babylonian beraitot which have no parallels.

Similarly, a statement ascribed in another beraita to Rabban Gamliel in discourse with R. Aqiva is construed by these scholars as quoting M. Pesahim 3.4: זה הכלל, תפח, תלטוש בצונן. The beraita (B. Pesahim 48b) reads:

תניא, אמר רבי עקיבא: דנתי לפני רבן גמליאל, ילמדינו רבינו בנשים זריזות או בנשים שאין זריזות? בעצים לחים או בעצים יבשים? בתנור חם או בתנור צונן? אמר לי: אין לך אלא מה ששנו חכמים, זה הכלל: תפח תלטוש בצונן.

This quote is adduced by both Albeck and Epstein as proof that M. Pesahim 3.4 was formulated in an exceptionally early period, since it is already quoted by Rabban Gamliel. Albeck writes, כלל זה הוא מזמן קדום וכבר הזכירו ר' גמליאל בברייתא שבבבלי מח, ב: אין לך אלא מה ששנו חכמים זה הכלל.[51] Many reasons can be adduced for *not* considering this beraita tannaitic, however, from considerations of style and its relationship to the Mishnah.[52] Auxiliary corroboration can perhaps be deduced from the portrayal of R. Aqiva as a self-abasing disciple of Rabban Gamliel, which is not historical, in terms of the picture presented in authentic tannaitic sources such as the following:

T. Berakhot 4.15 (pp. 21–22):

זה הכלל, כל שהוא ממין שבעה וממין דגן, רבן גמליאל או' מברך אחריו שלש ברכות. וחכמים או' ברכה אחת. מעשה ברבן גמליאל וזקנים שהיו מסובין בירייחו, הביאו לפניהם כותבות ואכלו. קפץ ר' עקיבא ברך אחריהן אחת, אמ' לו רבן גמליאל, עקיבא, למה אתה מכניס ראשך לבין המחלוקות. אמ' לו למדתנו אחרי רבים להטות, אע"פ שאתה או' כך וחביריך או' כך, הלכה כדברי המרובין.

T. Demai 5.24 (p. 93):

מעשה שנכנסו רבותינו לעיירות של כותים שעל יד הדרך, הביאו לפניהם ירק, קפץ ר' עקיבא ועשרן ודאי. אמ' לו רבן גמליאל, היאך מלאך ליבך לעבור על דברי חביריך, או מי נתן לך רשות לעשר. א' לו וכי הלכה קבעתי בישראל... רק שלי עשרתי. א' לו תדע שקבעתה הלכה בישראל, שעישרתה ירק שלך.

Historically, R. Aqiva was quite independent of Rabban Gamliel. It would be difficult to imagine him saying ילמדנו רבינו as quoted in some texts of the version of the beraita on B. Pesahim 48b, where Rabban Gamliel is made to quote the Mishnah, or otherwise presenting himself as his pupil (see n. 52).

We have seen that one of the ways that the Bavli alters beraitot which are paralleled in the Tosefta is by introducing language from the Mishnah.

---

[51] Ch. Albeck, *Shishah Sidrei Mishnah: Seder Moed,* additions (Tel Aviv, 1952), p. 447.

[52] See in detail, including the two textual versions of this beraita, *Tosefta Atiqta,* ch. 13.

Similarly, when the Bavli composes beraitot *de novo*, quotations from the Mishnah appear prominently. Consequently, it would not be correct to use these quotations placed in the mouth of tannaim as proof that the given mishnah is an ancient one, already quoted by early tannaim. Other attempts have been made to adduce evidence of ancient Mishnah material from Babylonian beraitot.[53]

In one case a surprising halakhic position ascribed to an early tanna serves as a first clue that an opinion presented in a Babylonian beraita may not be a genuine tannaitic opinion. Such is the opinion cited in the name of R. Yose Hag'lili, that benefit derived from *hametz*, other than eating it, is permitted during Passover. This position, indirectly suggested only in a Babylonian beraita, strikes a strange cord in terms of what we know about tannaitic halakhah.[54] A careful analysis of the sugya confirms this suspicion and leads to an explanation of how the beraita and its strange phrasing came into being.[55] It can no longer be credited with providing historically reliable information about halakhic opinions held in the tannaitic period.

It would appear that we can locate the literary parallel which served as the kernel for this beraita, though it does not bear the meaning which developed in the context of the Babylonian sugya:

Mekhilta, Bo, Parashah 16 (pp. 61–62)	B. Pesahim 28b

לא יאכל חמץ, לעשות את המאכיל כאוכל, או
אינו אלא לאוסרו בהנאה, כשהוא אומר לא
תאכל עליו חמץ למדנו שאסור בהנאה, הא מה
ת"ל לא יאכל חמץ, לעשות את המאכיל
כאוכל, דברי רבי יאשיה. רבי יצחק אומר
אינו צריך, ומה אם שרצים קלים עשה בהם
את המאכיל כאוכל, חמץ חמור אינו דין
שנעשה בו את המאכיל כאוכל, הא מה ת"ל

---

[53] Regarding passages which served as part of Hoffmann's original attempt to demonstrate the existence of early mishnayot, such as B. Pes 107b (Aggripas), see *Tosefta Atiqta*, introduction, and ch. 19.

[54] In contrast, R. Yose Hag'lili's position, cited elsewhere, that fowl is not included in the prohibition of Exod 23:19 is completely in keeping with tannaitic halakhah, and R. Aqiva agrees that there is no Torah prohibition of fowl with milk; R. Yishmael's pupil R. Yonatan is also in agreement (M. Hul 8.4; Mekhilta, p. 336; Sifrei Deuteronomy, p. 163; cf. Epstein, *Introduction to Tannaitic Literature*, p. 537). Furthermore, the position is quite logical in and of itself: לא תבשל גדי בחלב אמו יצא עוף שאין לו חלב אם. What was probably added by the Bavli was the conclusion that במקומו של רבי יוסי הגלילי היו אוכלין בשר עוף בחלב (B. Shab 130a, Yev 14a, Hul 116a). See *Talmud Arukh*, Text Volume, p. 17 n. 66.

[55] See *Tosefta Atiqta*, Pesah Rishon, chapter 7 additional note.

לא יאכל חמץ, לא בא הכתוב אלא לאסרו
בהנאה. רבי יוסי הגלילי אומר לא יאכל חמץ
היום, מגיד שלא אכלו ישראל מצה במצרים
אלא יום אחד בלבד.

רבי יוסי הגלילי או' ותמה על עצמך היאך
חמץ אסור בהנאה כל שבעה...

רבי יוסי הגלילי אומר: מנין לפסח מצרים שאין
חימוצו נוהג אלא יום אחד תלמוד לומר לא
יאכל חמץ וסמיך ליה היום אתם יצאים.

In the Mekhilta R. Yose Hag'lili's statement follows a discussion of the prohibition of benefit derived from *hametz*, but addresses another issue, the eating of matzah in Egypt one day only. This passage provides us with the earliest available example of this juxtaposition, in which the third-generation tanna R. Yose Hag'lili is not yet conceived as disagreeing with the law discussed in the preceding lines (by tannaim of the fourth generation!). He is simply recorded as assigning a different *derasha* to one of the verses—not enough in the tannaitic midrashim to establish rejection of the law which another (later) sage derived from this verse. The Bavli's (re)wording upgrades the statement by suggesting a direct (and opposite) halakhic position in the form of a dialectic challenge: תמה על עצמך היאך חמץ אסור בהנאה כל שבעה. In the context of the sugya this challenge is directed at sages of a later generation, R. Yehudah and R. Shimon, further indication that the context is not original. Higger, Epstein and Halivni have already described the artificial nature of the combination of various beraitot and late compositions in this sugya. We have taken their thinking one step further by viewing the statement attributed to R. Yose Hag'lili as a development of the original Mekhilta context.[56]

We can now round out and summarize as follows:

1. The prohibition of eating *hametz* is found several times in the Torah. In the Mekhilta we find R. Yose Hag'lili explicating Exodus 13:3–4, one of the superfluous verses (לא יאכל חמץ—היום), to mean that for the first Passover in Egypt *hametz* was prohibited for one day only.

2. Tannaim younger that R. Yose Hag'lili (R. Yoshiah and R. Yitzhak) are quoted in the Mekhilta, each of whom derives other laws from this verse—R. Yoshiah: feeding *hametz* to others; and R. Yitzhak: the prohibition of deriving benefit from *hametz*.

3. The passage in no way suggests that R. Yose Hag'lili permitted the

---

[56] See in detail *Tosefta Atiqta* (ibid.).

derivation of benefit from *hametz*. However, the fact that he interprets the verse differently from R. Yitzhak eventually led to such a conclusion.

4. According to an early amoraic tradition (R. Abbahu) found in Yerushalmi and Bavli parallels at the beginning of Pesahim chapter 2, biblical prohibitions against eating something automatically include a prohibition against deriving other benefit, unless and until an explicit verse indicates that benefit is permitted.[57] R. Yose Hag'lili's position in the Mekhilta passage does nothing to challenge this view.

5. The Mekhilta passage, containing the opinions of R. Yoshiah and R. Yitzhak, is quoted in the Yerushalmi sugya without, however, including R. Yose Hag'lili at all. It would appear that the Yerushalmi did not consider R. Yose Hag'lili's Mekhilta statement as germane at all to the issue of benefit derived from *hametz*.[58]

6. The Bavli contains no specific passage in which R. Yose Hag'lili permits benefit derived from *hametz*. The anonymous sugya at B. Pesahim 28b takes Exodus 13:3 as necessary for deriving the full prohibition of *hametz*, and also contains R. Yose Hag'lili's statement from the Mekhilta about the Egyptian Passover. The additional dialectic argument (ר' יוסי הגלילי או' ותמה על עצמך היאך חמץ אסור בהנאה כל שבעה) was probably ascribed to him because he made different use of that verse.

7. R. Yose Hag'lili would hardly have addressed such an argument to sages of the generation which followed him (R. Yoshiah and R. Yitzhak), and certainly not to sages of the generation after that (R. Yehudah and R. Shimon), whom he appears to address in a highly composite passage in the Bavli.

8. The anonymous sugya of the Bavli (Pesahim 32b), in line with the sugya at 28a–29a, assigned to R. Yose Hag'lili an absolute position that deriving benefit is permitted: כרבי יוסי הגלילי דאמר חמץ בפסח מותר בהנאה. This formulation (דאמר) is a clear indication that the opinion is a post-tannaitic extension or generalization, and in this case not a tannaitic quote at all.[59]

9. Were R. Yose Hag'lili's position permitting benefit derived from *ha-*

---

[57] R. Abbahu in the name of R. Elazar (Y. Pes 2.1 28c = Y. Orlah 3.1 62d ; B. Pes 21b and parallels). Hizkiah disagrees in both places. In the Yerushalmi, Hizkiah's question follows R. Abbahu. In the Bavli it is made to precede, and only in the Bavli does it specifically touch upon the laws of *hametz*.

[58] Furthermore, the Yerushalmi takes R. Yoshiah as a support for R. Abbahu and R. Yitzhak as a support for Hizkiah, while ascribing to both of them the clear stand that benefit from *hametz* is prohibited. R. Yitzhak requires the additional (*Nifal*) prohibition of Exod 13:3, while the general prohibition of eating *hametz* is sufficient for R. Yoshiah to prohibit the derivation of benefit also. R. Yose Hag'lili would certainly be categorized with R. Yoshiah.

[59] Cf. also רבי מאיר דאמר עדי חתימה כרתי רבי אלעזר דאמר עדי מסירה כרתי. See S. Friedman, *Talmud Arukh*, Text Volume, pp. 436–438 and literature quoted there.

metz already enunciated in historical, tannaitic sources, its complete omission from all Palestinian sources would be more than astounding, in light of the extended discussions of this prohibition in all of them.

In another case (B. Gittin 83b) the use of Babylonian Aramaic[60] within the beraita attributed to R. Yehoshua serves as the first clue that this may not be an authentic tannaitic statement. Assuming that the beraita is comprised only of the short text that precedes the Aramaic is inadequate stylistically. Actually this beraita is a re-adaptation of a *memra* of Rava's (B. Nedarim 70a–b).

B. Nedarim 70a–b	B. Gittin 83b
אמר רבא, דאמר קרא: ואם היו תהיה לאיש לקודמי הויה ראשונה, מקיש שניה לקודמי ונדריה עליה, מקיש שניה לקודמי הויה ראשונה, מה קודמי הויה ראשונה אב מיפר לחודיה, אף קודמי הויה שניה אב מיפר לחודיה.	תניא, א״ר יהושע: מקיש קודמי הויה שניה לקודמי הויה ראשונה, מה קודמי הויה ראשונה דלא אגידא באיניש אחרינא, אף קודמי הויה שניה דלא אגידא באיניש אחרינא.

In its original context the *heqesh* is a classical one—referring to two adjacent biblical words—and the reference to two *havayot* is transparent.[61] Furthermore, in context of the issue being discussed, it would be extremely surprising not to find any Palestinian parallel to R. Yehoshua's statement.

* * *

I would like to close with the famous beraita describing the history of the Hanukkah lights (B. Shabbat 21b):

תנו רבנן: מצות חנוכה נר איש וביתו. והמהדרין – נר לכל אחד ואחד. והמהדרין מן המהדרין, בית שמאי אומרים: יום ראשון מדליק שמנה, מכאן ואילך פוחת והולך ובית הלל אומרים: יום ראשון מדליק אחת, מכאן ואילך מוסיף והולך.

This beraita proclaims that the basic commandment is one light for each household; for the punctilious, one light for each person; for the most punctilious, the house of Shammai says that eight lights are lit on the first night and the number is progressively reduced to one over the course of the eight days of the festival, and the house of Hillel says that one light is lit on the first night, and the number is progressively increased to eight.

It would be difficult to consider this beraita in its present form an authentic tannaitic passage in its entirety,[62] providing the opinions of the house

---

[60] And not even Second Temple Aramaic as in M. Eduy 8.4, M. Avot 4.5, and T. Eruv 8.23 (p. 138) (R. Yehoshua!).

[61] See Rashi's attempt to address the difficulties of the Gittin passage on B. Git 83b, s.v. מקיש and s.v. לקודמי.

[62] See L. Ginzberg, *A Commentary on the Palestinian Talmud* (Hebrew; New York, 1941–1961), vol. 1, p. 279 n. 33; J. Tabory, *Jewish Festivals in the Time of the Mishnah and Talmud* (Hebrew; Jerusalem, 1995), p. 377.

of Shammai and the house of Hillel for the law of the most punctilious worshipers. At most the original form of this beraita could be taken to begin with the opinions of the house of Shammai and the house of Hillel, presenting the basic law as it should apply to everyone, eight lights down to one, or one light up to eight. The schematic evolution in the introduction, claiming that the original practice was one light only for each day, and that the house of Shammai and the house of Hillel were addressing only the most punctilious, is a Babylonian composition. This theory can be buttressed by a linguistic investigation of the phrase המהדרין מן המהדרין (the most punctilious).

Ben Yehuda lists this phrase under the root הדר, meaning "beauty."[63] In the *Piel* conjugation he lists a special sub-entry: "מהדר בדבר, משתדל לעשות הדבר ביופי, בהדור, בכל פרטיו ודקדוקיו," namely, punctilious observance. Our beraita is the only talmudic example adduced by Ben Yehuda for this sub-entry, and indeed no other exists throughout the entire range of tannaitic Hebrew.[64] It would therefore be best not to regard this word as authentic tannaitic Hebrew, but as a Babylonian coinage reflecting the Aramaic מהדר or מהדר בתר-א, which corresponds exactly to the meaning required in this passage. Here we will quote a nearby occurrence (B. Shabbat 23a), which is but one of many:

אמר רבי יהושע בן לוי: כל השמנים כולן יפין לנר, ושמן זית מן המובחר. אמר אביי: מריש הוה מהדר מר אמשחא דשומשמי, אמר: האי משך נהורי טפי. כיון דשמע לה להא דרבי יהושע בן לוי מהדר אמשחא דזיתא, אמר: האי צליל נהוריה טפי.

> Abbaye said: "Originally my master used to go out of his way to get sesame oil for the Sabbath lights ... now that he has heard R. Yehoshua ben Levi's statement in favor of olive oil, he goes out of his way to get olive oil."

The phrase מהדר א-, (which we have translated "go out of his way"), frequent in Babylonian Aramaic and equivalent to the Hebrew מחזר אחרי, is the source of המהדרין, and not הדר, meaning "beautiful," as found in the dictionaries.

Clearly המהדרין in our beraita is a calque of the Babylonian Aramaic usage in the sense of striving to fulfill a commandment in the best way.[65] The root הדר never has this meaning in authentic tannaitic sources, and it can

---

[63] E. Ben Yehuda, *A Complete Dictionary of Ancient and Modern Hebrew* (Jerusalem, 1980), p. 1046f. The Arukh too lists this phrase under the root הדר: see *Aruch Completum*, vol. 3, p. 186. Kohut defined the entry: ענינו ידוע מל״מ הדר, פר׳ תת כבוד ויקר לזולתו. Cf. R. Hananel on B. Shab 21b, s.v. ח״ר (ed. Metzger, p. 28): פי׳ המהדרין, מהדרי מצות, כדאמרינן ולהדור מצוה עד שליש במצוה. See below.

[64] I have dealt elsewhere with adjacent issues of הדר in the *Piel*.

[65] Cf. Rashi on B. Shab 21b: והמהדרין—אחר המצוה. Compare Rashi on B. Hul 139b, s.v. ה״ג: לפי שנאמר שלח תשלח ב׳ פעמים, שומע אני לחזור אחר המצוה הזאת עד שתבא לידו.

only be understood here as a Babylonian creation of pseudo-tannaitic Hebrew, under the influence of the Babylonian Aramaic dialect. This passage can therefore no longer serve as a source or proof that the original practice before the destruction of the Temple was to light one flame only on Hanukkah,[66] since at least the historical introduction to the beraita must be viewed as a Babylonian construction. Its purpose may have been to harmonize the description here of many Hanukkah lights with the fact that the Hanukkah light is usually mentioned in the singular.[67]

As for the phrase הידור מצוה in B. Bava Qamma 9b, even though it is usually ascribed to R. Zera, it is actually a coinage of the anonymous talmudic authors in their rewording of R. Zera's statement.[68] From context, it is clear that הידור מצוה means "beautifying the מצוה," and is not directly associated with המהדרין מן המהדרין.[69]

---

[66] J. Goldstein, *I Maccabees* (Garden City, 1976), p. 282.

[67] Especially in M. BQ 6.6, T. BQ 6.28 (p. 27), and B. Shab 21b–23b. The introduction is thus a sugya-like dialectic element such as found also in the Mishnah, e.g. M. Ber 1.1 (כל מה שאמרו חכמים עד חצות מצותן עד שיעלה עמוד השחר), which mediates between two tannaitic opinions (see *Tosefta Atiqta*, ch. 22), or M. Pes 1.1 ולמה אמרו שתי שורות) במרתף), which provides a dialectic leading to the inclusion of an older quote (ibid., ch. 2).

[68] Cf. *Yalkut Shimoni, Beshalah*, par. 245: תניא זה אלי ואנוהו התנאה לפניו במצות עשה לך ספר תורה נאה וכו', א"ר זירא הדור מצוה עד שליש במצוה. In the B. BQ 9a–b passage (already associated with המהדרין by R. Hananel [see n. 64, above]): א"ר זירא אמר רב הונא: במצוה — עד שליש. מאי שליש אילימא שליש ביתו, אלא מעתה, אי איתרמי ליה תלתא מצותא, ליתיב לכוליה ביתא? אלא אמר ר' זירא: בהידור מצוה — עד שליש במצוה. The phrase אלא א"ר פלוני following said rabbi's first statement is commonly the language of the anonymous editor of the Bavli. On rewording in the Bavli with אלא + name of amora, see S. Friedman, "A Critical Study of Yevamot X with a Methodological Introduction," *Texts and Studies, Analecta Judaica* (ed. H. Z. Dimitrovsky) 1 (1977), pp. 275–441, at p. 88 n. 62; A. Steinfeld, "On the Meaning of 'He Made the Decision Alone' and 'He Made the Decision Together with the Congregation,'" *Sidra* 9 (1993), p. 387 n. 7. That this phrase was authored by the anonymous editor is confirmed here by the reading of the Hamburg manuscript, אלא אימא הידור מצוה עד שליש, rather than אלא אמר ר' זירא, and similarly in MS Vat. 116: אלא אי (צ"ל: אי') הידור מצוה.

[69] Cf. R. Hananel on B. BQ 9a, s.v. זירא ר' אמר: אם נזדמן פי', במצוה שליש עד מצוה להידור לו לולב בכסף ולולב אחר מהודר בכסף וחצי יש עליך להוסיף שליש בדמיו ולהתנאות במצוה בלולב נאה; Y. Peah 1.1 15b: רב הונא אמר למצוה עד שליש מהו לכל המצות או שליש למצוה אחת סברין מימר לכל המצות עד שליש רבי אבון אמר אפילו למצוה אחת רב חביבא בשם רבנן דתמן מהו שליש לדמים היך עבידא לקח אדם מצוה וראה אחרת נאה הימנה עד כמה מטריחין עליו עד שליש תני רבי ישמעאל זה אלי ואנוהו וכי איפשר לו לאדם לנוות את בוראו אלא אנווה לפניו במצות אעשה לפניו לולב נאה דלא בעינן זה אלי ואנוהו; Rashi on B. Shab 133b: — סוכה נאה שופר נאה ציצית נאה תפילין נאין; and Rashi on Pes 99b: כדי שיאכל — לא יאכל דאחר נטילת האיסורין אין הידור מצוה ביפוי בשר מצה של מצוה לתיאבון משום הידור מצוה.

Conclusion

The model of the edited parallel provides a more realistic concept for talmudic literature than the model of independent parallels. Careful philological treatment, enhanced by greater access than ever available before to manuscript versions, encourages us in the judicious application of the model of editorial development in assessing synoptic parallels.

In this paper we have mentioned synoptic comparison of Mishnah and Tosefta, and have dealt with Babylonian beraitot paralleling the Tosefta, and beraitot occurring only in the Bavli. Elsewhere we have applied this model in additional areas: in lower-critical issues, explaining two text types found in many of the tractates of the Bavli, one conservative and one editorially creative;[70] in expanding awareness of the Erfurt manuscript of the Tosefta as an editorially creative text, building upon Lieberman's conclusions;[71] regarding dicta of the amoraim appearing in both Talmudim, where the Yerushalmi preserves a more original text of early Babylonian statements, and the Bavli creatively reworks them.[72]

The model of independent parallels was already used by the *geonim*, albeit apologetically, in order to combat the challenge presented by the existence of variant forms.[73] Regnant scholarship has exhibited a fascination with this idea. Under its influence a textual tradition of the Mishnah in Babylonia was posited, which was said to stand on equal footing with the Palestinian Mishnah.[74] This approach also accepted the Babylonian beraita as sometimes superior to its Palestinian tannaitic counterpart, and at other times gave unbridled authority to unique Babylonian beraitot as authentic representations of tannaitic statements and opinions, or was open to accepting the Erfurt manuscript's creative editing as authentic Tosefta, over the Vienna manuscript/printed edition family. The pervasiveness of the evolutionary process as perceived in the editorial model will also aid in

---

[70] Friedman, "On the Origin" (n. 15, above).

[71] *Tosefta Atiqta*, introduction. Lieberman furthered the development of the model of editorial treatment in his description of the doctored nature of the Erfurt manuscript of the Tosefta, which he likened to *tiqqune soferim*. At the same time, however, he continued to treat some of the Erfurt readings as independent traditions, and recognized in them the original Tosefta even when they could equally fit the evolutionary pattern. (In this connection, see S. Lieberman, *Tosefeth Rishonim* [Jerusalem, 1937–1939], vol. 4, pp. 12–13.) Compare, e.g., *Tosefta Ki-fshuta*, Nashim, p. 186 ll. 3–4; S. Friedman, "Variant Readings in the Babylonian Talmud—A Methodological Study Marking the Appearance of 13 Volumes of the Institute for the Complete Israeli Talmud's Edition," *Tarbiz* 68 (1998), p. 154 n. 96.

[72] *Talmud Arukh*, Text Volume, pp. 9–13.

[73] See "On the Origin" (n. 15, above), p. 99 and notes.

[74] See *Talmud Arukh*, Text Volume, p. 88 n. 104, and H. Fox cited there.

clarifying linguistic issues, where tracking development can go far beyond simply recording different traditions.[75] Spelling out the general relationship between the component works of the talmudic corpus, and modes of literary evolution discernible in synoptic parallels, will lead to the identification of institutional and conceptual evolution and development.[76]

---

[75] In other words, "good" representative manuscripts give only a partial and sometimes idealized picture. See Friedman, "Variant Readings" (n. 71, above), p. 150.

[76] See "Historical Aggadah" (n. 10, above).

BAVLI AND YERUSHALMI, THEMATIC STUDIES

Chapter 4

Halakhah le-Moshe mi-Sinai in Rabbinic Sources: A Methodological Case Study

Christine Hayes
Yale University

Introduction

In this paper I examine the use and meaning of the term *halakhah le-Moshe mi-Sinai* ("a law to Moses at Sinai") in the Mishnah, Tosefta, and Palestinian and Babylonian Talmudim (Yerushalmi and Bavli) in order to explore certain methodological issues currently debated in talmudic scholarship. Specifically, I argue that source critical and synchronic approaches to the study of talmudic texts need not be mutually exclusive; indeed, there is much to be gained from a judicious combination of the two.

The most recent work of Jacob Neusner[1] can be characterized as synchronic due to its assumption that individual rabbinic documents (Mish-

---

[1] Jacob Neusner, *Judaism: The Evidence of the Mishnah* (Chicago: University of Chicago Press, 1981); *Judaism in Society: The Evidence of the Yerushalmi* (Chicago: University of Chicago Press, 1983); *Judaism, The Classical Statement: The Evidence of the Bavli* (Chicago: University of Chicago Press, 1986); *Judaism and Scripture: The Evidence of Leviticus Rabbah* (Chicago: University of Chicago Press, 1986); *The Canonical History of Ideas: The Place of the So-Called Tannaite Midrashim: Mekhilta Attributed to R. Ishmael, Sifra, Sifre to Numbers and Sifre to Deuteronomy* (Atlanta: Scholars Press, 1990); *The Judaism Behind the Texts: The Generative Premises of Rabbinic Literature* (South Florida Studies in the History of Judaism [SFSHJ]; Atlanta: Scholars Press, 1993–94); *The Documentary Foundation of Rabbinic Culture: Mopping Up after Debates with Gerald L. Bruns, S. J. D. Cohen, Arnold Maria Goldberg, Susan Handelman, Christine Hayes, James Kugel, Peter Schaefer, Eliezer Segal, E. P. Sanders and Lawrence Schiffman* (SFSHJ 113; Atlanta: Scholars Press, 1995). See also Neusner, *Documentary Foundation*, xxii–xxv for an exhaustive list of works exemplifying the documentary method.

nah, Tosefta, Yerushalmi and Bavli) constitute wholes that should be studied independently. Although Neusner acknowledges the existence of diverse sources within the talmudic text,[2] he focuses on the level of the complete redacted work as the primary level about which positivistic statements can be made. My critique of this synchronic, or documentary, approach focuses on two of its main assumptions. First, the synchronic scholar maintains that the diverse source materials of the Talmud were so thoroughly reworked and recontextualized by the talmudic redactors as to neutralize their ability to provide information about the circles in which they originated—a claim that clearly has implications for our ability to use these texts for the purposes of historical or cultural reconstruction. Second, the synchronic scholar speaks of each rabbinic work, including the Talmudim, as a single unit, as though each were produced by a single (though corporate) authorship, giving testimony to a single community. In short, each rabbinic work is considered at the redacted level to be an authored text, shaped according to the ideology or philosophy of the final authors or redactors and bearing witness to the ideology of the period of redaction alone.

But, we may ask, do rabbinic documents in fact constitute integral wholes exhibiting the kind of editorial or thematic unity that Neusner proposes? The claim has a strong intuitive appeal, but is it borne out by the evidence? Does it make sense to privilege the period of the text's redaction as the only period "represented" by the text and thus the only period whose history is retrievable from it? In my recent book, I argued that such an approach ignores textual details that signal the texts' susceptibility to source critical analysis (and thus historical analysis) and employs models of authorship and redaction that are inappropriate for rabbinic texts or irrelevant for those engaged in historical study.[3]

Rabbinic documents signal their compositional complexity in many ways.[4] In a recent book, Richard Kalmin concluded that "the Bavli attests to a variety of rhetorical, terminological, institutional and attitudinal differences between early and later, Palestinian and Babylonian, and attributed and anonymous sources."[5] Kalmin argues persuasively that the presence of these differences attests to the existence of diverse sources within the talmudic text and a lack of editorial homogenization.[6] Similarly,

---

[2] *Documentary Foundation*, 28–37.

[3] See Christine Hayes, *Between the Babylonian and Palestinian Talmuds: Accounting for Halakhic Difference in Selected Sugyot from Tractate Avodah Zarah* (New York: Oxford University Press, 1997).

[4] See ibid., 11–13.

[5] Richard Kalmin, *Sages, Stories, Authors, and Editors in Rabbinic Babylonia* (BJS 300; Atlanta: Scholars Press, 1994), 11.

[6] Kalmin's case studies support his claim "that the Talmud preserves identifiable sources which were not fully homogenized by later editors, and contains

David Goodblatt's study of rabbinic instruction in Babylonia reveals that third-century and fourth- to fifth-century sages do not mention the same academic institutions. Goodblatt argues convincingly that the most likely explanation is that the terminology of the third-century sources has been accurately preserved, and that, generally speaking, the language of earlier amoraic generations has not been homogenized by the Bavli's editors.[7] Such evidence of chronological and geographical complexity calls into question the suitability of an exclusively or primarily synchronic approach to rabbinic literature. Indeed, source critical analysis of rabbinic texts would appear to be not precluded but mandated by the very nature of those texts.

The designation of the redactors/editors of various rabbinic documents as authors—a feature of the synchronic, or documentarian, approach—is also subject to question. Comparing rabbinic redactors to authors obscures the important differences between their respective activities, for it suggests a creative autonomy. In fact, the redactors of rabbinic texts were not creating texts *ex nihilo*, but were shaping and weaving an enormous corpus of inherited traditional materials. Of course they exercised freedom in recombining, recontextualizing, glossing and otherwise manipulating earlier traditions.[8] However, they were also constrained by the raw materials they received, by the agenda set in earlier combinations and contextualizations of traditions, by the community within which they worked and even by the genre of the work being produced. Furthermore, it must not be assumed that a reworked text loses its historical usefulness. As Richard Kalmin has argued, a set of sources may be heavily reworked, paraphrased and embellished and yet still faithfully convey historical information about, for example, the ideology or attitudes of an earlier period, while something only slightly reworked may in fact be less faithful.[9] It is only with the aid of

---

usable historical information regarding the centuries prior to its final editing" (ibid., xiii).

[7] David Goodblatt, "Towards the Rehabilitation of Talmudic History" in *History of Judaism: The Next Ten Years*, ed. Baruch M. Bokser (BJS 21; Chico, Calif.: Scholars Press, 1980), 31–44.

[8] See Shamma Friedman's discussion of the anonymous redactor's treatment of earlier source materials in "A Critical Study of Yevamot X with a Methodological Introduction" (Hebrew), *Texts and Studies, Analecta Judaica* (ed. H. Z. Dimitrovsky) 1 (1977): 275–441, esp. 288–301. See further Friedman, *Talmud Arukh: Bavli Bava Mezi'a VI* (New York: Jewish Theological Seminary of America, 1990), 1:7–23 for a discussion of the recombination and manipulation of source materials by the stam of the Talmud.

[9] Kalmin, *Sages*, chapter 3. Kalmin examines a passage from the Bavli in which several traditions paralleled in Palestinian sources concerning a Palestinian tanna

comparative study that we can assess the degree to which redaction has or has not affected the historical usefulness of its source materials.

Finally, the notion that each rabbinic document is a single unit authored by a single "authorship" entails the notion that each text has a unitary ideology which can be discerned through analysis. In several works, Neusner strives to discern the specific ideology or agenda of various rabbinic texts, the philosophy expressed by the redactional program of each document. However, this documentarian project is dependent upon a specific notion of what it is to be an editor or redactor, a notion that may not be appropriate for rabbinic texts. Neusner assumes that redaction entails the imposition of a uniform ideology upon a text's source materials. But there is no *prima facie* reason to accept such a definition and in the case of rabbinic literature it would appear that a different notion of editing/redaction is operative. In rabbinic literature we simply do not see a uniform and universal homogenization of earlier sources or a consistent attempt to replace the polyphony of the sources with the univocality of a single authorship.[10] We can only conclude that rabbinic notions of the role of a redactor or editor are different from those proposed by contemporary documentarians. Rabbinic editors were apparently concerned to preserve, not obliterate, distinctive layers within the text, to preserve heterogeneity.[11] A synchronic approach that ignores that heterogeneity and eschews source critical anal-

---

are woven together into a single narrative unit. The traditions are clearly heavily reworked and edited (see ibid., 64 for details), yet the basic portrait of a Palestinian dream interpreter as interpreting the symbolic dreams of non-rabbis is consistent with the portrait of dream interpreters found in the Yerushalmi and in Palestinian midrashic literature (and not with that found in materials of Babylonian origin). Thus, the editorial reworking of earlier material does not necessarily destroy the latter's historical usefulness.

[10] This is not to say that individual sugyot do not feature editorial shaping that is at times ideologically transparent. Shamma Friedman's analyses of sugyot from Yevamot and Bava Metzia (see the works cited in n. 8, above) identify the ideological interventions of the stammaitic layer of the Bavli. Nevertheless, such interventions do not necessarily entail homogenization, or the complete eclipse of an earlier polyphony; nor is it a universal or consistently pursued editorial practice. Further, I am not persuaded by Neusner's distinction between the "superficial contentiousness" of rabbinic documents and the deeper consensus it masks. In any event, the historian is concerned not with the "philosophical consensus" Neusner claims to discover within the text, but with the "superficial contentiousness" of the text, because it is precisely there that cultural and historical information will be found. Thus, the documentarian notion of "authorship" may be said to be not only inappropriate for rabbinic texts but irrelevant to the pursuits of the historian.

[11] Of course, often they do not. There are places where we can see a homogenizing trend, but this is by no means the overriding feature of talmudic redaction. Each case must be judged on its own merits.

ysis and historical reconstruction is reductionist. Despite the fact that source materials are subject to some process of redaction, several linguistic and literary features of rabbinic literature render implausible the notion of authored, synchronically leveled texts. These features indicate that some relatively reliable source critical and, ultimately, cultural-historical analysis of rabbinic texts beyond the level of redaction is possible.

Nevertheless, it is true that the composition and redaction of rabbinic works form an important determinant of each work's substance so that a work can be said to be more than the sum of its sources; and it is also true that the traditional sources are shaped by literary, rhetorical, and other concerns. These claims are supported by numerous comparative studies that examine what various rabbinic documents do differently with the material that is common to them. Different treatments (indeed, even similar treatments) of shared source materials (whether a mishnah, a beraita or a midrashic unit) or a shared term or legal concept can tell us something about the groups or communities that produced the documents being compared. The information gleaned may be linguistic, exegetical, cultural, or ideological.

We are left with one ineluctable and seemingly paradoxical conclusion. On the one hand, rabbinic texts are comprised of a variety of identifiable sources. On the other hand they are redacted works that exhibit editorial features. In some sense, then, they are integral wholes—even if rabbinic models of redaction and editing do not entail the kind of editorial or thematic unity advanced by modern-day documentarians. The nature of rabbinic documents *as redacted works that at times efface and at time preserve the heterogeneity of their source materials* justifies the judicious combination of both synchronic and source critical approaches in talmudic studies. The following study of the term *halakhah le-Moshe mi-Sinai* (henceforth HLMM) in the Mishnah, Tosefta, Yerushalmi and Bavli is intended to demonstrate the advantages of just such a combined approach.

In the first part of this study I will demonstrate the usefulness of a source critical approach by analyzing the use and conception of the term HLMM in the various sources contained in the Mishnah, Tosefta, Yerushalmi and Bavli. Within each rabbinic document we will observe distinctions between early and late, Palestinian and Babylonian, and attributed and anonymous sources. These chronological and geographical distinctions reinforce the claim that redactional homogenization in rabbinic literature is less than is sometimes claimed.

In the second part of this study I will demonstrate the usefulness of a synchronic approach by comparing the respective uses and conceptions of the term HLMM in each Talmud taken as a redacted whole. Our characterization of each document's use and conception of the term HLMM will be necessarily complex because of the diverse sources comprising these documents. Nevertheless, some distinctions between the two Talmudim, when characterized as wholes, indicate a shift in the use and meaning of the term HLMM between the two documents and, by extension, the two communities of scholars that produced these documents.

It is to be hoped that attention to the tandem operation of source critical (chronological and geographical) and synchronic factors in the composition of rabbinic texts, will lend greater precision and reliability to our historical conclusions. Source critical and synchronic approaches to rabbinic texts need not be viewed as mutually exclusive, but can operate simultaneously to unearth the full range of cultural, historical, and ideological data available within these texts.

* * *

The term HLMM is generally defined in a manner that reflects its post-talmudic usage. In the post-talmudic period, it became standard to view certain terms as equivalent to, and therefore designating, HLMM: e.g., *gemir, hilkheta, hilkheta gemiri lah, gemara gemiri lah, halakhah, halakhot* and *neemeru le-Moshe ba-Sinai* (some of these will be discussed below). As a consequence, the conception of HLMM that emerged in this period was based on a consideration of all passages in the classical sources that contained any of these terms, and was defined as a law given to Moses at Sinai that cannot be derived from Scripture, but can be traced through a line of transmission back to Moses who received it directly from God. HLMM and Torah law are mutually exclusive categories, so that verses adduced for a HLMM must be viewed as mere *asmakhtaot*. A HLMM requires no logical justification (*taam*), and there is a strong tendency to view HLMM as authoritative and not subject to dispute. Deviations from these general principles that may appear in the classical sources are generally dismissed as metaphorical rather than literal uses of the term HLMM. Halakhic commentators are divided on the question of a HLMM's authority (as equal to Torah law, rabbinic law or *sui generis*). Not all HLMMs were preserved; some were forgotten and, of these, some were later reestablished by rabbinic courts.[12]

The post-talmudic use and conception of the term HLMM just described does not correspond in every respect to the use and conception of the term in classical rabbinic literature. The assumption that terms such as *gemir, hilkheta, hilkheta gemiri lah, gemara gemiri lah, halakhah, halakhot* and *neemeru le-Moshe ba-Sinai* are equivalent to the term HLMM in classical rabbinic sources and the retrojection of post-talmudic definitions of a HLMM

---

[12] This synopsis is drawn from the *Entsiklopedyah Talmudit*, s.v. הלכה למשה מסיני, ed. M. Berlin and Sh. Zevin (Jerusalem: Hotsaat Entsiklopedyah Talmudit, 1947–2000), 9:365–387.

Halakhah le-Moshe mi-Sinai *in Rabbinic Sources* 67

are obstacles in the way of an objective evaluation of these sources. The present study is confined to an examination of passages in Mishnah, Tosefta, Yerushalmi and Bavli that explicitly employ the term HLMM (the phrase *neemeru le-Moshe ba-Sinai* will be considered separately; see below, pp. 111–114) and proceeds inductively to a general characterization of HLMM with an eye to chronological and geographical difference within texts and synchronic differences across texts. We begin with Mishnah and Tosefta before turning to the two Talmudim.

* * *

The term HLMM occurs in only three mishnaic texts: M. Peah 2.6, M. Yadayim 4.3 (|| T. Yadayim 2.7) and M. Eduyyot 8.7.[13] These three sources exhibit important similarities and differences in their use of the term HLMM.

---

[13] The term HLMM appears in tannaitic midrash only once—Sifra Tsav 11.6 (Weiss ed., 34d–35a). The passage is cited in B. Men 89a and B. Nid 72b and will be discussed below. In "Reflections on Classical Jewish Hermeneutics," *PAAJR* 62 (1996): 21–127, David Weiss Halivni points out that in contrast to the amoraim (particularly in Palestine), the tannaim make almost no use of the concept of HLMM (51). He adduces examples of laws described by amoraim as HLMM but derived exegetically by tannaim. For example, in Y. Shev 1.7 33b || Y. Suk 4.1 54b the amora R. Yohanan asserts that the willow and water libation rites are HLMM, although the tanna Abba Shaul provides a biblical derivation for the first, and the tanna R. Akiva provides a biblical derivation for the second; in B. MQ 3a R. Yohanan states that the law of the ten saplings (discussed below) is a HLMM while R. Akiva derives it from Scripture. See further B. Yoma 80a. But note the exception in Y. Meg 1.11 71d; Halivni, op. cit., p. 61).

Shmuel Safrai, "Halakhah le-Moshe mi-Sinai: Historyah o Teologyah?" in *Mehqerei Talmud*, ed. Y. Sussman and D. Rozental (Jerusalem: Magnes, 1993), 1:11–38, attributes the scarcity of HLMM in tannaitic literature to genre. The halakhic midrashim are by definition concerned with the derivation of law from Scripture (11) and thus it is not surprising that there is only one reference to HLMM in this entire corpus. Likewise, one could argue that the Mishnah is in general not concerned with the source (whether biblical, rabbinic, or HLMM) of its rulings. Halivni, however, explains the scarcity of the term HLMM in tannaitic sources as part of the trend away from reliance on oral tradition and towards exegesis in the tannaitic period, and the increased use of the term in amoraic sources as part of the subsequent shift away from exegesis. According to Halivni, pre-tannaitic religious authority relied on oral tradition to overcome the imperfections and discrepancies in Scripture that were the result of its composite nature. Tannaitic authorities later abandoned this reliance on oral tradition in favor of exegetical solutions ("Reflections," 89); with the canonization of Scripture, theological notions of the latter's perfect and all-encompassing nature developed, with the result that laws taught purely as oral instruction given to Moses at Sinai were derived exegetically from the Scriptural text (49). Exegetes maintained that Scripture itself could yield all that

M. Peah 2.6

מעשה שזרע ר' שמעון איש המצפה לפני רבן גמליאל ועלו ללשכת הגזית ושאלו
אמר נחום הלבלר מקובל אני מרבי מיאשא שקבל מאבא
שקבל מן הזוגות שקבלו מן הנביאים הלכה למשה מסיני
בזורע את שדהו שני מיני חטין
אם עשאן גורן אחת נותן פאה אחת שתי גרנות נותן שתי פאות

[2.5 He who sows his field with one kind of seed, though he makes up of it two threshing-floors, need give only one *peah*. If he sows it of two kinds, then even if he makes up of it only one threshing-floor, he must give two *peot*. He who sows his field with two species of wheat and makes up of it one threshing-floor, gives one *peah*; but if two threshing-floors, he gives two *peot*.]

2.6 It once happened that R. Simeon of Mizpah sowed [his field with two species of wheat and the case came] before Rabban Gamliel. They went up to the Chamber of Hewn Stone and inquired [as to the law]. Nahum the Scribe said: "I have received a tradition from R. Measa, who received it from Abba, who received it from the Pairs, who received it from the prophets, a *halakhah le-Moshe mi-Sinai* that a man who sows his field with two species of wheat and makes up of it one threshing-floor, gives only one *peah*, but if two threshing-floors, he gives two *peot*." [=2.5]

M. Peah 2.5 contains a tripartite law concerning the obligation of *peah*. A field sown with one kind of seed requires one *peah*, with two kinds of seed requires two *peot*—regardless of the number of threshing-floors (i.e., quantity of grain produced). The third clause constitutes an exception to the general principle that prevails in the two preceding clauses. If a field is sown with two species of wheat, the number of *peot* for which one is obligated *is* determined by quantity. Thus, while quantity is not generally a factor in the obligation of *peah*, in this exceptional case it is. Mishnah 2.6 contains an incident in which R. Shimeon of Mizpah asks about precisely such an exceptional case. The answer of Nahum the Scribe (1st c. CE) is reported as a HLMM transmitted from tradent to tradent until reaching Nahum the Scribe from his own teacher (R. Measa who received it from Abba who received it from the Pairs, who received it from the prophets, a HLMM). This HLMM mirrors the wording of the anonymous third clause of the previous mishnah.

---

once had been viewed strictly as oral law (41). According to Halivni, exegesis reached its apex in the halakhic midrashim of the tannaim (89). The amoraic period, however, witnessed an erosion of confidence in exegesis, attested to by the fact that after the Talmud no new laws were derived directly from Scripture. Instead, in the amoraic and post-talmudic period there was a trend toward HLMM, and by the Middle Ages there was a renewed belief in divine oral instruction revealed alongside the Written Torah (ibid.). We will return to some of these ideas—particularly the erosion of confidence in exegesis—in the course of this study.

The following observations about the term HLMM can be made on the basis of this text. First, in the view of the mishnah's editors a HLMM can be posited as the source of an anonymous clause of the Mishnah. In other words, that a law appears in the Mishnah does not preclude the possibility that it is held to be a HLMM. Second, the clause that is declared to be a HLMM constitutes an exception to a general rule. For now, we may hypothesize that it is precisely the exceptional and anonymous nature of the law that leads to its identification as a HLMM, in order to lend it greater authority (this hypothesis will be explored further below). Third, we see that a HLMM concerns a detail of a Torah law, i.e., it provides specific and practical information as to how a Torah law is to be carried out. A fourth observation concerns the literary features of the passage. We see that a declaration that law X is a HLMM is accompanied by a chain (albeit gapped) of transmission featuring tradents, stretching back to Moses. The term *mequbbal* is used to describe the process of transmission from tradent to tradent. The presence of a chain of transmission and the term *mequbbal* implies a fairly literal understanding of the term HLMM. In other words, Nahum the Scribe appears to be saying that this halakhah was received by Moses orally and handed down orally until reaching Nahum himself.

M. Yadayim 4.3 (cf. T. Yadayim 2.7)

בו ביום אמרו עמון ומואב מה הן בשביעית
גזר ר״ט מעשר עני וגזר ר' אלעזר בן עזריה מעשר שני . . .
נמנו וגמרו עמון ומואב מעשרין מעשר עני בשביעית
וכשבא ר' יוסי בן דורמסקית אצל רבי אליעזר בלוד אמר לו
מה חדוש היה לכם בבית המדרש היום
אמר לו נמנו וגמרו עמון ומואב מעשרים מעשר עני בשביעית
בכה רבי אליעזר ואמר (תהלים כה) סוד יי ליראיו ובריתו להודיעם
צא ואמר להם אל תחושו למנינכם מקובל אני מרבן יוחנן בן זכאי
ששמע מרבו ורבו מרבו עד הלכה למשה מסיני
שעמון ומואב מעשרין מעשר עני בשביעית

On that day they said: "What is the law for Ammon and Moab in the seventh year?"
R. Tarfon decreed poor tithe and R. Elazar b. Azariah decreed second tithe . . . (Each side advances various logical arguments in support of its view.) The votes were counted and they decided that Ammon and Moab should give poor tithe in the seventh year.
When R. Yose b. Durmasqit visited R. Eliezer in Lod he said to him: "What new thing occurred in the house of study today?"
He said to him: "They voted and decided that Ammon and Moab must give poor tithe in the seventh year."
R. Eliezer wept and said: *"The counsel of the Lord is with those who fear him and his covenant, to make them know it* (Psalms 25:14). Go and tell them: Do not be

anxious about your vote. I received a tradition from R. Yohanan b. Zakkai who heard it from his teacher, and his teacher from his teacher, and so back to a HLMM, that Ammon and Moab must give poor tithe in the seventh year."

In this passage tannaim debate the tithing law that applies to Ammon and Moab in the seventh year. Are these regions to give poor tithe or second tithe? A number of logical arguments (omitted here) are presented by first-century CE tannaim on both sides of the debate and when a vote is taken, it is determined that Ammon and Moab are to render poor tithe in the seventh year. R. Yose b. Durmaskit reports this legal innovation to R. Eliezer who weeps in relief and declares that the rabbis need not be apprehensive about their ruling since he has it on tradition as a HLMM that Ammon and Moab give poor tithe in the seventh year.

The following observations about the term HLMM can be made on the basis of this text. First, we have already hypothesized that HLMM may be a device for conferring authority upon a law of unstable authority (the exceptional third clause in M. Peah 2.6). That hypothesis appears to be supported by M. Yadayim 4.3, in which the authority of a hotly disputed rabbinic legal innovation is confirmed by R. Eliezer's report of a corresponding HLMM. The text is explicit on this point: the assertion that the rabbis' ruling accords with a HLMM is intended to allay anxiety about, and strengthen confidence in, the rabbinic ruling in question.[14] Second, it appears that a HLMM may be forgotten and subsequently arrived at independently through the argumentative give-and-take of later rabbinic authorities. Thus it is possible for a rabbinic legal innovation to be at one and the same time a HLMM, although the ancient origin of the law may be lost to human memory completely (in this case, it was known only to R. Eliezer). Third, this passage strongly implies that a HLMM does not require logical justification. If it had been generally known that there was a HLMM regarding the legal issue in question then the lengthy arguments and logical deductions from other cases and principles would not have been necessary. In addition, R. Eliezer's assertion that the law is in fact a HLMM is clearly intended to establish the law as correct, indisputable and incontrovertible. Thus, this passage strongly implies that the authority of a HLMM is absolute—it requires no justification and is not subject to dispute. Fourth, unlike M. Peah 2.6, where a HLMM provides specific and practical information concerning the observance of a Torah law, M. Yadayim 4.3 fea-

---

[14] For a discussion of rabbinic and non-rabbinic evidence that sabbatical year observance outside the land of Israel was difficult to uphold see Safrai, "Halakhah," 24 n. 54, and Shmuel Safrai, "Mitsvat Shevi'it bi-Metsi'ut she-le-ahar Hurban Bayit ha-Sheni," *Tarbits* 36 (1966-67): 304–306.

tures a HLMM which corresponds to a rabbinic legal innovation.[15] Finally, M. Yadayim 4.3 shares notable literary features with M. Peah 2.6. R. Eliezer's declaration that law X is a HLMM is accompanied by a chain of transmission (R. Eliezer received the tradition from R. Yohanan b. Zakkai, who received it from his teacher, and so back to a HLMM) and employs the terms *mequbbal* and, in this case, *shama mi-* to describe the transmission from tradent to tradent. Here again, the presence of a chain of transmission—however vague or imprecise—and the terms *mequbbal* and *shama mi-* implies a fairly literal understanding of the term HLMM.[16]

M. Eduyyot 8.7

אמר רבי יהושע מקובל אני מרבן יוחנן בן זכאי
ששמע מרבו ורבו מרבו הלכה למשה מסיני
שאין אליהו בא לטמא ולטהר לרחק ולקרב
אלא לרחק המקורבין בזרוע ולקרב המרוחקין בזרוע . . .
רבי יהודה אומר לקרב אבל לא לרחק
רבי שמעון אומר להשוות המחלקת
וחכמים אומרים לא לרחק ולא לקרב אלא לעשות שלום בעולם
שנאמר (מלאכי ג) הנה אנכי שלח לכם את אליהו הנביא וגו'
והשיב לב אבות על בנים ולב בנים על אבותם

R. Joshua said: "I have received a tradition from R. Yohanan b. Zakkai, who heard it from his teacher, and his teacher from his teacher, a HLMM that Elijah will not come to pronounce impure or pure, to put away or to bring near, but to put away those brought near by force and to bring near those put away by force" . . .
R. Judah says: "To bring near, but not to put away."
R. Shimon says: "To reconcile disputes."
And the sages say: "Neither to put away nor to bring near, but to make peace in the world, for it is said, *Behold, I send to you Elijah the prophet . . . and*

---

[15] This seemingly paradoxical declaration that a rabbinic legal innovation is a HLMM leads some scholars to state that the term HLMM is not intended literally in this passage since, so it is assumed, a law cannot be both a HLMM and a rabbinic ruling (see Safrai, "Halakhah," 16–17, 22–23). Thus, R. Eliezer means to say only that the law is *as clear and certain* as a HLMM. While such metaphorical usages do occur, primarily in the Yerushalmi, there is little internal evidence that the term HLMM in M. Yad 4.3 is purely metaphorical. Rather, the text appears to claim that a HLMM can be lost to human memory, but through divine providence (hence R. Eliezer's citation of Ps 25:14) or rabbinic ingenuity reinstated as a law of the rabbinic court. It must be conceded however, that the term HLMM may be a purely *literary* device for conferring authority on a rabbinic law that was subject to dispute, much like the literary deployment of a *bat kol* (Heavenly voice) in several rabbinic texts to settle a legal question or to signal the "correct" side of a debate. See the discussion of this issue below.

[16] But see the previous note.

he shall turn the heart of the fathers to the children and the heart of the children to their fathers (Malachi 3:23–24)."

R. Joshua (2nd-generation tanna) reports a tradition he has received as a HLMM to the effect that Elijah will come to put away those brought near by force and to bring near those put away by force (i.e., he will rectify certain unjust and arbitrary genealogical rulings). R. Joshua's statement is disputed by R. Judah, R. Shimon (3rd-generation tannaim) and finally by the sages, all of whom present different conceptions of Elijah's intended activity.

This passage has some points of contact with the two mishnaic passages already examined but also differs from them in significant ways. First, the HLMM in M. Eduyyot 8.7 does not convey information pertaining to the performance of a Torah law. Nor does it confirm an independently established rabbinic law. On the contrary, it conveys a purely aggadic tradition regarding Elijah.[17] Second, R. Joshua's assertion that the tradition he presents is a HLMM does not establish that tradition as correct, indisputable and incontrovertible (as was the case in M. Yadayim 4.3), and three alternative views are advanced. According to this text, the authority of a HLMM is not necessarily absolute, nor are its contents immune to dispute.[18] Third, the sages support their opposing view with a passage from Malachi, implying that the authority of a HLMM is inferior to (or certainly no greater than) that of a prophetic text,[19] and that a HLMM can be set aside or rejected. Finally, M. Eduyyot 8.7 exhibits the literary features seen in the Peah and Yadayim texts: the claim that a tradition is a HLMM is accompanied by a chain of transmission and the terms *mequbbal* and *shama mi-*. As in the previous cases these features imply a fairly literal understanding of the term HLMM.

The term HLMM occurs in two toseftan texts.[20] T. Yadayim 2.7 is a compressed version of M. Yadayim 4.3, and is for our purposes sufficiently par-

---

[17] Insofar as such traditions are purely speculative, we have a third example of HLMM being used to lend authority to a teaching whose authority is weak for one reason or another.

[18] This may be a function of the aggadic rather than halakhic nature of the tradition reported here. On the other hand, it may be that R. Joshua's tradition is disputed because later tradents/the stam reject his claim that the tradition is a HLMM. Were they convinced that his teaching was a HLMM they may not have disputed it. However, the text is most easily construed as one in which the notion of a HLMM as absolutely authoritative is simply lacking.

[19] The authority of a HLMM relative to that of the biblical text and biblical exegesis will be considered in our discussion of the amoraic material.

[20] T. Hal 1.6 employs the related phrase "matters said from Mount Horeb," equivalent to "matters said [to Moses] at Sinai" (e.g. T. Peah 3.2), which will be discussed below.

allel to the latter text as to render unnecessary any separate analysis. The other text is T. Sukkah 3.2:²¹

ערבה הלכה למשה מסיני
אבא שאול אומר מן התורה שנאמר וערבי נחל שתים ערבה ללולב וערבה למזבח

The willow ritual is a HLMM.
Abba Shaul says: "[It is] from the Torah, as it is written, *And willows of the brook* (Leviticus 23:40)—which means two: a willow for the lulav and a willow for the altar."

The stam asserts here that the willow ritual performed on Sukkot is a HLMM. This is immediately followed by Abba Shaul's assertion that the willow ritual is derived from the Torah. It is most likely that these two views are presented as alternatives, in opposition to one another, rather than as mutually supportive claims.²² Nevertheless, the larger context suggests that the stam's assertion and Abba Shaul's tradition are not directed at one another so much as they are directed at a third position—that of the Boethusians, who rejected the willow-ritual altogether as described in the immediately preceding passage.

The following observations can be made on the basis of T. Sukkah 3.2. First, the stam's assertion that the willow ritual is a HLMM is clearly an attempt to confer authority on a practice whose observance is rejected by sectarians. Thus, this passage is yet another example of HLMM as a device for bolstering the authority of a law, belief or practice whose authority is disputed or unstable for one reason or another. Second, although the stam's assertion and Abba Shaul's teaching are directed primarily against the Boethusian rejection of the willow ritual, their conjunction here suggests that biblical exegesis and HLMM are at least alternative, if not mutually exclusive, sources of law (i.e., if something is HLMM it is not derived from Scripture and vice versa). Third, it is clear from this passage that the source of a particular law (whether biblical, HLMM, or rabbinic) can be subject to dispute. Finally, this text deviates from the literary pattern common to the three mishnaic texts. The stam's declaration that the willow ritual is a HLMM is not accompanied by a chain of transmission or by terms implying transmission from tradent to tradent (*mequbbal, shama mi-*). This raises a question: Does the term HLMM bear a literal connotation (as is likely in the three mishnaic cases), or is it primarily rhetorical and metaphorical, intended only to designate a tradition of great antiquity?

* * *

---

²¹ T. Peah 3.2 employs the term *she-neemeru le-Moshe ba-Sinai* ("which were said to Moses at Sinai," henceforth NLMB), which will be discussed below, pp. 111–114.

²² Certainly the amoraim in both the Yerushalmi and the Bavli see these as conflicting claims.

The preceding analysis of Mishnah and Tosefta identified the following, at times contradictory, characteristics of HLMM (numbers 4 and 5 are contradictory as are numbers 7 and 8):

(1) A HLMM may be posited as the source of a law, belief or practice whose authority is unstable because that law, belief or practice is exceptional (M. Peah 2.6) or disputed by other rabbis (M. Yadayim 4.3 ‖ T. Yadayim 2.7; M. Eduyyot 8.7) or by sectarians (T. Sukkah 3.2).[23]

(2) A HLMM may be forgotten and subsequently arrived at independently through the argumentative give-and-take of later rabbinic authorities who may be unaware of the ancient origin of the law (M. Yadayim 4.3 ‖ T. Yadayim 2.7). This raises the possibility that any rabbinic law or anonymous mishnaic ruling may correspond to a HLMM.

(3) A HLMM (a) may convey a ruling detailing the proper way to observe a Torah law (M. Peah 2.6); (b) may be identical to a rabbinic legal innovation (M. Yadayim 4.3); or (c) may convey an aggadic rather than a strictly halakhic tradition (M. Eduyyot 8.7).

(4) A HLMM is absolutely authoritative: it requires no logical justification, is not open to dispute and cannot be set aside or overturned (M. Yadayim 4.3 ‖ T. Yadayim 2.7 and, implicitly, M. Peah 2.6).

(5) A HLMM is *not* absolutely authoritative: it is open to dispute and can be set aside or overruled (M. Eduyyot 8.7). (Note that number 5 contradicts number 4.)

(6) A HLMM is distinct from Scripture as a source of law. If a law is said to be a HLMM it is not derived from Scripture and vice versa (implied by T. Sukkah 3.2).

(7) The claim that a law, belief, or practice is a HLMM may be accompanied by a chain of transmission (however gapped or vague) leading back to Moses at Sinai and by terms indicative of the process of transmission (*mequbbal, shama mi-*). This implies a fairly literal understanding of the term HLMM (M. Peah 2.6, M. Yadayim 4.3 ‖ T. Yadayim 2.7). It must be conceded, however, that even in these cases the term may be primarily metaphorical, indicating that a law is certain, correct, or ancient.

---

[23] Safrai rejects the idea (advanced by Geiger) that HLMM arose as a strategy invoked to bolster the authority of laws disputed by sectarians (particularly the oral law of the Pharisees disputed by the Sadducees). He argues that there are many laws in tannaitic literature that lack a scriptural basis and would appear to require support, yet receive none ("Halakhah" [n. 13, above], 17–18). Safrai is certainly correct—there are many disputed rabbinic traditions that are not designated as HLMM. Nevertheless, I am less concerned to pinpoint the occasion for the rise of the term HLMM than I am to describe its function as perceived by the amoraim who built upon tannaitic precedent. Thus, my assertion that the category HLMM may be invoked to bolster the authority of a law, belief, or practice whose authority is unstable is not a genetic claim but a purely descriptive one.

Halakhah le-Moshe mi-Sinai *in Rabbinic Sources*   75

(8) The claim that a law, belief, or practice is a HLMM may be simply asserted without a chain of transmission or terms indicative of the process of transmission (T. Sukkah 3.2). It may be that in such cases the term is not intended literally, but metaphorically designates a tradition of great antiquity (T. Sukkah 3.2). (Note that number 8 contradicts number 7.)

This last point requires further discussion. Whether HLMM is employed literally or metaphorically by the tannaim is disputed by scholars. Halivni views M. Peah 2.6 as the only case in which HLMM is certainly a literal reference to a historical Mosaic tradition. He maintains that the other two mishnaic passages employ HLMM hyperbolically to mean reliable or old, "as if" a HLMM.[24] However, this conclusion is partly driven by the retrojection of post-talmudic conceptions of a HLMM, and thus begs the question. That tannaitic usage of the term HLMM does not conform to post-talmudic assumptions regarding HLMM (e.g., undisputed, absolutely authoritative, non-biblical and non-rabbinic, halakhic rather than aggadic, etc.) does not necessarily mean that the term HLMM is used metaphorically in the tannaitic sources. It is more likely that the discrepancies between the tannaitic usage of the term HLMM and post-talmudic characterizations of HLMM are due to the fact that the tannaitic conception of a HLMM differs from the post-talmudic conception.[25] For this reason, I have tried to identify the characteristic features of a HLMM as found in the tannaitic sources, without attempting to harmonize the discrepancies that occur among the sources themselves or between these sources and later talmudic and post-talmudic conceptions of HLMM.

Safrai is aware that modern scholars troubled by the designation of a Second Temple or rabbinic law as HLMM[26] interpret the term metaphorically: it is *as if* this law were a HLMM. Safrai rejects the metaphorical interpretation of M. Yadayim 4.3 (in which HLMM indicates only that the law is certain or ancient) in favor of a literal interpretation.[27] However, Safrai then argues that the rabbinic concept of HLMM was not historical so much as theological and was intended to express the idea of a single continuous revelation encompassing both the legal innovations of the rabbis and the revelation to Moses at Sinai (29). For the rabbis, HLMM is an ideological assertion that the Oral Torah draws from, has its roots in, and is nourished

---

[24] Halivni, "Reflections" (n. 13, above), 53.

[25] That this is the more likely explanation is supported by the fact that the term HLMM clearly evolved over time, as Halivni himself observes (ibid., 69).

[26] As in M. Peah 2.6 and M. Yad 4.3, respectively.

[27] Safrai, "Halakhah," 16–17. Safrai believes there is no way to determine whether M. Peah 2.6 uses the term literally or metaphorically. According to Safrai, the term HLMM in M. Eduy 8.7 is not meant literally because the tradition in question is open to dispute—but this is also a retrojection of later definitions of HLMM upon the tannaitic sources.

by the Written Torah (35). Even disputes over details of the law can be said to belong to that which was revealed to Moses (see T. Peah 3.2 and M. Hallah 1.6), while tradent chains are simply expressions of the continuity of learning rather than historical records of transmission.[28] Paradoxically, in order to make the case that HLMM should be understood literally as designating a law that is Sinaitic, Safrai redefines the rabbinic notion of "Sinaitic" in a metaphorical manner: "Sinaitic" does not refer, Safrai suggests, to a law that was actually, historically revealed to Moses at Sinai and handed down orally. Rather, it refers to a law that has "its roots" in the Sinaitic revelation. But a theological or ideological linguistic usage of this type is by definition metaphorical, not literal. Thus, despite his assertion that tannaitic texts employ the term HLMM literally, Safrai advances a description of the tannaitic usage of the term that is strongly metaphorical.

Summary: The tannaitic sources, despite their small number, present an extraordinarily complex portrait of the term HLMM. In just four texts, the term HLMM is used in a variety of ways that conflict not only with later (i.e., post-talmudic) usage, but with one another. It should further be noted that the fundamental heterogeneity of the three mishnaic sources was preserved in the process of the Mishnah's redaction, suggesting that the process of redaction was not one that imposed ideological unity or that flattened or destroyed the distinctive elements of the various traditions serving as sources for the text in its final form.

Palestinian and Babylonian amoraim inherited this small but conflicted tannaitic corpus regarding HLMM. In the following analysis of the talmudic deployment of the term HLMM we will see that the amoraic sources contain very little that cannot be traced—even if only in embryonic form—to the tannaitic sources. In other words, taken together the tannaitic sources contain the seeds of nearly everything that will emerge in the amoraic material. Nevertheless, the two Talmudim subject the material they inherited in common, to different treatments. Analyzing the texts from both a source critical and synchronic perspective will reveal chronological and geographical distinctions within each Talmud as well as distinctions between

---

[28] Safrai supports his argument with aggadic texts (some quite late) that feature what Halivni would call the maximalist position—that all of the Written and Oral Torah derives from the Sinaitic revelation. However, while aggadic texts can inform our interpretation of halakhic texts, they are not determinative, particularly when they date to a much later period. Very often halakhic and aggadic texts respond to the same cultural issue or problem, but in very different ways, as we shall see below. Thus, aggadic notions of a continuous revelation do not necessarily represent the halakhic usage of the term HLMM in tannaitic texts. Further, the use of technical terms of transmission (*mequbbal* and *shama mi-*) strongly implies a literal understanding of the phrase HLMM as indicating a law revealed to Moses and handed down orally.

the two Talmudim. It is hoped that this exercise will show the merit of both source critical and synchronic approaches to the study of the talmudic material.

I. Source Critical Analysis of the Talmudim

The term HLMM appears in 11 distinct sugyot of the Yerushalmi, and in 26 distinct sugyot of the Bavli.[29] Source critical analysis of these sugyot reveals certain ideological differences between early and late, Palestinian and Babylonian sources.[30] It must be conceded that 37 sugyot is a very

---

[29] Translations of Yerushalmi are based on the text of the first printed edition (Venice). Significant variants, particularly from the Leiden ms., are noted. Translations of the Bavli are based on the standard printed edition, occasionally emended in light of manuscript or other evidence. Significant variant readings are cited in the notes.

The total number of Yerushalmi sugyot containing the term HLMM is actually 12, due to a parallel sugya. A complete list follows: Y. Ber 5.1 8d; Kil 2.2 27d; Shev 1.7 33b ‖ Suk 4.1 54b; Ter 2.1 41b; Or 3.8 63b; Shab 1.6 3b, 10.4 12c; Meg 1.11 71d, 4.9 75c; Hag 1.2 76b; Naz 7.3 56c. For compilations of HLMM see Halivni, "Reflections" (n. 13, above), 51 n. 47, and Safrai, "Halakhah" (n. 13, above), 14. It should be noted that these lists vary and often include laws not explicitly labeled HLMM by the talmudic sources themselves. This study is confined to texts that explicitly refer to a HLMM, or employ the term HLMM or a certain equivalent (e.g., some cases of NLMB indicate a HLMM).

As for the Bavli, the total number of sugyot is actually 27, due to a parallel sugya. The complete list follows: B. Shab 28b, 62a, 79b; Eruv 4a ‖ Suk 5b; Eruv 97a; Pes 110b; Yoma 80a; Suk 34a, 44a; Taan 3a; Meg 19b, 24b; MQ 3b; Ned 37b; Naz 56b; Qid 38b–39a; BB 12b; Mak 11a; AZ 36b; Zev 110b; Men 29b, 32a–b, 35a–b, 89a; Nid 45a, 72b.

[30] In this study, I follow Richard Kalmin's definition of Palestinian and Babylonian sources, presented most recently in *The Sage in Jewish Society of Late Antiquity* (London and New York: Routledge, 1999). Kalmin writes: "[T]he term 'Palestinian sources' refers to statements attributed to, as well as stories involving, Palestinian rabbis, preserved in the various rabbinic compilations of late antiquity: the Bavli, Yerushalmi, and midrashic collections. The term 'Babylonian sources' refers to statements by, and stories involving, Babylonian sages found in the same rabbinic compilations" (28). I employ the term "early" to describe tannaim, Palestinian amoraim of the first two or three generations, and Babylonian amoraim of the first three generations. I employ the term "late" to describe Palestinian amoraim from the fourth and fifth generations (and occasionally the third, which functions as something of a transition between early and late) and Babylonian amoraim from the fourth generation on. I assume, following Shamma Friedman in "Yevamot X" (n. 8, above), that the stammaitic layer of the Talmud is late, or post-amoraic (see Friedman's discussion, 293–301). This assumption finds support in the strong correspondence between stammaitic and later amoraic views. In general, the stammaitic layer appears to be the work of the sugya's redactor(s).

small number of sources. At times a particular phenomenon will be observed in just one or two cases. This would constitute very weak evidence of shifts over time. However, it is to be hoped that the cumulative weight of several differences among various sources is a powerful argument for chronological and geographical difference within the gemaras.

Early and late, Palestinian and Babylonian sources differ as to the status and authority of a HLMM. By status, I mean the position of HLMM in relation to Scripture: Is HLMM identical to or distinct from the written revelation recorded in Scripture? By authority, I mean the authority of HLMM relative to the authority of Scripture: Is the authority of HLMM greater than, lesser than, or equal to the authority of Scripture? As regards status, Babylonian sources—whether early or late, attributed or stam—are consistently presented in both Talmudim as drawing a distinction between HLMM and Scripture as mutually exclusive sources of law. By contrast, later Palestinian sages do not draw this distinction. (The mixed view of the stam of the Yerushalmi will be addressed below.) As regards authority, early Palestinian (and possibly early Babylonian) sources draw a distinction between Scripture and HLMM. According to the evidence of both Talmudim, later Palestinian and Babylonian sources and the stam of both Talmudim assign a high level of authority to HLMM, identical in certain important respects to the authority of Scripture.

Y. Sheviit 1.7 33b ∥ Y. Sukkah 4.1 54b attributes two statements to an early Palestinian amora, R. Yohanan (PA 2).[31] In the first instance we read, "R. Zeira (PA 3) in the name of[32] R. La (PA 3), R. Yissa (PA 3) in the name of R. Yohanan: The willow ritual is a HLMM."[33] This statement is immediately followed by the observation, "And this is not in accordance with Abba Shaul (tanna), for Abba Shaul said, 'The willow ritual is a *devar Torah* (a scriptural law; plural: *divrei Torah*)'"—derived exegetically from Leviticus 23:40. Likewise, in the second instance we read, "R. Ba (PA 4), R. Hiyya (PA 3) in the name of R. Yohanan: The willow ritual and the water libation (on Sukkot) are HLMM." This statement is immediately followed by the statement, "And this is not in accordance with R. Akiva (tanna), for R. Akiva said, 'The water libation is a *devar Torah*'"—derived exegetically from Numbers 29:19, 31, and 33. These passages clearly set in opposition the categories HLMM and *devar Torah* as distinct and mutually exclusive sources of law. R. Yohanan, a relatively early Palestinian amora, is said to hold that the willow ritual and the water libation ritual are HLMM, in op-

---

[31] PA=Palestinian Amora, BA=Babylonian Amora, and the number following these designations indicates the sage's generation.
[32] Leiden ms. omits "in the name of."
[33] This teaching is presented stam in T. Suk 3.2.

position to older tannaitic traditions (cf. T. Sukkah 3.2) that assert a biblical source for these practices.

Admittedly, the distinction between HLMM and Scripture is only explicitly signalled by the anonymous redactor. Can we assume, then, that the statement attributed to R. Yohanan expresses this distinction independent of its redactional context? The assumption is not unreasonable, since elsewhere R. Yohanan is said to draw a distinction between HLMM and Scripture as sources of law. In Y. Orlah 3.8 63b, he is represented as viewing HLMM and Scripture as distinct sources of law. The mishnah to which the gemara is attached deals with the application of certain agricultural rules outside the land of Israel and states: "The prohibition of new produce applies everywhere *min ha-Torah* (according to Scripture); [the application of the prohibition of] *orlah* [outside Israel] is a halakhah, and [the application of the prohibition of] *kilayim* [outside Israel] is rabbinic (*mi-divrei soferim*)." In the gemara, R. Yohanan is cited as saying that the term *halakhah* employed by the mishnah means HLMM. Thus, whatever the mishnah's intended meaning, it appears that in the statement attributed to R. Yohanan, Scripture, HLMM and rabbinic authority are seen as three distinct sources of law.

This depiction of R. Yohanan and other early Palestinian authorities appears also in the Bavli. B. Qiddushin 38b–39a, like its Yerushalmi parallel in Y. Orlah 3.8 63b, presents R. Yohanan as viewing HLMM and Scripture as distinct sources of law in connection with the mishnah's identification of three agricultural laws as deriving from Scripture, halakhah, and rabbinic authority, respectively. Further, the Bavli contains two aggadic traditions in which tannaitic authorities are depicted as maintaining a distinction between HLMM and Scripture. In the famous story of R. Akiva's schoolhouse (B. Menahot 29b, discussed below, pp. 98–100) R. Akiva does not offer a biblical derivation for a particular law, asserting instead that the law is a HLMM. Similarly, B. Menahot 89a ‖ B. Niddah 72b, also discussed below (p. 101), couples R. Elazar b. Azariah's rejection of R. Akiva's exegetical gymnastics with the assertion that the law in question is a HLMM. While these traditions are likely reworked by Babylonian tradents and editors, their depiction of a (very) early Palestinian view of the status of HLMM is consistent with the depiction of the early amora, R. Yohanan, that appears in the Yerushalmi.

By contrast, two other texts suggest that later Palestinian authorities viewed HLMM and Scripture as equivalent rather than distinct and mutually exclusive categories. M. Hagigah 1.2 describes a dispute between the house of Hillel and the house of Shammai over the minimum amount required to fulfill the obligation of the festal offering and the pilgrimage offering, the former maintaining that one *maah* of silver fulfills the obligation of the pilgrimage offering and two pieces of silver (=two *maot*) that of the festal offering. In the gemara (Y. Hagigah 1.2 76b), R. Yohanan states that this view (one *maah*/two *maot*) is *devar Torah*. R. Yose (PA 3) teaches before R. Yohanan that any amount is permitted according to Scripture, but the sages established a minimum of one *maah*/two *maot*. To this point, the sugya is consistent with what we have seen previously. R. Yohanan and R. Yose, both early sages, are represented as viewing Scripture, HLMM and rabbinic authority as distinct and mutually exclusive sources of law. Immediately following, a late Palestinian amora, R. Yose b. R. Bun (PA 5), points to two teachings by R. Yohanan that might appear to be in conflict. Here, R. Yohanan declares the prescribed minima of one *maah*/two *maot* to be biblical in origin, while elsewhere he has stated that prescribed minima in general are HLMM. R. Yose b. R. Bun asserts that these statements are not contradictory because HLMM and Scripture are equivalent, or essentially indistinct, as sources of law. Thus, according to this 5th generation amora, R. Yohanan can in all consistency maintain (a) that prescribed minima in general are HLMM and (b) that the minima for these two offerings are biblical. The two designations—biblical and HLMM—amount to the same thing.[34] R. Yose b. R. Bun ascribes the equation of HLMM and Scripture to R. Yohanan, even though (a) in earlier strata of this very sugya and in other sugyot[35] it is evident that these terms refer to distinct sources of law; and (b) R. Yohanan himself is represented as maintaining that distinction in the two texts discussed above.

A second example, this time involving the stam, may be found in Y. Nazir 7.3 56c regarding the anonymous and exceptional mishnaic ruling that the days of impurity as a gonorrheic and the days of sequestration for scale-disease do not diminish a nazirite's term of naziriteship (unlike the days of impurity while contaminated by a corpse). The gemara opens with a statement by R. Elazar b. Pedat (PA 3) that this ruling is a HLMM.[36] This statement is followed by a stammaitic passage that puts forward biblical passages from which the law in question is said to derive. There is no suggestion that the derivation of this law from Scripture in any way challenges R. Elazar's claim that the law is a HLMM, suggesting that in the eyes of the stam, HLMM and Scripture are not mutually exclusive categories.[37]

---

[34] The precise nature of this equivalence is not clear from the discussion in the sugya.

[35] See Y. Shev 1.7 33b ‖ Y. Suk 4.1 54b; and Y. Or 3.8 63b, which uses *min ha-Torah* instead of *devar Torah*.

[36] We shall return to a more detailed discussion of R. Elazar b. Pedat's statement below.

[37] It is not certain, however, that the stam's silence should be construed as approval. It may be that a third example appears in Y. Meg 1.11 71d. In this sugya, the stam cites Exod 13:9 as a source for the law that only the hide of a pure animal may be used for a Torah scroll. This law appears as one of a number of laws, many of

In these seven sources from the Yerushalmi and Bavli, early Palestinian authorities (tannaim, R. Yohanan and R. Yosi) maintain a distinction between HLMM and Scripture as sources of law, a distinction that is not upheld by a later Palestinian sage or source—R. Yose b. R. Bun in one case and the stam in another. The stam's position, however, is rather mixed. In Y. Nazir 7.3 56c the stam appears to equate a HLMM with Scripture, but in Y. Sheviit 1.7 33b ‖ Y. Sukkah 4.1 54b and Y. Orlah 3.8 63b the stam faithfully preserves the view of early Palestinian sages that the two are distinct sources of law. It is possible that the stam conflates HLMM and Scripture as sources of law (as in Y. Nazir 7.3 56c), and the latter two exceptional cases are simply examples of the redactional preservation of early sources, even when those sources do not align with the view of the redactor.

The Babylonian evidence is entirely consistent on this issue. Although we lack any relevant attributed sources, the stam of the Bavli always distinguishes HLMM and Scripture as distinct and mutually exclusive sources of law.[38] In some cases, the stam imposes this distinction on tannaitic and amoraic sources not directly concerned with this question. For example, several beraitot in B. Sukkah 34a (‖ Y. Sheviit 1.7 33b and Y. Sukkah 4.1 54b) expound Leviticus 23:40 in various ways, but since none derives the willow ritual of Sukkot from this verse the stam assumes that the general view of the rabbis must be that the law is a HLMM. A related case is B. Taanit 3a, which focuses on the water libation ritual of Sukkot. When no biblical authority can be found for determining the duration of the ritual, the stam finally asserts that the performance of the water libation throughout the seven days of the festival is founded on a tradition (*hilkheta*). This claim is then supported by the tradition of R. Yohanan, that the water libation ritual is a HLMM. B. MQ 3b features R. Yohanan's teaching in a different context, where again the stam constructs the discussion around Scripture, HLMM and rabbinic authority as mutually exclusive sources of law ("Is X a HLMM? Is it not rather biblical?").

In B. Shabbat 28b, the gemara sets about determining the practical application of a rabbinic teaching recited by R. Joseph (BA 3). Various options are considered and rejected because they are either biblically derived or a HLMM. Clearly, the stam assumes that Scripture, HLMM and rabbinic teachings are distinct and mutually exclusive categories. In B. Yoma 80a, the assumption that HLMM and Scripture are distinct sources of law leads the stam to emend a tradition attributed to R. Yohanan. Finally, in B. Eruvin

which are explicitly labelled HLMM, leading traditional commentators to assume that all the laws listed in the sugya are HLMM (e.g., Rambam). If we accept this assumption, we might conclude that in the eyes of the stam, HLMM and Scripture are not distinct and mutually exclusive sources of law, since the stam cites a biblical source for the law. However, it is not clear that the law is in fact a HLMM.

[38] One possible exception is discussed in n. 39.

4a (cf. B. Sukkah 5b), the stammaitic redaction organizes its source materials around the distinct categories of Scripture and HLMM. The stam discusses the claim that certain laws are HLMM and argues that since biblical exegesis yields some of these laws, then only that which is not biblically derived is HLMM.[39]

The combined evidence of the two Talmudim paints a consistent portrait: The Bavli's redactional voice coincides with early Palestinian sources (tannaitic and early amoraic) that would maintain a distinction between HLMM and Scripture as mutually exclusive sources of law. The conflation of HLMM and Scripture as sources of law occurs only among later Palestinian sources.[40] The picture changes when we consider the perceived authority of a HLMM. Only early sources differentiate the authority of HLMM and Scripture. By contrast, late sources—both Palestinian and Babylonian, attributed and stammaitic—tend to equate the authority of HLMM and Scripture. In these sources HLMM is perceived to be equal to Scripture in one of four key ways: (a) HLMM is not open to change or abolition, (b) HLMM can serve as a basis for legal analogies, (c) HLMM has no logical justification, and (d) HLMM is decided stringently in cases of doubt.

(a) Early and late sources differ on whether a HLMM, like Scripture, is open to change or abolition. For example, Y. Hagigah 1.2 76b features a debate over the status of the minima prescribed for various laws. R. Yohanan (PA 2) holds that prescribed minima are HLMM while R. Yose (PA 3), R. Yonah (PA 4) and R. Hoshaiah (PA 3) hold that prescribed minima are rabbinic. R. Yosi b. R. Bun (PA 5) explains the view of R. Hoshaiah: R. Hoshaiah believes prescribed minima to be rabbinic and not HLMM precisely because they are open to change by rabbinic courts. Thus, the passage attests to the view among transitional and later Palestinian authorities that a HLMM, like Scripture, is not open to change by rabbinic authorities and that any law subject to change is by definition a rabbinic law rather than a HLMM. In an interesting postscript the stam notes that in the view

---

[39] In the course of its discussion, the stam cites a tradition attributed to R. Isaac (PA 3) according to which a particular law is a *devar Torah*. R. Isaac's tradition is cited in support of the stam's view that the law is a HLMM, suggesting that here *devar Torah* and HLMM are taken by the stam of the Bavli as equivalent terms. This would seem to undermine my claim that only later Palestinian sages and the Yerushalmi stam equate HLMM and Scripture. However, the tradent who applies the term *devar Torah* to the law discussed in this sugya is a 3rd generation Palestinian authority (transitional generation, not strictly early or late). It may be that this sugya signals the Bavli's faithful preservation of a Palestinian source according to which HLMM and Scripture are not distinct sources of law. The language of the tradition was not modified in line with Babylonian usage.

[40] The third generation of Palestinian sages is transitional and includes representatives of the early view (R. Yose) and the late view (R. Isaac).

of some, R. Yohanan retracted but R. Yonah and R. Yonatan say he did not, and bring evidence to this effect. In short, even when the problem of alteration by rabbinic authorities is explicitly raised an early authority still did not see fit to equate HLMM and Scripture.

It may be significant that the three Palestinian amoraim allied against R. Yohanan in this passage (R. Yosi, R. Yonah and R. Hoshaia), are all of Babylonian origin. Babylonian sources from at least the third generation on (we lack clear evidence for earlier Babylonian sages) also espouse the view that prescribed minima must be rabbinic, rather than scriptural or HLMM, apparently because they are subject to change by rabbinic authorities.[41] In B. Yoma 80a, a discussion of prescribed minima opens with a tradition attributed to R. Elazar (another Babylonian who eventually emigrated to Palestine, where he is counted among the third generation of Palestinian amoraim), according to which prescribed minima are open to change by rabbinic courts (cf. the tradition attributed to R. Hoshaia in Y. Hagigah 1.2 76b cited above). The implication of this tradition is that prescribed minima are rabbinic rather than HLMM. Later in the sugya R. Yohanan is said to hold that prescribed minima *and penalties* are HLMM. The addition of penalties to the view attributed to R. Yohanan elsewhere (Y. Hagigah 1.2 76b; B. Eruvin 4a) is significant because it prompts the stammaitic objection, "but penalties are biblical!" followed by the proposed emendation of R. Yohanan's statement: "Rather, read 'R. Yohanan said: the prescribed minima *for* penalties' are HLMM;[42] it was also taught thus [in a beraita]: 'the minima required for penalties are HLMM.'" As Epstein already noted, Bavli beraitot that lack a Palestinian parallel, and that repeat an amoraic statement that has been generated through emendation or inference by the stam, are not, in all likelihood, genuine.[43] In this case, it is likely that the ideological *tendenz* of the stam and the dialectical needs of the sugya have led to this revision of R. Yohanan's statement and the creation of the beraita

---

[41] It is not clear whether later Palestinian authorities first viewed HLMM to be unalterable and communicated this new view to Babylonian sages from whence it came to dominate Babylonian thinking on the subject, or whether Babylonian sages held this view and communicated it to Palestinian sages who spent time in Babylonia. For this reason I will merely point out the correspondence between late Palestinian and Babylonian views without indicating influence in one direction or the other.

[42] On this reading (attested in most mss. and editions), the emendation of R. Yohanan's tradition is introduced by the stam. JTS ms. 0218 reads: "Rabbi Yudan said." On this reading, the emendation of R. Yohanan's tradition is introduced by a late Palestinian sage (Rabbi Yudan=PA 4). However, R. Yudan is not mentioned again in the Talmud, suggesting that this reading is unlikely (see R. Rabbinovicz, *Diqduqei Soferim* [1959 reprint of Munich: Huber, 1867–97; henceforth *DS*], 5:259 n. *ayin*).

[43] J. N. Epstein, *Mavo le-Nosah ha-Mishnah* (Jerusalem: Merkaz, 1948), 2:681.

that supports that revision. The revision brings R. Yohanan's statement into line with the later Palestinian and Babylonian view that prescribed minima, being subject to change, cannot be HLMM. R. Yohanan is here made to say that only prescribed minima for penalties are HLMM, leaving open the possibility that all other prescribed minima are rabbinic.[44] R. Yohanan as remade by the stam of the Bavli maintains that a HLMM is like Scripture in its being insusceptible to alteration by a rabbinic court.

Susceptibility to alteration is the topic of a further set of sources in which the same distinction between early and late, Palestinian and Babylonian sources is apparent. Y. Sheviit 1.7 33b ‖ Y. Sukkah 4.1 54b discusses an exceptional law presented in M. Sheviit 1.6: If ten saplings are spread out evenly within a certain area, it is permitted to plow the entire space for their sake in a pre-Sabbatical year right up until the New Year. Normally such plowing is prohibited (lest the plowing appear to benefit the growth of the produce of the seventh year, when certain agricultural labors are prohibited). Although this exceptional law is not labeled a HLMM, its juxtaposition to a discussion of two laws (the willow ritual and the water libation ritual of Sukkot) explicitly labeled HLMM[45] implies that the law of the ten saplings is also understood to be a HLMM (this is certainly the assumption of the remainder of the sugya). A Babylonian-born émigré, R. Hiyya b. Abba (PA 3), is said to have asked R. Yohanan (PA 2) how it is that the law

---

[44] Like the Palestinian sources, Babylonian sources can be differentiated chronologically. In B. Eruv 4a, R. Hiyya b. Ashi (BA 2) is said to have stated in the name of Rav that prescribed minima and certain other matters are HLMM. The Bavli stam objects, Aren't they biblical? and then cites a tradition by R. Hanan (PA 3) in support of the derivation of prescribed minima from Scripture. The stam itself answers the objection: prescribed minima are not, in fact, Scripture. They are *hilkheta* and the biblical verses adduced here are only *asmakhtaot*. It is not clear if *hilkheta* here means HLMM or rabbinic law (see Rashi), but the idea of biblical verses serving as props or mnemonics for laws strongly suggests that the term *hilkheta* here refers to rabbinic law. Thus, despite an early Babylonian tradition that prescribed minima are HLMM (and a Palestinian tradition ascribing them to Scripture) the Bavli stam maintains that prescribed minima are only rabbinic. Unfortunately, however, there is no indication that the early Babylonian sages R. Hiyya b. Ashi and Rav held their view despite the fact that prescribed minima are subject to change by rabbinic courts. Thus, we cannot state with confidence that this text attests to an early Babylonian view that HLMM is not equal to Scripture, and that HLMM is subject to alteration while scriptural law is not.

[45] Third- and fourth-generation Palestinian authorities report R. Yohanan's designation of the willow ritual and water libation ritual of Sukkot as HLMM. It bears emphasizing that this tradition is reported by late Palestinians, even though it is not, in general, consistent with late Palestinian views. The preservation of early opinions by later tradents, even when these opinions contradict later opinion, is an argument for the preservation of source materials by the Talmudim.

of the ten saplings is ignored in contemporary practice so that even fields without saplings are plowed late in the pre-Sabbatical year. In other words, a later Palestinian sage, perhaps influenced by Babylonian traditions, assumes that, like Scripture, a HLMM should not be open to alteration by rabbinic authorities.[46]

The sugya presents two solutions to the objection raised by R. Hiyya b. Abba, one a harmonizing modification of R. Yohanan's original statement according to which the HLMM contained its own "amendment clause" as circumstances might require. In a second solution, R. Ba bar Zavda (PA 3) cites a tradition by the late tanna/early amora, R. Honia of Bet Hauran (=R. Nehuniah of Bet Hauran in the Bavli), that declares all three rituals—the willow ritual, the water libation ritual and the ten saplings law—to be prophetic in origin (and thus classed with rabbinic rather than scriptural law).[47] In keeping with this declaration, the stam suggests that the designation HLMM (assigned by R. Yohanan) is metaphorical, rather than literal (see below, pp. 105–106, for a detailed discussion of this solution).

The foregoing analysis of Y. Sheviit 1.7 33b ‖ Y. Sukkah 4.1 54b provides the following data: Early Palestinian authorities may have considered the exceptional law regarding ten saplings to be a HLMM. Later Palestinian authorities, with extensive Babylonian connections, argue that the susceptibility of this law to alteration indicates that it cannot be a HLMM because a HLMM, like Scripture, is not open to alteration by rabbinic authorities.

---

[46] Y. Shev 1.1 33a cites a beraita (see T. Shev 1.1) indicating that R. Gamliel lifted the prohibition against plowing prior to the start of new year.

[47] It is surprising to find such an early Palestinian sage (R. Honia) subscribing to the view that these laws are prophetic/rabbinic. Early (i.e., tannaitic) Palestinian views of the water libation ritual and the willow ritual claim either that they are biblical or that they are HLMM. Indeed, according to T. Suk 3.2, rejection of these rituals as biblical or HLMM was characteristic of sectarians. R. Akiva and Abba Saul ground these two rituals in Scripture while the stam of the Tosefta asserts that they are HLMM. Only in this sugya of the Yerushalmi is it claimed that R. Honia viewed these laws as prophetic. See, however, the Vatican printed edition in which R. Ba bar Zavda states in the name of R. Honia that the willow ritual and water libation ritual are HLMM and only the law of the ten saplings is an institution of the prophets. This reading is more consistent with Palestinian tradition as attested in other sugyot. Nevertheless, it is in all likelihood a correction based on the Bavli. In the Bavli's version of the tradition of R. Honia (B. Suk 44a) all three rituals are said to be HLMM. The Bavli's version is itself best understood as a conflation of distinct Palestinian traditions, for which see below, pp. 105–106. It bears emphasizing that the amora reporting R. Honia's tradition in the Yerushalmi is R. Ba bar Zavda, a Palestinian who spent time in Babylonia learning with Babylonian sages. His version of R. Honia's teaching corresponds to and supports the Babylonian conviction (evident in a sugya to be discussed below) that these laws are neither biblical nor HLMM.

They conclude that the law is of prophetic origin (i.e., it is "rabbinic" rather than "Scriptural" law) and harmonize earlier Palestinian sources to this view.[48]

These distinctions among early and late, Palestinian and Babylonian sources appear also in a Babylonian sugya that parallels Y. Sheviit 1.7 33b. B. Moed Qatan 3b differs in detail from the Palestinian sugya just discussed, but in certain important respects it is similar. First, Palestinian sages report that the laws concerning the ploughing of fields in the pre-Sabbatical year were abrogated by R. Gamliel and his court. Second, the stam points out that according to R. Assi reporting in the name of R. Yohanan in the name of R. Nehuniah of Bet Hauran, these laws (along with the water libation ritual and willow ritual) were a HLMM.[49] The stam clearly assumes that this is a problem—a HLMM cannot be abrogated or modified by a rabbinic court. After some further dialectical twists and turns, involving the citation of a wide range of early Palestinian sources, Rav Ashi proposes the following resolution: R. Gamliel viewed the laws of ploughing as a halakhah (meaning here, HLMM) but understood such halakhot to be valid only while the temple stood, and not subsequently. In this sugya, as in its Palestinian parallel, later Palestinian and Babylonian sages and the stam of the Bavli maintain that a HLMM is not open to change by rabbinic authorities and employ various techniques to legitimate what appears to be just such a change.[50]

(b) Early and late sources may differ over whether a HLMM can serve as a basis for legal analogies, but our sources are so few that it is difficult to make strong claims of certainty. B. Makkot 11a cites a tannaitic dispute over analogies that involve a HLMM. Both tannaim maintain that since Exodus 13:9 juxtaposes the Torah scroll and tefillin, it is permitted to draw an analogy from the one to the other. They differ, however, over the anal-

---

[48] The parallel sugya of the Bavli (B. Suk 44a) will be discussed below (pp. 104–106). The Babylonian sugya features the same revision of earlier Palestinian sources, but the motivation there is not explicit. For that reason, I do not include it here as evidence for the view that early and late authorities differ over a HLMM's susceptibility to change by rabbinic authorities.

[49] Cf. Y. Shev 1.7 33b ‖ Y. Suk 4.1 54b where the same sage says these three rulings are prophetic.

[50] This is, I have claimed, in contrast to early Palestinian sages who would not maintain that a HLMM is immune to change or abrogation. Just such a view is attributed to a Palestinian sage in B. Mak 11a. It is asserted there that sewing tefillin with gutstring is a HLMM. Rav reports that his uncle R. Hiyya (a fifth-generation tanna) sewed his tefillin with flaxen thread but the halakhah is not in accord with his practice. Assuming that R. Hiyya believed the gutstring requirement to be a HLMM, we may have evidence that among some early Palestinians, a HLMM was not incontrovertible.

ogy that may be drawn. According to one tanna, the analogy includes HLMMs. Thus, since it is a HLMM to use gut-string to sew up tefillin, one should also use gutstring to sew together a Torah scroll.

In Y. Peah 2.6 17a (‖ Y. Hagigah 1.8 76d) an analogy drawn from a HLMM is revised in light of the assertion by Shmuel (BA 1) as cited by R. Zera (PA 3) that analogies are not made on the basis of "halakhot." Despite this early tradition, the stam goes on to draw an analogy on the basis of this very HLMM, suggesting that what was disputed in tannaitic and even early amoraic times was no longer questioned in later, or stammaitic times: a HLMM is equivalent to the Torah in so far as analogical inferences are concerned.[51]

(c) Sources differ on whether a HLMM, like Scripture, ever has a logical justification (*taam*). In Y. Shabbat 1.6 3b, R. Elazar b. Pedat (PA 3) identifies the exceptional ruling in the Mishnah as a HLMM (see pp. 93–94, below). A *taam* for this ruling is then provided in a beraita. Similarly, in Y. Shabbat 10.4 12c R. Elazar b. Pedat again identifies an exceptional ruling in the Mishnah as a HLMM, despite the fact that a *taam* is provided by the mishnah itself. In neither case does the stam comment on the provision of a logical justification for a law identified as a HLMM. Is this silence to be construed as the stam's implicit approval, or merely as its faithful preservation of earlier sources even though they run counter to the view of the redactor? It is difficult to know, but Y. Megillah 1.11 71d suggests that the stam does not in general maintain that a HLMM has a *taam*. In the latter text, five laws are explicitly said to be HLMM. In the midst of this list R. Ba b. R. Hiyya bar Ba and R. Hiyya (both PA 3) in the name of R. Yohanan, report that a particular technique for sewing parchments into a Torah scroll, enjoined so that the scroll not tear, is a halakhah. We may assume, on the basis of the general context as one in which HLMMs are being discussed, that *halakhah* here does indeed mean "HLMM." In what appears to be an insertion by the stam, the tradent is said to correct himself (literally, he struck himself on the head), saying: "If it is a halakhah, then why the justification 'that it not tear,' and if it is for the reason that the scroll not tear, then why say it is a halakhah?!" In other words, the designation HLMM and the presence of a logical justification are incompatible. In this regard, then, HLMM is like Scripture—neither has a logical justification. If we assume this to be the position of the stam, then in all likelihood, Y. Shabbat 1.6 3b and Y. Shabbat 10.4 12c should be understood as simply preserving,

---

[51] In view of the assertion (found also in Y. Peah 2.6 17a) that analogies cannot be drawn from special dispensations or personal deeds (i.e., from exceptional and individual cases), it may be that the early sages objected to drawing analogies from a HLMM because they perceived HLMM to cover exceptional or special cases (in keeping with tannaitic usage of HLMM). It may be that later amoraim did not perceive HLMM as indicating exceptional or special case laws.

but not endorsing, the views of earlier sources (see discussion below, pp. 93–95).

The incompatibility of HLMM and logical justification is apparent in Babylonian sources. B. Megillah 19b parallels Y. Megillah 1.11 71d, just discussed. This time a Babylonian amora Rav Hiyya bar Ashi (BA 2) reports R. Yohanan's tradition of a HLMM that prescribes sewing a Torah scroll in a manner that will prevent tearing. He, too, according to the stam, reconsiders and apparently retracts in light of the fact that a *taam* is provided for the law. Thus, an early Babylonian amora who gives a logical justification for a HLMM is "corrected" by the stam. Likewise, in B. Pesahim 38b a tannaitic tradition is reinterpreted by the stam because of the latter's assumption that a HLMM has no logical justification. This tradition is not subject to the same reinterpretation in its Palestinian contexts (T. Hallah 1.6; cf. T. Peah 3.2).[52] Thus, we find that tannaitic, transitional Palestinian and early Babylonian sages do not deem HLMM and logical justification to be mutually exclusive (as are Scripture and logical justification). By contrast, the stam of the Bavli does see them as incompatible. While the stam of the Yerushalmi holds the same view in at least one sugya, it is not clear that it holds this view consistently.

(d) Early and late, Palestinian and Babylonian sources differ over whether HLMM is decided stringently in cases of doubt. M. Orlah 3.7 states that doubtful cases involving *orlah* fruit are decided stringently in the land of Israel and leniently in Syria. The Mishnah adds that the prohibition of *orlah* outside the land of Israel is a halakhah (as opposed to a scriptural ruling). This explains the leniency in doubtful cases, since only doubtful cases of scriptural law are decided stringently. The Yerushalmi (Y. Orlah 3.8 63b) records diverging opinions (Babylonian vs. Palestinian) over the meaning of the term *halakhah* in the Mishnah. Shmuel (BA 1) states that halakhah here means a voluntary provincial legal practice while R. Yohanan (PA 2) states that halakhah here means HLMM. That R. Yohanan designates this law a HLMM despite the fact that doubtful cases are decided leniently implies that R. Yohanan differentiates HLMMs from Scripture, since doubtful cases of scriptural law are always decided stringently. A later Palestinian sage (R. Yose, PA 3) objects to R. Yohanan: How can this law be a HLMM when doubtful cases are decided leniently? Clearly, this slightly later Palestinian sage (a Babylonian émigré) does not differentiate HLMM and Scripture, and maintains that doubtful cases of a HLMM, like doubtful cases of scriptural law, are to be decided stringently.[53]

---

[52] We may speculate that one factor accounting for the Bavli's failure to explicitly identify the laws in M. Shab 1.6 and 10.4 as HLMM is that logical justifications were known for both.

[53] R. Yohanan is represented as responding that this particular HLMM was

Halakhah le-Moshe mi-Sinai *in Rabbinic Sources* 89

The same chronological and geographical distinctions are attested in the Bavli's parallel to this sugya, at B. Qiddushin 38b–39a. Indeed, the same opening dispute appears in the Bavli, but now with Babylonian tradents. Thus, Rav Judah (BA 2) says in the name of Shmuel (BA 1) that the term *halakhah* in M. Orlah 3.8 refers to a voluntary provincial practice, while Ulla (BA 3) states in the name of R. Yohanan (PA 2) that it refers to a HLMM. In the subsequent dialectic, various Babylonian authorities assert in rather strong terms that there is no mandatory *orlah* prohibition outside Israel. Levi (a Palestinian émigré to Babylonia contemporaneous with Shmuel) tells Shmuel that he would eat doubtful *orlah* outside Israel, and R. Awia (BA 4) and Rabbah bar bar Hanah (BA 3) are said to have supplied each other with doubtful *orlah*. The keen scholars of Pumbeditha are reported to have said that there is no *orlah* prohibition in the diaspora. When Rav Judah informs the Palestinian R. Yohanan of the views of these scholars, Yohanan curses their offspring. The stam of the Bavli defends the scholars of Pumbeditha by asserting that early tannaim also taught that there is no *orlah* in the diaspora (the view is traced back to R. Elazar the Great). When a tradition is cited in which R. Elazar does not in fact hold such a view, the stam simply emends the problematic teaching! The Bavli then concludes just as the parallel sugya in the Yerushalmi concluded:

> R. Assi said in R. Yohanan's name: "[The prohibition of] *orlah* in the diaspora is a HLMM."
> R. Zera said to R. Assi: "But we learned, 'Doubtful *orlah* is forbidden in the land [of Israel] but permitted in Syria.'"
> He was astonished for a moment, then he answered him: "Perhaps it (the HLMM) was given thus: 'Doubtful [*orlah*] is permitted in the diaspora, certain [*orlah*] is forbidden.'"

When R. Assi (PA 3) reports R. Yohanan's view it is challenged by R. Zera (PA 3)—how can the prohibition of *orlah* in the diaspora be a HLMM when doubtful cases are decided leniently?! HLMMs are comparable to Scripture, and doubtful cases should be decided stringently! R. Assi is taken aback at first, but then responds that this particular HLMM specified that doubtful cases should be decided leniently, even though leniency is not generally the rule for doubtful HLMMs.[54] With this answer, R. Yohanan's view is brought into line with the later Palestinian and Babylonian view of HLMM as equivalent to Scripture.

Both Talmudim attest to the same phenomenon: an early Palestinian amora distinguishes HLMM from Scripture in regard to the rules for re-

---

given with the specification that doubtful cases would be decided leniently, and R. Yose praises the brilliance of this response. It is likely that this response is not original to R. Yohanan.

[54] In the Yerushalmi parallel discussed above it is R. Assi (=R. Yose) who poses the challenge to R. Yohanan, and R. Yohanan who answers.

solving doubtful cases. Babylonian sources (as it happens, primarily the stam) equate HLMM with Scripture in this regard, as do Palestinian sages of a transitional generation (R. Zera and R. Yose). The stam of both Talmudim (particularly the Bavli) organizes its sources in such a way as to bring early Palestinian tradition into line with later Palestinian and Babylonian views.

In summary: our source critical analysis of sugyot featuring HLMM reveals a chronological tendency to conflate and equate the authority of HLMM and Scripture. In Palestinian sources this shift in authority coincides with a shift in status: early Palestinian sources view Scripture and HLMM as distinct sources of law and do not equate their authority. Unlike scriptural laws, HLMMs are open to change by rabbinic authorities, are excluded from analogies, may have logical justifications and are decided leniently in cases of doubt. Later Palestinian sources appear to conflate Scripture and HLMM as sources of law. This change in status may account for the elevation of the authority of HLMM in later Palestinian sources. Like scriptural laws, HLMMs are not open to change by rabbinic authorities, are included in analogies, do not have logical justifications, and are decided stringently in cases of doubt. The third generation of Palestinian amoraim represents something of a transition between these two conceptions of HLMM, with some tradents adopting the earlier position and others adopting the later position.

The same chronological distinction obtains in Babylonian sources. The few early sources we have do not equate the authority of HLMM and Scripture as regards analogies or logical justification. But late Babylonian sources, like later Palestinian sources, do equate the authority of HLMM and Scripture. It is interesting to note, however, that the Bavli equates the authority of HLMM and Scripture, even though it reverts to the older Palestinian perception of HLMM and Scripture as distinct sources of law. This suggests that Oral Torah had acquired in Babylonia an elevated status in its own right. Finally, the chronological and geographical distinctions isolated here support the proposition that the Talmud is a variegated "thick" document that preserves a range of source materials accessible to the critical scholar, in contrast to the "thin" relatively undifferentiated document hypothesized by documentarians.[55]

---

[55] Cf. Kalmin, *Sages*, 214. Source critical analysis of the Bavli also reveals a difference between attributed and stammaitic sources in the area of terminology. The attributed sources use the term HLMM almost exclusively, while stammaitic sources within the same sugya will refer to one and the same law as a *halakhah* or *hilkheta*. The following texts attest to this difference:

1. B. Suk 5b. "According to R. Judah [the minimum height of the sukkah] is learned as a traditional law (*hilkheta gemiri lah*, henceforth HGL), for R. Hiyya b. Ashi (BA 2) stated in the name of Rav: '[The laws relating to] prescribed minima, in-

II. Synchronic Analysis of the Talmudim

Source critical analysis of the Palestinian and Babylonian talmudic materials regarding HLMM reveals the preservation of distinctive sources,

terpositions and partitions are HLMM.'" (Cf. the parallel in B. Eruv 4a, which employs *hilkheta* in a similar manner.)

2. B. Suk 34a (cf. B. Suk 44a). "Whence do the rabbis derive [the law of the willow ritual] for the sanctuary? They learned it as a traditional law (HGL), for R. Assi (PA 3) said R. Yohanan (PA 2) said in the name of R. Nehuniah from the Plain of Bet Hauran: 'The law of the ten saplings, the willow ritual and the water libation are HLMM.'" (Cf. the parallel in B. Taan 3a, where R. Ami conveys R. Yohanan's tradition, and *gemara gemiri lah* appears as a ms. variant.)

3. B. Nid 72b. "R. Elazar b. Azariah said to R. Akiva . . . 'The prescribed minima of half a log of oil for a thank offering, a quarter log of wine for a nazirite and the eleven days between one menstrual period and the next are HLMM.'" The stam subsequently asks: "But are these traditional laws (*halakhot*)?! Are they not in fact Scripture? For it was taught . . ." After a lengthy midrashic exposition the stam concludes: "According to R. Akiva they are derived from Scripture (*qeraei ninhu*) but according to R. Elazar b. Azariah they are traditional laws (*hilkhata*)."

4. B. Mak 11a. The stam states that one party to a tannaitic dispute draws an analogy from a verse in Exodus in which Torah is mentioned alongside tefillin: "Just as in the case of tefillin there is a HLMM to the effect that gut-string is used for sewing them, so the entire Torah (i.e., a Torah scroll) may be sewn with gut-string." The other party to the dispute is said by the stam to reject this analogy, on the principle that "analogies do not extend to *hilkhotav* (traditional laws)." Here the stam uses both HLMM and *halakhot* in its reconstruction of tannaitic views.

In all of these cases the stam voice employs *halakhah/hilkheta* while the named tradents cited by the stam use HLMM. Less clear is the following case:

5. B. Men 32a–b. Conflicting traditions regarding the mezuzah are reported: "R. Minyomi b. Hilkiah on his own authority said that [writing] the mezuzah on ruled lines is a HLMM. Tannaim differ on this, for it is taught: R. Jeremiah says in the name of Rabbi: 'Tefillin and mezuzot may be written from memory, and ruled lines are not necessary.' The halakhah (*hilkheta*) is that tefillin need not be written on ruled lines, the mezuzah must be written on ruled lines, and both may be written from memory." It is possible that the stam's *hilkheta* refers to the HLMM of R. Minyomi b. Hilkiah (so Rashi), which is being "corrected" or at least integrated with the tradition attributed to R. Jeremiah. The idea of correcting a report of a HLMM may have disturbed later scribes and may account for the insertion of the phrase "on his own authority" after R. Minyomi's name (lacking in Munich 95), to indicate that he did not have a reliable tradition as to the HLMM. However, it is equally possible that *hilkheta* here simply means "law" and the stam is spelling out what the law is.

There are only two instances in which the stam employs the phrase HLMM. In B. AZ 36b we read, "But [the prohibition against] an Israelite man having intercourse with a non-Israelite woman is a HLMM, for a master has said: If [an Israelite] has intercourse with a heathen woman, zealots may attack him." It may be that the lack of a clear reference to HLMM in the tannaitic source in the passage necessi-

underscoring the heterogeneity of rabbinic texts and militating against the documentarian notion of a redactional voice that flattens source materials and results in documents that are not susceptible to historical analysis and reconstruction beyond the level of redaction. Nevertheless, it may be said that rabbinic texts are more than the sum of their parts, that each text can be viewed as a whole, albeit a complex whole that cannot be characterized without reference to the place and function of its disparate and diverse component parts. Synchronic characterizations of rabbinic texts enable us to compare entire texts with one another so as to reveal distinctions among the communities of scholars who produced these texts. What follows is a synchronic analysis and comparison of Yerushalmi and Bavli materials concerning HLMM designed to demonstrate the possibilities and limitations of analysis and comparison of these texts as redacted wholes. This discussion will be organized around the characteristics of HLMM isolated

---

tated the stam's use of the term in this case. A second exception occurs in B. MQ 3b, in which the pattern just described (HLMM in attributed amoraic sources and some form of *halakhah* in the stammaitic sources) is disturbed. Here the stam does employ the term *hilkheta* three times in reference to a HLMM, but also uses HLMM ("was it not a HLMM, as in fact R. Assi said . . . etc."; cf. case 2, above, where the same attributed tradition is introduced by the stam as HGL). Further, terms like *hilkheta* and *hilkheta gemiri lah*, characteristic of the stam, are found in some attributed sources in this same sugya: R. Yitzhak (PA 3) once, R. Nahman b. Isaac (BA 4) once and R. Ashi (BA 6) four times. The latter two sages are relatively late Babylonian tradents. It may be, therefore, that *hilkheta* and *hilkheta gemiri lah* represent not just normal stammaitic usage but also later amoraic usage. In any event, the stam's preference for HGL as opposed to HLMM is not seriously undermined by these exceptional sugyot. We are dealing here with tendencies, not strict dichotomies.

In an appendix to "Reflections" (n. 13, above), Halivni discusses the terms *halakhot, halakhah, hilkheta, gemiri, gemara gemiri* and *hilkheta gemiri* and concludes that (1) the stammaim interpreted *halakhah* as a HLMM, though the amoraim do not; (2) the stammaim are inclined to interpret all instances of *hilkheta* as references to Sinai (though on occasion amoraim do also); and (3) *gemiri, gemara gemiri* and *hilkheta gemiri* can refer to a HLMM (but do not always). Halivni includes within the scope of his study passages in which the term HLMM does not appear explicitly, but may be implied if we assume that post-talmudic conceptions of HLMM are fully operative in the talmudic text. Although the present analysis does not make this assumption and is strictly confined to sugyot in which the designation HLMM is explicit, there is nevertheless a strong correspondence between Halivni's conclusions and the conclusions presented here.

The diachronic differences in terminology isolated here further support the view that documentarian theories of the Talmudim as reflecting a single, late editorial voice simply do not account for the data as well as does the theory that diversity is the result of genuine historical processes.

in the tannaitic sources (see above, pp. 74–75), thus allowing for a three-way comparison of Mishnah, Yerushalmi and Bavli.

* * *

(1) In tannaitic sources a HLMM may be posited as the source of a law, belief, or practice whose authority is unstable because that law, belief, or practice is exceptional (M. Peah 2.6) or disputed by other sages (M. Yadayim 4.3 ‖ T. Yadayim 2.7; M. Eduyyot 8.2) or sectarians (T. Sukkah 3.2).

Yerushalmi: Palestinian sages were apparently sensitive to the fact that in the tannaitic sources the term HLMM was used to shore up the authority of a law, belief, or practice whose authority was unstable for one reason or another. In at least two-thirds of the eleven sugyot featuring HLMM in the Yerushalmi the term is invoked in precisely this manner.[56]

Exceptional and disputed mishnayot. On five occasions the following general principle attributed to R. Elazar b. Pedat (PA 3, Babylonian-born émigré, disciple of R. Yohanan) is cited: "Every time they teach (variant: we learn) *be-emet* in the mishnah, [the ruling that follows is] a HLMM." *Be-emet [ameru]* occurs seven times in the Mishnah,[57] and in regard to five of these the Yerushalmi cites this tradition attributed to R. Elazar.[58] The force of R. Elazar b. Pedat's principle becomes clear when we examine the *be-emet* clauses of the five mishnayot to which his tradition attaches. In each case, the term *be-emet* introduces an exceptional ruling, a special case that deviates from the general rule set out earlier in the Mishnah. The correct translation of *be-emet* in these cases is "nevertheless, however." For example:

- Y. Shabbat 1.6 3b. The mishnah states: "A tailor may not go out with his needle near nightfall [of the Sabbath] lest he forget and [be guilty of] carrying out [on the Sabbath]; nor a scribe with his pen. And one may not search his garment [for vermin], nor read by the light of the lamp. *Neverthless (be-emet)* it was said that the hazzan may see [by lamplight]

---

[56] Compare Halivni, "Reflections" (n. 13, above), 60–61 and 67. Halivni argues that the "increasing inclination toward ascribing all oral tradition to *Halakhah le-Moshe mi-Sinai* on the part of the early Palestinian Amoraim was motivated by the desire of the students of R. Judah the Prince to enhance the authority of the Mishnah . . . support for the Mishnah's authority was provided by the concept of *Halakhah le-Moshe mi-Sinai*" (60). According to Halivni, because Rabbi's Mishnah encountered greater opposition in Palestine, the need to defend and justify the Mishnah was greater than it was in Babylonia where it was accepted without resistance—accounting for the greater tendency toward HLMM in the Yerushalmi than in the Bavli (67). I am not here making a global claim about the authority of the Mishnah as a whole, but rather about the authority of individual laws that were weak for one reason or another.

[57] M. Kil 2.2, Ter 2.1, Shab 1.3, 10.4, Naz 7.3, BM 4.11, BB 2.3.

[58] All but M. BM 4.11 and BB 2.3.

where the children are reading, though he himself must not read . . ." The gemara reads: "R. Elazar said: 'Every time we learn *be-emet* (nevertheless), [the ruling that follows is] a HLMM.'"

The rule regarding the hazzan, introduced by *be-emet* constitutes a specific exception to the general rule of the mishnah. Exceptional cases and special exemptions require some degree of legitimization. R. Elazar b. Pedat's principle provides this legitimization by asserting that exceptional cases like this one are to be understood as HLMMs. R. Elazar is apparently familiar with the tannaitic precedent of invoking the term HLMM in order to bolster the authority of exceptional cases, and sufficiently well-versed in mishnaic idiom to know that *be-emet* signals an exceptional case. As a result he proposes that every *be-emet* clause (i.e., every clearly labelled exception) is a HLMM and is therefore legitimate and authoritative despite its exceptional status.

The other four sugyot that cite R. Elazar's general principle are:

• Y. Kilayim 2.2 27d, regarding the minimum amount of diverse seed to create liability under the law of *kilayim*. The mishnah indicates that 1/4 *qab* of diverse seed in every *seah* of seed is the minimum for liability, and then states an exception to this rule: "Nevertheless (*be-emet*), garden seeds which are not eaten combine [to create liability when they are] 1/24 of the volume] sown in a space of 50 cubits square."

• Y. Terumot 2.1 41b. Separating terumah from ritually pure produce on behalf of that which is ritually impure is prohibited *ab initio*. However, the mishnah indicates certain exceptional cases, introduced by *be-emet*, in which this prohibition does not apply (a circle of pressed figs, a bunch of greens and a heap of produce).

• Y. Nazir 7.3 56c. The days of defilement of a gonnorheic and the days of quarantine for scale-disease do not diminish a nazirite's term of naziriteship, a deviation from the rule that applies in cases of certain and even doubtful corpse impurity.

• Y. Shabbat 10.4 12c. The mishnah contains a general rule to the effect that if one intends to carry out an object on the Sabbath either in front of him or behind him and the article works its way around to the other side, one is not culpable for violating the Sabbath laws against carrying. Nevertheless (*be-emet*), a woman wearing an apron is liable.

In all of these cases *be-emet* introduces an exceptional law in the Mishnah, whose authority is bolstered by R. Elazar's assertion in the Yerushalmi that each is a HLMM. It should also be noted that in two further cases an exceptional ruling in the Mishnah is said in the gemara to be a HLMM, even though these rulings are not introduced by the term *be-emet*. Y. Sheviit 1.7 33b ‖ Y. Sukkah 4.1 54b discusses a mishnaic exception found in M. Sheviit 1.4–6. As we have seen, the Mishnah establishes that one may not plough an orchard of mature trees right up to the end of the 6th year.

This determination is followed by an exception: in the case of ten saplings spread evenly over a space of 50 cubits square, the entire area may be ploughed for the sake of the saplings, right up to the new year. In the gemara this law is considered in conjunction with two other laws that are said to be HLMM. Y. Orlah 3.8 63b deals with a mishnaic list of agricultural rules that are exceptional because they apply outside the land of Israel. R. Yohanan in the gemara identifies one of these rules as HLMM.

These last two cases, in combination with the five *be-emet* cases, indicate that the Yerushalmi adopts and continues the strategy attested in tannaitic sources of deploying the term HLMM in order to lend authority to an exceptional ruling. In addition, the Yerushalmi follows tannaitic precedent in using HLMM to bolster the authority of contested or disputed practices. The Yerushalmi to M. Megillah 4.9 consists of one line: "R. Yose b. Bibai (Venice printed ed. = Bibi = R. Yose b. R. Bun [PA 5])[59] taught: 'That tefillin should be square and black is a HLMM.'" The mishnah to which this statement attaches discusses deviant or sectarian practices regarding the tefillin: "He who makes his tefillin round, it is dangerous and does not fulfill the religious obligation; if he put it on his forehead or on the palm of his hand, that is the way of heresy (*minut*). If he covered it with gold or put it on his sleeve, that is the way of outsiders (*hitsonim*)." The tradition of R. Yose b. R. Bun, itself a conflation of older Palestinian traditions, can be understood as an effort to legitimize rabbinic practices regarding tefillin in the face of deviant and sectarian practices.[60]

Thus, in a full eight out of eleven sugyot featuring the term HLMM the Yerushalmi follows the tannaitic precedent of legitimizing an exceptional mishnaic ruling or disputed practice.[61] This phenomenon is further illuminated by the lengthy sugya that attaches to M. Peah 2.6—one of the three mishnaic passages to employ the term HLMM and to do so in regard to an anonymous and exceptional ruling. The gemara opens as follows (Y. Peah 2.6 17a): "R. Zeira [PA 3] in the name of R. Yohanan: "If a halakhah comes to you and you do not know its nature, don't be quick to dismiss it, for many laws were transmitted to Moses on Sinai (NLMB) and all of them are

---

[59] See Albeck, *Mavo la-Talmudim* (Tel Aviv: Dvir, 1970), 395–6.

[60] Halivni, "Reflections" (n. 13, above), notes that the observance of the law of tefillin is known to have been lax in talmudic times (55). That the rabbinic laws pertaining to tefillin may have been a subject of rebellion is suggested by M. Sanh 11.3 (93). Halivni suggests that designating the laws of tefillin as HLMM may have been intended to elevate their importance and draw adherents to the custom (55).

[61] It can even be argued that in the three remaining sugyot, HLMM legitimizes a rabbinic ruling that lacks a Scriptural basis and is therefore of unstable authority: in Y. Ber 5.1 8d the rule of eleven days between one menstrual period and the next; in Y. Meg 1.11 71d various rules regarding the preparation of tefillin and Torah scrolls (see below); and Y. Hag 1.2 76b concerning prescribed minima.

embedded in the Mishnah." This statement is followed by R. Avin's (PA 3)[62] observation that were it not for Nahum the Scribe's explanation that the exceptional ruling in M. Peah 2.6 was a HLMM we would not have known that it was a HLMM. The subsequent aggadic passage glorifies the Oral Torah, describing it as more precious or beloved than the Written Torah. This sugya also contains the hyperbolic midrashic exposition attributed to R. Joshua b. Levi (cf. Y. Megillah 4.1 74d) to the effect that Scripture, Mishnah, Talmud, Aggada, even what an experienced student will teach before his teacher, were already said to Moses at Sinai (NLMB). The passage betrays a rabbinic anxiety over the authority of anonymous mishnaic rulings—particularly those of an exceptional nature. Lacking both an attribution and a clear Scriptural basis, such rulings are weak and easily questioned. This sugya asserts that just as the anonymous, exceptional ruling regarding the *peah* requirement for a field sown with two species of wheat is a HLMM, so too many anonymous statements of the Mishnah are HLMM.[63] Consequently, mishnaic statements whose nature (perhaps: source, authority, rationale) is unknown should not be quickly dismissed or controverted, for these very statements may be oral HLMM, and the Oral Law is in some sense more precious and beloved than the Written. The sugya employs hyperbolic rhetoric in praise of the Oral Law in order to establish this claim and instil a measure of respect for the authority of oral tradition. Significantly, this very sugya appears also in Y. Hagigah 1.8 76d in connection with the famous mishnah that describes certain laws as hovering in the air, lacking all Scriptural support, others as mountains hanging by a hair (i.e., many laws and only slight Scriptural basis) and others as having strong Scriptural support. The mishnah's description of laws hovering in the air and lacking Scriptural support—however honest—was surely anxiety-producing. The Yerushalmi's assertion that many such laws are HLMM and that oral tradition is more beloved than written revelation can be seen as directly addressing that anxiety by urging respect for and observance of those elements of tradition lacking clear Scriptural warrant (cf. Y. Megillah 1.7 70d and Y. Megillah 4.1 74d, discussed below).

Bavli: In contrast to the Yerushalmi, the Bavli minimizes the use of HLMM as a strategy to confer authority upon a *specific* law, tradition, or practice of unstable authority. Instead, the Bavli uses the term in aggadic passages that explore and legitimize the *general* authority of the rabbis themselves.

---

[62] Probably R. Avin (=Avun or Bun) bar Kahana; see Albeck, *Mavo*, 219.
[63] The text literally says NLMB, but since it is commenting directly on M. Peah 2.6's HLMM it is clear that here at least NLMB = HLMM. Elsewhere, however, the equivalence of the two terms cannot be assumed, as will be seen below.

First, the *be-emet* tradition, when it does appear in the Bavli, appears in a somewhat modified form. In the printed edition of B. Shabbat 92b the gemara comments on the exceptional *be-emet* clause in M. Shabbat 10.4 and contains this single statement: "It was taught: Every *be-emet* is the halakhah," which may of course simply mean "the established law" rather than HLMM. Further, it must be noted that this statement is not found in mss. and early editions.[64]

The Bavli makes no comment on the term *be-emet* in any other sugya. Indeed, in the case of M. Nazir 7.3 (see B. Nazir 56b) there is no identification of the exceptional clause as a HLMM; rather, the law's derivation from Scripture is shown. It would appear, then, that the identification of exceptional mishnaic rulings as HLMM is not generally adopted in the Bavli. Whether this use of the term featured in the Mishnah and Yerushalmi was simply overlooked, passively ignored or actively rejected, we cannot determine.

In only three instances does the Bavli cite a tradition employing the term HLMM to confer authority upon a specific law, tradition, or practice, and in one case—B. Qiddushin 38b–39a (cf. Y. Orlah 3.8 63b)—R. Yohanan's identification of a particular mishnaic exception as a HLMM is countered by various Babylonian authorities. In the other two cases—B. Nedarim 37b and B. Avodah Zarah 36b—it may be supposed that the term HLMM is proposed in order to bolster the authority of a weak or unstable rabbinic ruling. B. Nedarim 37b cites R. Isaac (PA 3) to the effect that certain scribal traditions regarding the phrasing and recitation of Torah (*miqra soferim*) are HLMM, while B. Avodah Zarah 36b contains the stammaitic assertion that the prohibition of public non-marital intercourse between an Israelite male and a non-Israelite female is a HLMM. However, the instability of these traditions is not indicated in the relevant sugyot themselves.

Thus, the Bavli's use of the term HLMM to ground the authority of specific laws or practices is minimal. However, we do find the term in three aggadic passages devoted to a general legitimization of the rabbis'

---

[64] See Halivni, "Reflections" (n. 13, above), 62 n. 67, and Safrai, "Halakhah" (n. 13, above), 13 n. 11. In B. BM 60a we find the following tradition as part of the gemara commenting on an exceptional mishnaic ruling introduced by *be-emet:* "R. Elazar said: 'From this it may be concluded that wherever *be-emet* is stated, that is the halakhah.'" Although the general principle is ascribed to R. Elazar as in the Yerushalmi, its formulation and substance have been modified. As in B. Shab 92b, R. Elazar is represented as asserting not that the exceptional mishnaic ruling is a HLMM but that it is the halakhah—the established law (so Rashi; see Halivni, ibid., 62). However, here also, the tradition does not appear in some mss. and early editions (Safrai, ibid.).

authority to interpret Torah for all Israel. The first of these passages is B. Bava Batra 12b:

> R. Avdimi from Haifa (PA 3) said: "Since the day when the Temple was destroyed, prophecy has been taken from the prophets and given to the wise." Is then a wise man not also a prophet? What he meant was this: although it has been taken from the prophets, it has not been taken from the wise.
> Amemar (BA 5–6) said: "A wise man is even superior to a prophet [followed by a biblical proof] . . ."
> Rav Ashi (BA 6) said: "The proof is that a great man makes a statement and then it is found that the same rule was a HLMM."

Here the rabbis stake their claim to authority: a Palestinian tradition describing the sages as the successors to the prophets is elaborated by Babylonian rabbis who assert that sages are superior to the prophets. Proof of the sages' excellence is the occasional correspondence between a great rabbi's statement and a HLMM. The term HLMM is used heuristically, as a benchmark of authenticity and correctness against which the authority of the rabbis is to be measured.

Two further passages—early Palestinian sources adopted by the Bavli's redactors—exploit the reputation of R. Akiva as a zealous midrashist in an effort to allay anxiety over the midrashic enterprise. As I have argued elsewhere,[65] the rabbis were sensitive to the fact that midrashic exegesis inspired resistance and rebellion because of its generation of interpretations far removed from, if not antithetical to, the contextual meaning of a biblical passage. Some talmudic texts express simple anxiety over midrashic excess and the ridicule it arouses in non-rabbis; but in other texts, anxiety gives way to exuberance as the rabbis confront the vision of their own strangeness, only to embrace and even celebrate it.

The classic example of rabbinic self-acceptance in the face of radical doubt is the amoraic tradition of B. Menahot 29b in which Moses listens befuddled and uncomprehending to R. Akiva's complex midrashic expositions of Torah:

> Rav Judah said in the name of Rav: "When Moses ascended on high he found the Holy One, blessed be He, engaged in attaching crownlets [decorative squiggles] to the letters [of the Torah]. He said to Him, 'Lord of the Universe, why should you bother with this!?'[66] He answered, 'There is a man who is destined to arise at the end of many generations, named Akiva b. Joseph, and to expound upon each squiggle heaps and heaps of laws.' [Moses] said to him, 'Lord of the Universe, show him to me.' He replied, 'Turn around.' Moses went and sat down behind eight rows [in R. Akiva's

---

[65] Christine Hayes, "Displaced Self-Perceptions: The Deployment of *Minim* and Romans in Bavli Sanhedrin 90b–91a," in *Religious and Ethnic Communities in Later Roman Palestine*, ed. Haim Lapin (Bethesda: University Press of Maryland, 1998), 249–289.

[66] Lit., "Who constrains your hand [to do such a trivial and unnecessary task]?"

schoolhouse, with the least skilled students], but he could not understand what they were saying. His strength left him.[67] But when they came to a certain topic and the disciples said to him [R. Akiva], 'Rabbi, whence do you know it?' he replied to them, 'It is a law given to Moses at Sinai!' And Moses was comforted.[68]

Thereupon he returned to the Holy One, blessed be He, and said to Him, 'Lord of the Universe, You have such a man and You are giving the Torah by me?!' He replied, 'Be silent, for such is my decree.'[69]

[Moses] said to him, 'Lord of the Universe, You have shown me his Torah, now show me his reward.' He replied to him, 'Turn around.' And Moses saw them weighing out R. Akiva's flesh in the marketplace.[70] Moses said to Him, 'Lord of the Universe, that was his Torah and this is his reward!?' And He replied, 'Be silent, for such is my decree.'"[71]

This story, at once humorous and tragic, enables the rabbis brilliantly to voice their simultaneous admiration for and anxiety over the midrashic virtuosity of earlier greats, of which R. Akiva is the premier example. The opening lines sound one of the primary themes of the story: the derivation of mounds of laws from the slimmest biblical details (cf. M. Hagigah 1.8). God's participation in this project—by encoding the text in such a manner that the complex exegesis of the rabbis can proceed—implies his endorsement of it. God tells Moses that R. Akiva will expound these minute calligraphic details so as to yield heaps of laws. Incredulous, Moses asks God to show him R. Akiva at work. Granted a vision of R. Akiva's schoolhouse where the biblical text is expounded to yield these heaps of law, Moses is at a complete loss to understand. Moses, the very one to whom God entrusted his Torah and the first to teach Torah to Israel does not recognize that Torah in the hands of a master exegete some 1500 years later. Moses' non-recognition—a figure for the rabbis' own aching suspicion that midrashic techniques have rendered the Torah unrecognizable—depresses him, until R. Akiva comes to a certain topic. When the students ask R. Akiva the source of this particular law he does not supply a tortuous derivation from Scripture. This law, he says, is a law given to Moses at Sinai and does not emerge from exegesis of Scripture. In other words, there are some things that even a R. Akiva would not attempt to derive from Scripture, and at this Moses heaves a sigh of relief. It is following R. Akiva's *refusal* to expound that Moses praises the latter's great wisdom. The story therefore expresses great ambivalence about extreme methods of midrashic exegesis.[72]

---

[67] An expression used to indicate despair or depression.
[68] Or: "his mind was set at ease."
[69] Or: "so it has occurred to me to do."
[70] A reference to his martyrdom at the hands of the Romans.
[71] See n. 69.
[72] Thus, in all likelihood the story originates in circles opposed to the exegetical pyrotechnics traditionally associated with R. Akiva and his school.

These methods may be part of a divine plan, but the truly wise man knows when to refrain from creating tortured scriptural derivations by means of them (and we can all breathe easier when he does!).

Moses never does understand the proceedings of the schoolhouse, the complex exegetical processes by which a vast structure of laws and teachings had come to rest upon at times "insignificant" calligraphic details in the biblical text. Indeed, R. Akiva's midrashic virtuosity makes Moses quite nervous—and in this respect Moses surely reflects the anxiety of the rabbinic author(s) of the story. On the other hand, the depiction of God as partner to R. Akiva's midrashic excesses suggests that the authors' anxiety is not absolute. Portraying God as R. Akiva's partner betokens at least a desire on the part of the author(s) to believe that despite the yawning gulf that appears to separate the teachings of the rabbis from the divine Torah of ancient Israel, there is an organic unity between them. Midrashic exegesis may engender an agonizing sense of distance and difference between the Torah and rabbinic halakhah, but midrash is also the bridge that connects the two, and in Moses' mouth are placed words of praise and approbation for R. Akiva. In this story, the amoraic rabbis assert their faith in the power and creative possibilities inherent in the midrashic method despite—or rather because of—their equally explicit anxiety over the often odd and unintuitive nature of its results.[73]

This text betrays an exegetical self-consciousness, an awareness that the rabbis' own methods of interpretation involve unintuitive and non-contextual readings that can provoke ridicule, resistance and ultimately rejection of their authority. However, in these texts the rabbis grapple with their anxiety and emerge victorious, overcoming their radical doubt with grandiose assertions of divine approval of the midrashic method and the complex of law and lore resulting from it: the Oral Torah. The term HLMM stands in opposition to the excessive and convoluted biblical exegesis (concerning which the rabbis felt no slight anxiety) and designates laws for which no Scriptural basis can be found.[74]

---

[73] Compare Yaakov Elman, "It is No Empty Thing: Nahmanides and the Search for Omnisignificance," *The Torah U-Madda Journal* 4 (1993): 1–83 at 3 for an interpretation that highlights another aspect of the conflicted nature of this passage.

[74] Halivni's description of the erosion of confidence in exegesis throughout the amoraic period and beyond ("Reflections" [n. 13, above], 29, 83, 89) is consonant with the argument advanced here and elsewhere (see n. 65, above): midrashic excess generated anxiety in the amoraic period and led to (1) a decline in exegetical activity as the source of new law; (2) hyperbolic assertions of the exegetical authority of the rabbis in theory, despite the more conservative exercise of rabbinic authority in practice; and (3) the composition of rhetorical passages that extol and praise the Oral Torah as more beloved and precious than the Written Torah and that which is derived from it (again, despite the more conservative exercise of rabbinic

Similarly, in B. Menahot 89a (‖ B. Niddah 72b) the assertion that a particular law is a HLMM is intended to counter the midrashic zeal of R. Akiva. The sugya opens with a beraita in which R. Akiva attempts to derive from Scripture the half log of oil required for a thank offering. The derivation is complex and convoluted, and revolves around the repetition of the phrase "with oil" in the biblical text. R. Elazar b. Azariah is said to respond to this display of midrashic virtuosity with the contemptuous remark: "Akiva, even if you repeat the words 'with oil' the whole day long I shall not listen to you; rather, the half log of oil of the thank offering, the quarter log of oil of the nazirite and the eleven days between menstrual periods are HLMM." R. Elazar b. Azariah simultaneously articulates and responds to the same anxiety evident in B. Menahot 29b—one can carry midrashic exegesis too far and so undermine rabbinic authority and prestige. At a certain point one must renounce the effort to derive everything from Scripture. Such a renunciation is symbolized by the simple assertion that a particular law is a HLMM, not to be found in the Written Torah. Here again, HLMM is an abstract category that functions as a literary device, a counter or foil to the portrait of the overzealous sage producing contrived and counterintuitive interpretations of Scripture.

The Yerushalmi and Bavli differ markedly in their employment of HLMM to confer authority upon specific laws, traditions, or practices whose authority is unstable in some way. Nearly 80% of the laws identified in the Yerushalmi as HLMM are laws or traditions whose authority is unstable. By contrast, only 40% of the sugyot featuring HLMM in the Bavli employ the term to identify specific laws of possibly unstable authority, and the majority of these (12 of 16) involve just two cases: tefillin and the water libation/willow ritual. Two other identifications of exceptional laws as HLMM are presented in the name of Palestinian tradents. In short, the Bavli relies heavily on Palestinian precedent when it does identify exceptional laws as HLMM. In general, the Bavli's redactors tend to reduce the use of HLMM as a label for a specific exceptional law. For example, the Bavli's redactor modifies or excludes altogether R. Elazar b. Pedat's identification of certain exceptional rulings as HLMM.

Clearly, the close association of HLMM with assertions of authority was known to the Bavli's redactors. Even if they did not use the term to bolster the authority of specific exceptional laws as frequently as did the redactors of the Yerushalmi, they did incorporate into the Bavli early

authority in developing and extending the Oral Torah). In short, anxiety over rabbinic authority, particularly in regard to exegesis of Scripture, led to an increase in the hyperbolic praise for and assertion of that authority in theory, but a reduction in its actual use. See further below (p. 116), and see Halivni, ibid., pp. 59–60 for the view that Palestinian traditions that extol the Oral Law are connected with the greater amoraic reliance on HLMM rather than on exegesis.

aggadic traditions that employ the term "HLMM" in an exploration and legitimation of rabbinic authority generally. These traditions about early tannaim were not selected for inclusion in the Yerushalmi by that text's redactors (though this may be a function of genre: the Bavli in general contains a good deal more aggadah than does the Yerushalmi). Thus, in both Talmudim, HLMM is connected with assertions of authority, but the specific nature of the connection differs markedly. The Yerushalmi's use is concrete and halakhic while the Bavli's use is rhetorical and aggadic, and often raises as much anxiety as it allays. A similar conclusion emerges from a comparative analysis of the forgotten/reestablished strategy in the Bavli and Yerushalmi, to which we now turn.

* * *

(2) A HLMM may be forgotten and subsequently arrived at independently through the argumentative give-and-take of later rabbinic authorities who may be unaware of the ancient origin of the law.

Yerushalmi: The Yerushalmi employs a forgotten/reestablished strategy on five occasions in order to reconcile conflicting traditions regarding the source of a particular law, but in a manner that differs from the tannaitic precedent in M. Yadayim 4.3 in which a law established by the rabbis is identified as a HLMM that had been forgotten. In the Mishnah, the phrase "HLMM" is used literally: the law in question was given as a HLMM, later forgotten and then reestablished through the give-and-take of scholarly debate. However, in the Yerushalmi the reestablished law is not always explicitly identified as a HLMM in a literal sense—as is the case in the tannaitic precedent—but is said to be precious and to endure *like* that which was said to Moses at Sinai (=NLMB). For example, in Y. Peah 1.1 15b R. Gamliel reports the view that one should give no more than one-fifth of his possessions in charity. The stam wonders how R. Gamliel can report on a ruling that was instituted only later, at Usha. We then read:

> R. Yose b. R. Bun in the name of R. Levi: "That was the halakhah as they received it, but they forgot it and later authorities arose and agreed with the earlier [authorities], in order to teach you that any matter to which a court devotes itself will endure as if it were said to Moses at Sinai (כמה שנאמר למשה בסיני)." This is in agreement with what R. Mana said: "*For it is no trifle for you [but it is your life]*" (Deuteronomy 33:27). If it is a trifle for you then it is because you did not labor in it. When is it your life? When you labor in it.

The tradition attributed to R. Levi (PA 3) and reported by R. Yose b. R. Bun (PA 5) is introduced in order to explain the fact that pre-Ushan R. Gamliel cited a tradition attributed to the Ushan court. R. Levi's solution is to assert that this law was in fact a pre-Ushan halakhah (not necessarily a HLMM), but it was forgotten and (re)established later by the Ushan sages. In such cases the ruling survives because it is as precious as that which was said to Moses at Sinai (NLMB).[75]

The forgotten/reestablished strategy employed in the Yerushalmi reconciles contradictory claims as to the source of the law—even when none of these claims actually identifies the law as a HLMM. The passage just cited (up to the exegesis of R. Mana [PA 5]) is found in two more sugyot concerned with reconciling conflicting claims as to the source of a particular law. In the first, Y. Shabbat 1.7 3d (‖ Y. Ketubbot 8.11 32a), neither party to the dispute claims that the law is a HLMM. Here, the forgotten/reestablished strategy of R. Yose b. R. Bun in the name of R. Levi resolves conflicting claims regarding the law of the impurity of Gentile lands: does this law emanate from R. Yose b. Yoezer and R. Yose b. Yohanan, or from the house of Hillel and the house of Shammai? In Y. Sheviit 1.7 33b ‖ Y. Sukkah 4.1 54b the strategy is applied to the laws of the willow ritual, the water libation ritual, and the ten saplings. These laws *are* said by R. Yohanan (PA 2) to be HLMM (though the law of the ten saplings is only implicitly identified as a HLMM by the stam), but R. Hunia (=Nehuniah) of Bet Hauran (cited by R. Ba bar Zavda) holds them to be "rulings of the prophets." In each case, the later reestablishment of a law known earlier but forgotten prompts the stam's invocation of R. Levi's tradition: the dedication of the court ensures that the law endures as if it were said to Moses at Sinai (NLMB).

The phrase "as if it were said to Moses at Sinai (כמה שנאמר למשה בסיני)" is not equivalent to a declaration that the law is a HLMM. It has a purely metaphorical meaning in these cases and indicates that a tradition is so precious (as precious as that which was revealed to Moses at Sinai) that it ultimately survived, even though it was temporarily forgotten. It may be that the original context of the tradition of R. Levi cited by R. Yose b. R. Bun involved a law which was held by some to be a HLMM, and by others to be a later ruling (e.g. the case in Y. Orlah). On this point we can only speculate, however. Whatever the origin of the tradition, it was apparently applied to other cases featuring conflicting claims over the source of a law—whether

---

[75] The latter part of this same sugya provides biblical examples of persons who managed to arrive at and fulfill certain laws or instructions as given to Moses at Sinai, despite their having no knowledge that they had been said to Moses at Sinai. Both Bezalel and Joshua are said to have done "all that the Lord had commanded Moses." The verse is interpreted to mean that God told Moses, and not Bezalel and Joshua, what was expected of the latter two. Nevertheless, even though Bezalel and Joshua never heard these instructions from God or Moses, each arrived independently at the content of God's speech as reported to Moses at Sinai. Unlike the first part of the sugya, the second part employs the phrase NLMB in an entirely literal sense. Even if ignorant of the words said to Moses at Sinai, a diligent person can hit upon the actual content of revelation. Indeed, a final midrash indicates that God ensures lack of error in such cases.

HLMM or not. Thus, in two respects, the Yerushalmi's use of the forgotten/reestablished strategy differs from that of the Mishnah in M. Yadayim 4.3 (cf T. Yadayim 2.7). First, in the Yerushalmi the strategy is not confined to cases involving a HLMM (or what is eventually declared to be a HLMM). Second, the law in question is not identified literally as a HLMM; rather, its reestablishment after being forgotten indicates that, like the revelation to Moses at Sinai, the law was precious and thus able to endure.

Bavli: The Bavli's use of this strategy is minimal at best, occurring in only two sugyot. In B. Yoma 80a and B. Sukkah 44a the strategy appears in the most skeletal form, and in the latter case it is explicitly rejected. Following the stam's fictive claim that minima prescribed for penalties were given as a HLMM, B. Yoma 80a features the anonymous ("others say") and contradictory claim that these minima were fixed by the court of Jabetz. The stam objects on the basis of Leviticus 27:34 that Scripture prohibits the introduction of any new law after Sinai. The stam resolves this problem with the simple line: "Rather, they were forgotten and then they established them anew." Unlike the Yerushalmi sugyot examined above, this sugya employs a forgotten/reestablished strategy in a most literal sense, and thus closely resembles the mishnaic precedent in M. Yadayim 4.3: the prescribed minima for penalties were given as a HLMM but were forgotten and subsequently reestablished by the court of Jabetz. Entirely lacking is the Yerushalmi's shift into metaphor, i.e., whatever a diligent court labors to (re)establish is as precious and enduring as that which was said to Moses at Sinai.

The only other Bavli sugya to feature the forgotten/reestablished strategy—B. Sukkah 44a—ultimately rejects it. B. Sukkah 44a opens with Rav Zevid (BA 5) stating in the name of Rabbah[76] (BA 2) that the willow ritual is rabbinic. This Babylonian amoraic tradition sets the theme for the entire sugya, and all contrary sources will be harmonized to this claim in some way. First, the stam points out contradictory traditions (Abba Saul's claim that the willow ritual is scriptural and R. Assi's statement in the name of R. Yohanan that the ten saplings law, the willow ritual and the water libation ritual are HLMM).[77] The contradiction is resolved by *oqimta*: Rabbah meant

---

[76] Following DS 6:135 n. *tsadde*, a correction from "Rava." On this reading, it is an early Babylonian amora who states that the willow ritual is rabbinic.

[77] R. Assi states in the name of R. Yohanan who had it from R. Nehuniah of the Plain of Bet Hauran: "The laws of the ten saplings, the willow ritual and the water libation ritual are HLMM." Only in the Bavli does this tradition add the law of the ten saplings to the willow ritual and the water libation ritual (B. Suk 34a, 44a; Taan 3a; MQ 3b; Zev 110b [not all of these cite R. Nehuniah]). In the Yerushalmi, only the willow ritual and water libation ritual are explicitly designated HLMM by R. Yohanan. That R. Yohanan holds the ten saplings law to be a HLMM is strongly implied by Y. Shev 1.7 33b, as we have seen. Babylonian tradents, aware of the juxta-

that the performance of the willow ritual *inside* the sanctuary is Pentateuchal while the performance of the ritual *outside* the sanctuary is rabbinic. There is an implicit equation of Scripture and HLMM here since this one *oqimta* answers the objection raised by the traditions of both Abba Saul and R. Yohanan. Shortly after this section, we read:

> You may conclude that it was R. Yohanan who said that it [the willow ritual] is one of the institutions of the prophets, since R. Abbahu said in the name of R. Yohanan, "The willow rite is one of the institutions of the prophets." You may conclude it.
> R. Zera said to R. Abbahu: "Did then R. Yohanan say so? Did not[78] R. Yohanan in fact state in the name of R. Nehuniah of the Plain of Bet Hauran that the ten saplings law, the willow ritual and the water libation were HLMM?"
> The other was dumbfounded for a while (cf. Daniel 4:16) and then he answered: "They were forgotten and the prophets reinstituted them."
> But could R. Yohanan say so?[79] Did not R. Yohanan in fact state: "What I said was yours were in fact theirs"?[80]
> Rather, this is no difficulty since one statement refers to the sanctuary [HLMM] and the other to the provinces [institution of the prophets].

The stam infers that R. Yohanan himself actually believed the willow ritual to be an institution of the prophets (i.e., rabbinic in the sense of non-Pentateuchal, and therefore open to alteration). This inference is supported by the stam's citation of R. Abbahu's (PA 3) statement in the name of R. Yohanan: The willow ritual is an institution of the prophets. To this R. Zera (PA 3) is said to object: "Did then R. Yohanan say so? Did not R. Yohanan in fact state in the name of R. Nehuniah of Bet Hauran that 'the law of the ten saplings, the willow ritual and the water libation ritual were HLMM'?" The Bavli's version of R. Yohanan's statement appears to be a conflation of Palestinian traditions. In Y. Sheviit 1.7 33b ‖ Y. Sukkah 4.2 54b, R. Honia/R. Nehuniah of Bet Hauran declares that all three rituals—the willow ritual, the water libation ritual and the ten saplings law—are prophetic in origin.[81] In the same sugya, R. Yohanan declares the willow ritual and the water

---

position of these topics and traditions among Palestinians, drew their conclusions and made the implicit explicit. See below, pp. 105–106, for a discussion of the development of this tradition.

[78] Munich ms. reads here, "Did not R. Assi say that R. Yohanan in fact stated in the name of . . ."; DS 6:135, n. *gimmel*.

[79] Munich ms. omits this phrase.

[80] The meaning of this phrase is obscure (witness the varied suggestions of Rashi, R. Hananel and Tosafot), but it is probably intended as a retraction of one claim or the other (e.g., what I said was a HLMM was in fact a prophetic institution, or vice versa).

[81] But see n. 47, above, for the reading of the Vatican printed edition according to which the first two are HLMM.

libation ritual to be HLMM. These traditions are combined in the Bavli, where R. Assi (or R. Ammi) says that R. Yohanan said in the name of R. Nehuniah of Bet Hauran that all three rituals are HLMM.

The first proposed solution for R. Yohanan's self-contradiction is the forgotten/reestablished strategy—the strategy adopted in the Yerushalmi parallel: These three laws were HLMM, but they were forgotten and later reestablished by the prophets. This solution is rejected, and ultimately the two views here attributed to R. Yohanan are reconciled by the *oqimta* employed earlier in the sugya: R. Yohanan held that the willow ritual inside the sanctuary was a HLMM while the willow ritual outside the sanctuary was an institution of the prophets. Through this *oqimta*, early Palestinian traditions are brought into line with the Babylonian view that the willow ritual must be prophetic (i.e., rabbinic) rather than scriptural or HLMM.

Divergent redactional attitudes towards the forgotten/reestablished strategy are apparent in these parallel sugyot. The Bavli and the Yerushalmi share the same redactional goal: the conversion of the willow ritual from a HLMM to a rabbinic law. In order to achieve this goal, both must "unseat" the Palestinian tradition attributed to R. Yohanan that the rite is a HLMM. Both Talmudim cite a contradictory tradition to the effect that the willow rite is an institution of the prophets (i.e., it is rabbinic). In both Talmudim this tradition prevails, and R. Yohanan's contrary tradition is harmonized to it by one or another means. The Yerushalmi employs its version of a forgotten/reestablished strategy: these laws are only metaphorically HLMM. The Bavli considers and rejects such a strategy, adopting an *oqimta* instead.

We see from these examples that the Bavli's use of the forgotten/reestablished strategy more closely resembles the Mishnah's than the Yerushalmi's. It reconciles conflicting claims about the source of the law, one of which is that the law is a HLMM, and it employs the term HLMM in a literal sense. However, the Bavli's use of the strategy is extremely minimal—it appears in only two passages that feature a HLMM, and in one of those the strategy is rejected outright in favor of an *oqimta*. Further, in another two of the five cases in which the Yerushalmi invokes the forgotten/reestablished strategy, the Bavli employs an *oqimta* without even considering the forgotten/reestablished strategy. In B. Shabbat 15a–b (‖ Y. Shabbat 1.7 3d) regarding the impurity of heathen lands, conflicting claims as to the source of the law are reconciled by an *oqimta* painstakingly negotiated by the stam:

> They (R. Yose b. Yoezer and R. Yose b. Yohanan) came and decreed suspension [for terumah that contacted] a clod of earth [from Gentile land], and nothing at all [for terumah that contacted] the atmosphere [of Gentile land]; then the rabbis of the eighty years [i.e., of the generation 80 years prior to the destruction] came and decreed suspension in both cases; then at Usha

Halakhah le-Moshe mi-Sinai *in Rabbinic Sources*   107

they came and decreed burning in regard to a clod of earth, and as for the atmosphere they left the law as it was.

In B. Moed Qatan 3b (‖ Y. Sheviit 1.7 33b) the laws of ploughing before the sabbatical year (including the law of the ten saplings) are attributed to the house of Shammai and the house of Hillel and are said to be HLMMs. The conflict is resolved by *oqimta* (viz., the HLMM was a thirty-day restriction while the law as issued by the house of Hillel and the house of Shammai was for a longer period). Furthermore, the Bavli does not employ the forgotten/reestablished strategy in connection with the other three laws that feature this strategy in the Yerushalmi.[82]

Thus, while the Yerushalmi adopts the forgotten/reestablished strategy and transforms it into metaphor, the Bavli all but ignores and rejects it. This is all the more remarkable in view of two facts: (1) the motif of forgetting laws is found frequently in the Bavli. There are passages that feature a sage who forgets or fears he will forget a specific halakhah, prooftext or even all of his learning; or the people Israel as a whole forgetting Torah; or a law being forgotten in Israel were it not for the efforts of a particular individual;[83] (2) the forgotten/reestablished strategy is found elsewhere in the Bavli but in primarily aggadic or hyperbolic contexts (unlike the Yerushalmi where it does not appear outside the halakhic contexts discussed here), and never in connection with the term or concept of HLMM. For example, in two passages the forgotten/reestablished strategy is part of the polemical artillery of Babylonians trumpeting their superiority over their Palestinian counterparts. In B. Sukkah 20a we read:

> What is marzuble?—R. Abba said, "Bags filled with foliage." R. Simeon b. Lakish said, "Reed matting." And Resh Lakish is consistent [in this view], since Resh Lakish said, "May I be an expiation for R. Hiyya and his sons.[84] For in ancient times when the Torah was forgotten from Israel, Ezra came up from Babylon and established it. [Some of] it was again forgotten and Hillel the Babylonian came up and established it. Yet again [some of] it was forgotten, and R. Hiyya and his sons came up and established it. And thus said R. Hiyya and his sons: 'R. Dosa and the Sages did not dispute about the reed-mats of Usha, that they are susceptible to [ritual] uncleanliness, or of

---

[82] B. Ket 50a (‖ Y. Peah 1.1 15b) regarding the maximum amount of one's possessions that may be distributed for charitable purposes, B. Shab 14b (‖ Y. Ket 8.11 32a) regarding the impurity of heathen glassware, and B. Naz 56b (‖ Y. Peah 2.6 17a) regarding the two species of wheat, do not record contradictory traditions over the source of the law at all, and thus no solution is required or proposed.

[83] B. Pes 66a, 69a, 106b; Suk 20a; Ned 41a; BB 9b, 21a; Ket 22a; Qid 57a; Sanh 82a, 96a; AZ 52b; Zev 59a, 70b; Men 7a, 99a; Hul 82a, 103b, 107b.

[84] In other words, "May I make atonement for, and so relieve them of, any punishments awaiting them after death"—an expression of respect and admiration; cf. B. Qid 71b.

Tiberias that they are not susceptible. About what do they dispute? About those of other places.'"

Likewise, in B. Pesahim 66a the people of Bathyra (in northern Palestine) forget whether or not slaughtering the Paschal lamb overrides the Sabbath. Hillel the Babylonian establishes the law through argumentative give-and-take and rebukes the people of Bathyra for their indolence which caused the law to be forgotten. The Bavli's use of the strategy here conforms to tannaitic precedent in certain respects: a forgotten law is reestablished by virtue of the argumentation and deliberation of the sages. The same idea appears in B. Ketubbot 103b ‖ B. Bava Metzia 85b where R. Hanina boasts to R. Hiyya, "Were the Torah, God forbid, to be forgotten in Israel, I would restore it by means of my dialectical arguments." Even in the clearly hyperbolic claim in B. Temurah 16a that 1700 *kal vehomer* and *gezerah shavah* arguments and scribal specifications were forgotten during the period of mourning for Moses, we find the idea that rabbinic dialectic can make good the loss: "R. Abbahu said, 'Nevertheless, Othniel son of Kenaz restored them as a result of his dialectics'" (cf. B. Yoma 80a).

These examples suggest that the Bavli employs a forgotten/reestablished strategy for primarily rhetorical purposes that include grandiose claims on behalf of rabbinic authority or in praise of a particular sage or Babylonian sages generally. Unlike the Yerushalmi, the Bavli rarely employs the forgotten/reestablished strategy (with or without the term HLMM) in a strictly halakhic context.

*   *   *

(3) A HLMM (a) may convey a ruling detailing the proper way to observe a Torah law (M. Peah 2.6); (b) may be identical to a rabbinic innovation (M. Yadayim 4.3); or (c) may convey an aggadic rather than a strictly halakhic tradition (M. Eduyyot 8.2).

In general, the Yerushalmi and Bavli conform to tannaitic precedent in this regard, identifying as HLMM rulings concerning Torah laws as well as certain clearly post-biblical or rabbinic innovations.[85] Both Talmudim contain traditions citing the general principle that prescribed minima for the observance of Torah laws are HLMM,[86] though this principle is subject to dispute and revision. Both Talmudim contain traditions that identify details of the preparation of tefillin, mezuzot and Torah scrolls as HLMM,[87] although a comparison of Palestinian and Babylonian traditions regarding

---

[85] In the latter case, of course, the post-biblical or rabbinic origin of the law in question is implicitly denied by the declaration that it is a HLMM.

[86] B. Eruv 4a ‖ B. Suk 5b, cf. Y. Hag 1.2 76b.

[87] Y. Meg 1.11 71d, and 4.9 75c; B. Shevu 28b; B. Shab 62a, 79b; B. Eruv 97a; B. Meg 19b, 24b; B. Ned 37b; B. Men 35a–b.

tefillin highlights the "creativity" of the latter. Tannaitic sources describe the square shape of tefillin as a HLMM, while a late Palestinian amora (R. Yosi b. R. Bun, PA 5) states that the rule that tefillin are square and black is a HLMM. The Bavli cites the Palestinian traditions describing the shape and color of tefillin as HLMM, but in addition includes Babylonian traditions describing other details as HLMM. For example, B. Eruvin 97a: "Rav Judah son of Rav Shmuel b. Shilat (BA 3; but in Munich and Oxford mss., just R. Judah, BA 2) said in the name of Rav: 'The shape of the knot of the tefillin is a HLMM.'" This tradition is expanded in B. Shabbat 62a:

> Abbaye (BA 4) said, "The *shin* of tefillin [stamped out of the leather side of the capsule] is a HLMM." Abbaye also said, "The *dalet* of tefillin [formed by the knot in the strap of the head phylactery] is a HLMM." Abbaye also said, "The *yod* of tefillin [formed by the knot in the strap of the hand phylactery] is a HLMM."[88]

Finally, with the exception of B. Pesahim 110b, in which a Palestinian tradition recommending avoidance of things that occur in pairs is said to be a HLMM, neither Talmud identifies aggadic teachings as HLMM.

* * *

(4) In tannaitic sources, a HLMM is absolutely authoritative: it requires no logical justification, is not open to dispute and cannot be set aside or overturned (M. Yadayim 4.3 ‖ T. Yadayim 2.7 and, implicitly, M. Peah 2.6), versus

(5) In tannaitic sources, a HLMM is *not* absolutely authoritative: it may be disputed and can be set aside or overruled (M. Eduyyot 8.7).

As we saw above (p. 90), the tendency in both the Yerushalmi and the Bavli is towards a strengthening of the authority of HLMM, and the equation of that authority with the authority of Scripture in certain respects. Although both Talmudim preserve sources that attest to a shift in attitudes over time, the final redactors of both texts tout the authority of HLMM. The passage in Y. Peah 2.6 17a ‖ Y. Megillah 4.1 74d ‖ Y. Hagigah 1.8 76d which extols that which was said to Moses at Sinai (NLMB) as more beloved and precious than Written Torah may be understood in this light. In the Bavli, a story involving tannaitic protagonists employs the term HLMM to express the very idea of incontrovertibility: In B. Niddah 45a, R. Akiva's students are astonished to hear him give a ruling contrary to the accepted halakhah, but learn that unless a law is a HLMM it is subject to reversal based on logi-

---

[88] It must be noted, however, that in the Munich ms. the third of Abbaye's traditions is absent and the second appears in brackets. The Tosafot debate both of the final two traditions, which suggests that the creative Babylonian tendency to multiply HLMMs in connection with tefillin may have extended into the manuscript traditions. For a discussion of this phenomenon in connection with the manuscripts of Bava Metzia, see Sh. Friedman, *Talmud Arukh*, 1:26.

cal and legal considerations.[89] Thus, the term HLMM here connotes that which cannot be overturned or contradicted but enjoys absolute authority.

Practices contrary to a HLMM are not tolerated in B. Shabbat 79b ‖ B. Menahot 32a–b and B. Menahot 35a–b, and are explained away. In the former text, R. Meir is said to write the mezuzah upon one kind of parchment despite a HLMM to the effect that a mezuzah should be written upon a different kind of parchment. The gemara's explanation—that in this case the HLMM sets out only the preferred, not the mandatory, way of doing things—is clearly based on the stam's assumption that practices contrary to a HLMM are in general not allowed. In B. Menahot 35a–b, R. Isaac (PA 3) states that the straps of the tefillin must be black, in keeping with a HLMM. This is followed by reports of a conflicting tradition (the straps may be green, black, or white, but not red) and conflicting practices (the tefillin straps of various rabbis are said to be various colors). The variant practices are explained away easily enough and the conflicting tradition is resolved by *oqimta* (the HLMM refers to the outside of the strap only and the conflicting tradition concerns the inside of the strap)—an indication that a HLMM cannot be overturned or set aside. The only exception to the picture of HLMM as authoritative and incontrovertible is a brief notation in B. Makkot 11a. After discussing the HLMM that tefillin must be sewn together with gut-string, Rav remarks: "We saw the phylacteries in the household of my beloved [uncle, R. Hiyya], and they were sewn with flaxen thread. But the halakhah is not in accordance with his practice." Although the passage contains a report of non-observance of a HLMM by a Palestinian sage, it does not endorse the behavior reported.

*   *   *

(6) In tannaitic sources, a HLMM is distinct from Scripture as a source of law. If a law is said to be a HLMM it cannot be derived from Scripture, and vice versa (implied by T. Sukkah 3.2).

The evidence of the Yerushalmi is mixed, as we saw above (pp. 78–80). Two sources (Y. Sheviit 1.7 33b ‖ Y. Sukkah 4.1 54b and Y. Orlah 3.8 63b) depict relatively early Palestinian authorities as maintaining a distinction between HLMM and Scripture as sources of law. By contrast, two further sources (Y. Hagigah 1.2 76b and Y. Nazir 7.3 56c) suggest that at a later period HLMM and Scripture were viewed as equivalent rather than distinct and mutually exclusive categories.

The Bavli, however, clearly assumes with early Palestinian sources that HLMM and Scripture are distinct and mutually exclusive sources of law.

---

[89] See the text critical comments and interpretation in Halivni, "Reflections" (n. 13, above), 54.

This distinct status does not prevent the Bavli from equating HLMM and Scripture in terms of authority, as we saw above (p. 90).

* * *

(7) In tannaitic sources, the claim that a law, belief, or practice is a HLMM may be accompanied by a chain of transmission (however gapped or vague) leading back to Moses at Sinai and by terms indicative of the process of transmission. This implies a fairly literal understanding of the term HLMM (M. Peah 2.6, M. Yadayim 4.3 ‖ T. Yadayim 2.7),
versus
(8) The claim that a law, belief, or practice is a HLMM may be simply asserted without a chain of transmission or terms indicative of the process of transmission (T. Sukkah 3.2).

In neither Talmud is the declaration that a particular law is a HLMM ever accompanied by a chain of transmission or terms indicative of the process of transmission; the claim that a law, belief, or practice is a HLMM is simply asserted. Are we to suppose, then, that the amoraic notion of HLMM is less literal, and more metaphorical than that of tannaitic sources?

In most cases it is not possible to determine if the conception of a HLMM is literal or metaphorical, but on occasion there are details in the surrounding context that provide helpful clues. Turning first to the Yerushalmi, a literal conception of HLMM is apparent in Y. Peah 2.6 17a (‖ Y. Hagigah 1.8 76d). The mishnah has identified one of its rulings as a HLMM. In the gemara, R. Zeira (PA 3) says in the name of R. Yohanan: "If a halakhah comes to you and you do not know its nature, do not dismiss it, for many matters of law were transmitted to Moses on Sinai (NLMB) and all of them are embedded in the Mishnah." In effect, this tradition defines a HLMM as a matter of law transmitted to Moses on Sinai (NLMB)—a very literal conception indeed.[90] In other sugyot, however, NLMB is probably not intended literally. As we have seen (pp. 102–104, above), the Yerushalmi on several occasions employs a tradition attributed to R. Levi and reported by R. Yose b. R. Bun (BA 5) according to which any matter forgotten and later reestablished by the diligence of rabbinic authorities will endure as if it were said to Moses at Sinai (NLMB).[91] In these cases, the term

---

[90] A literal conception of the related phrase NLMB can be found in Y. Meg 1.7 70d, in which the establishment of a new law (the observance of Purim) by Esther and Mordechai appears to contradict Torah verses that indicate that no new law shall appear after the Mosaic revelation. One solution to this problem is to propose that even the book of Esther was said to Moses at Sinai. Since it is clear that this solution is intended to attribute the law of Purim observance to Moses himself, we must construe the phrase NLMB quite literally.

[91] Y. Shev 1.7 33b ‖ Y. Suk 4.1 54b; Y. Peah 1.1 15b; Y. Shab 1.7 3d ‖ Y. Ket 8.11 32a.

NLMB connotes something as precious and therefore enduring as that which actually was said to Moses at Sinai (NLMB).[92]

The Bavli too contains only simple assertions that a particular law or tradition is a HLMM (i.e., no tradent chains or terms of transmission) and, again, in most cases there is no way to determine on the basis of function or context whether the attribution is a literal or metaphorical one. In four sugyot, however, there are contextual clues that indicate that the term HLMM is used literally. In B. Yoma 80a the claim that prescribed minima are a HLMM is understood by the stam to mean that they preceded the court of Jabetz—thus HLMM most likely refers literally to a law spoken to Moses. In B. Nazir 56b, Nahum the Scribe's tradent chain for the HLMM reported in M. Peah 2.6 is cited by Rav Nahman bar Isaac (BA 4) as proof that intermediate names in chains of transmission—in this case Joshua and Caleb—may be omitted. Clearly, this fourth-generation Babylonian amora takes literally the notion of a law given to Moses at Sinai and handed down from tradent to tradent. In B. Avodah Zarah 36b the prohibition of public nonmarital intercourse between an Israelite male and a Gentile female is cited by the stam as a HLMM. From the continuation of the sugya it is clear that the motivation for this statement is the justification of the zealous act of Phinehas in Numbers 25, in the lifetime of Moses. Thus, the term HLMM is likely intended literally here too, as it is in the stam of B. Sukkah 44a (see the discussion of this text above, pp. 104–106). In all four of these cases, the literal understanding of HLMM is held by a late Babylonian amora or the stam.[93]

By way of comparison, the use of NLMB in the Bavli differs entirely from its use in the Yerushalmi. This can be seen in the following examples featuring early Babylonian and Palestinian (especially tannaitic) sages:

- B. Rosh ha-Shanah 32a (cf. B. Megillah 21b): "To what do these ten kingship verses correspond? . . . R. Joseph said: 'To the Ten Commandments that were NLMB.'"

---

[92] It is likely that the tradition of R. Joshua b. Levi found in Y. Peah 2.6 17a ‖ Y. Hag 1.8 76d and Y. Meg 4.1 74d to the effect that Scripture, Mishnah, Talmud and Aggadah were already all said to Moses at Sinai (NLMB), should also be understood as a hyperbolic metaphor, occuring as it does in passages concerned with grounding the authority of an unstable law or tradition. Both Halivni ("Reflections" [n. 13, above]) and Safrai ("Halakhah" [n. 13, above]) assume a basic equivalence of HLMM and NLMB, and their discussions of HLMM draw upon sources that contain either of the two phrases. Although they are clearly related, however, the two terms are not always equivalent, as will become apparent in the discussion to follow. For this reason, I do not conflate the terms but treat them separately.

[93] The only clearly non-literal understanding of HLMM to appear in the Bavli is held by early Palestinian authorities. For example, in a beraita featuring R. Akiva and his students in B. Nid 45a, the term probably means only "incontrovertible."

- B. Sanhedrin 99a: "Even as the school of Ishmael taught: *Because he has despised the word of the Lord* (Numbers 15:31)—this applies to one who despises the words spoken to Moses at Sinai (NLMB), namely, *I am the Lord thy God* . . . , etc. (i.e., the Ten Commandments)."

In these cases, NLMB reports a concrete fact of the biblical revelation *as recorded in the biblical text*, not as preserved by oral tradition (its meaning in the Yerushalmi). According to the biblical narrative itself, the Ten Commandments *were* spoken to Moses at Sinai. The Bavli's use of NLMB is consistent: it refers to the revelation at Sinai, the contents of which are explicitly or implicitly indicated in Scripture. Thus, every occurrence of NLMB in the Bavli is accompanied by a biblical prooftext or allusion, demonstrating that the law or tradition in question was actually said to Moses at Sinai. For example, in B. Shabbat 70a the tanna R. Nathan identifies the verse that intimates the 39 categories of labor prohibited on the Sabbath and said to Moses at Sinai (NLMB). The claim that God communicated the 39 categories of labor to Moses simply reports a "fact" of the biblical narrative. B. Hullin 42a cites a tannaitic tradition from the school of R. Ishmael identifying the verse that intimates the 18 defects that render an animal *terefah* and that were NLMB. In B. Makkot 32b R. Simlai's (PA 2) assertion that 613 precepts were NLMB is proven by *gematriyah* of Scripture, and in B. Keritot 6b a lengthy midrash introduced by Rav Huna (BA 2) is cited in support of R. Yohanan's (PA 2) claim that 11 kinds of spices were NLMB.[94]

It is apparent from these examples that the Bavli and Yerushalmi differ markedly in their deployment of the term NLMB. In the Yerushalmi, the term can overlap with HLMM, but is most often employed metaphorically

---

[94] B. Pes 38b is an exception that proves the rule. This passage features a "Babylonian beraita" (for a discussion of this phenomenon see Shamma Friedman, "The Baraitot in the Babylonian Talmud and the Parallels in the Tosefta," in *Atara l'Haim: Studies in the Talmud and Medieval Rabbinic Literature in Honor of Professor Haim Zalman Dimitrovsky*, ed. D. Boyarin et al. [Jerusalem: Magnes, 2000], 163–201), in which R. Eliezer reacts to a particular rabbinic ruling by declaring "By the covenant! These are the very words which were said to Moses at Sinai (NMLB)." No scriptural verse is cited and the most likely explanation of R. Eliezer's words is that the ruling arrived at by the rabbis was also believed to have been given to Moses at Sinai as an oral tradition. This is the only time the Bavli "cites" a source in which NLMB refers to an oral tradition that does not appear in the written record of the revelation at Sinai. It is not surprising then, that the passage is immediately followed by the stammaitic suggestion that R. Eliezer's statement was actually a rhetorical question: "By the covenant! Are these the very words which were said to Moses at Sinai?" Of course not, is the implied response, and R. Eliezer never intended to say that this law was NLMB, as can be proven by the fact that the law has a logical justification. Thus, the one time the Bavli cites a source in which NLMB is employed in a manner that violates the Bavli's understanding of the term, the stam promptly reinterprets the source and eliminates the contradiction.

(it is introduced by *kemah* or found in hyperbolic contexts). In the Bavli, NLMB is not at all equivalent to HLMM. HLMM always signals a law or tradition *not* intimated in the biblical text, while NLMB always signals a law or tradition that *is* intimated (or even explicit) in the biblical text. NLMB is never metaphorical, but refers precisely to the contents of revelation as documented in Scripture. It is interesting that this understanding of NLMB is held primarily by early Palestinian authorities, especially tannaim; yet, despite its Palestinian provenance, this use of NLMB to refer to the actual contents of the revelation at Sinai as explicitly recorded or intimated in Scripture does not appear in the Yerushalmi, which instead adopts the metaphorical understanding of NLMB espoused in later Palestinian sources. Rather, the early Palestinian understanding of NLMB noted here is espoused by some Babylonian authorities (Rav Joseph, Rav Huna), and is ultimately adopted by and preserved in the Bavli. Here then is another instance of a correspondence between early Palestinian and Babylonian sources, as distinct from late Palestinian sources (cf. above, p. 82).

Summary

My synchronic analysis of the two Talmudim reveals that there is not a single, uniform relationship between Mishnah/Tosefta and the Talmudim. At times, there is a strong correspondence between the tannaitic documents and both Talmudim, at other times a correspondence between the tannaitic documents and only one or the other Talmud. In the case of HLMM, synchronic analysis enables the following comparative observations:

1. The Yerushalmi follows tannaitic precedent as found in the Mishnah and Tosefta in its use of HLMM to bolster the authority of exceptional or disputed halakhot and contains the observation that many HLMMs are embedded in the Mishnah. In the Bavli, HLMM is less often used to bolster the authority of a specific exceptional or disputed halakhah, though it appears in aggadic passages that seek to bolster rabbinic authority generally. In these texts featuring tannaim, the abstract category HLMM serves as a counterbalance to the kind of tortured biblical exegesis that undermined confidence in rabbinic leadership—among rabbis and non-rabbis alike. HLMM is a way to claim authority for the Oral Law generally without resort to the midrashic pyrotechnics of earlier generations. In short, unlike the Palestinian texts the Bavli shies away from the practice of grounding the authority of unstable laws in either HLMM or complex midrashic exegesis—perhaps because *both* strain credulity—although it does allow itself to employ the concept of HLMM for broad-based claims of rabbinic authority. These findings are consistent with my findings in two recent studies, both of which uncover, particularly in the Bavli, some kind of amoraic

ambivalence towards—i.e., a simultaneous rabbinic acceptance of and resistance to—an earlier rabbinic idea, strategy, or technique.[95]

2. There is in general, a greater correspondence between Mishnah/Tosefta and Bavli than there is between Mishnah/Tosefta and Yerushalmi. Although the Bavli's use of the forgotten/reestablished strategy is minimal, it nevertheless closely mimics tannaitic usage (which is literal) rather

---

[95] The two studies to which I refer identify amoraic discomfort with and reduced exercise of some aspect of rabbinic authority, coupled with hyperbolic and rhetorical assertions of that very authority. In a paper entitled "The Abrogation of Torah Law: Rabbinic Taqqanah and Praetorian Edict," in *The Talmud Yerushalmi in Graeco-Roman Culture*, ed. P. Schäfer (Tübingen: Mohr, 1998), 643–674, I look at tannaitic rulings (later termed *taqqanot*) that contradict or overturn Torah law—obviously a bold exercise of rabbinic authority. I show that in several instances the amoraim go on to neutralize or deny the innovative or contradictory nature of these tannaitic taqqanot. The amoraic neutralization or denial of rabbinic enactments that contradict biblical law is less pronounced in the Yerushalmi than in the Bavli. The Bavli adopts various strategies in order to redescribe all of the taqqanot that it identifies as ostensibly contradicting Torah law, as not in fact contradicting Torah law. By contrast, the Yerushalmi is quite prepared to admit that at least some taqqanot are indeed innovations that contradict provisions of biblical law. In matters of practical halakhah, then, the Bavli exhibits a more conservative attitude towards the exercise of rabbinic authority, despite grandiose assertions in hyperbolic and highly rhetorical passages of the power of the rabbis and their Oral Torah over the Written Torah.

In a second paper, entitled "Displaced Self-Perceptions: The Deployment of *Minim* and Romans in Bavli Sanhedrin 90b–91a" (see n. 65, above), I analyze an aggadic passage from the Bavli in order to make the claim that rabbis of late antiquity felt a deep ambivalence towards non-contextual or extreme midrashic methods of exegesis. I argue that the rabbis are indeed aware of a distinction between contextual and non-contextual methods of interpretation, that self-consciousness about, and discomfort with, extreme midrashic techniques are not only a post-talmudic phenomenon, as has been argued by others, but can be found already in the talmudic period, and that rabbinic authors introduce or exploit the presence of *minim* and Romans in certain traditions in order to voice and thus grapple with their own ambivalence and radical doubt concerning non-contextual methods of exegesis. I conclude that the reactions to non-contextual exegesis attributed to these non-rabbis are displaced expressions of radical doubt and anxiety on the part of the rabbis themselves. Nevertheless, rabbinic expressions of doubt go hand-in-hand with hyperbolic praise of the great midrashic masters of the past and their extreme methods—indicating a basic rabbinic ambivalence. The amoraim simultaneously accepted and resisted extreme midrashic methods, as evidenced by two types of texts: those that focus on the dangers inherent in a non-contextual program of exegesis (characterized by expressions of anxiety, embarrassment, or general discomfort) and others that focus on the creative possibilities inherent in such a program (characterized by expressions of exuberance and confidence that overcome this anxiety).

than the Yerushalmi's usage (which is metaphorical). Like Mishnah/Tosefta, the Bavli views HLMM and Scripture as distinct sources of law—a view that is not consistently represented in the Yerushalmi and not espoused by the stam.

Finally, both Talmudim employ the term HLMM in a literal fashion at times, and in this both resemble Mishnah/Tosefta. Nevertheless, the Bavli's use of the related term NLMB is always literal, while the Yerushalmi's is overwhelmingly metaphorical. In this respect too the Bavli more closely resembles Mishnah/Tosefta, and it is probably no accident that the NLMB traditions cited by the Bavli are primarily tannaitic.

The present study, in combination with the two studies cited in n. 95, suggests a general cultural difference between the communities of rabbis who produced the Yerushalmi and the Bavli. The Bavli exhibits a pronounced anxiety over rabbinic authority and eschews techniques and strategies that threaten to undermine confidence in rabbinic authority or credibility, such as the use of HLMM to bolster specific unstable laws, extreme forms of exegesis of Scripture, and the issuance of legislation contrary to Torah law. This anxiety had two results: an increase in the hyperbolic praise for and assertion of oral tradition and rabbinic authority in theory, but a reduction in the actual exercise of that authority (in the use of HLMM, the issuance of innovative rabbinic decrees and the midrashic derivation of new laws).

Conclusion

This study has uncovered a chronological shift in the Palestinian conception of HLMM.[96] Early Palestinian sources tend to distinguish HLMM and Scripture as sources of law and employ the term HLMM (and the related term NLMB) in a literal fashion. Later Palestinian sources and the stam of the Yerushalmi tend to conflate HLMM and Scripture as sources of law and to employ the term HLMM (and the related term NLMB) in a metaphorical fashion. In general, when early and late Palestinian views diverge, the stam of the Yerushalmi favors the later view with the result that these views tend to characterize the Yerushalmi as a whole.

By contrast, Babylonian sources and the Bavli as a redacted document betray a clear and strong preference for the early Palestinian conception of HLMM. When early and late Palestinian views diverge, attributed Babylonian sources and the stam of the Bavli tend to adopt the earlier view, with the result that these views tend to characterize the Bavli as a whole. This pattern of general conservatism accounts for some significant differences

---

[96] It should be remembered that there are some important and broad continuities between early and late Palestinian sources—such as the use of HLMM to legitimate exceptional, disputed or unstable laws.

between the Yerushalmi and the Bavli on the question of HLMM. Unlike the Yerushalmi, the Bavli distinguishes HLMM and Scripture as sources of law and employs the term HLMM (and the related term NLMB) in a literal fashion.

But in one important respect the Bavli abandons its usual pattern of conservatism. As regards the *authority* of HLMM, the Bavli does not adopt the early Palestinian view as it does in every other instance of difference between early and late Palestinian views. Instead the Bavli adopts the view of the later Palestinian sources endorsed by the stam of the Yerushalmi, and conflates the authority of HLMM and Scripture in several ways (a HLMM is not open to alteration by rabbinic authorities, logical justification, or analogical reasoning, and is decided stringently in cases of doubt). Despite the elevation of a HLMM's authority, however, the Bavli rarely employs HLMM to bolster the authority of exceptional, disputed or unstable traditions—and here also the Bavli breaks with Palestinian precedent, this time both early and late.

This aberration in the Bavli's relation to Palestinian precedent (i.e., its preference for later rather than earlier Palestinian sources as regards the authority of HLMM and its reduced use of HLMM to bestow authority on unstable laws or institutions) is likely symptomatic of an increasing Babylonian anxiety over authority claims that are not based directly on Scripture, as I have argued above and elsewhere. At all events, it is only through the judicious combination of source critical and synchronic approaches that the full complexity of the redacted documents of rabbinic literature can be brought to the attention of, and utilized by, the historian.

Chapter 5

Rabbinic Portrayals of Biblical and Post-biblical Heroes

Richard Kalmin
Jewish Theological Seminary

Ancient rabbis generally emphasize the greatness of biblical heroes and compare them favorably to even the most important rabbis.[1] The dominant rabbinic attitude is that present-day heroes suffer by comparison to the greats of Israel's biblical past.[2] The following passage in the Mekhilta de-R. Yishmael exemplifies this view:

> You find that the prayers of the righteous are answered in the morning. Where do we find the morning of Abraham? As it is said, *And Abraham arose early in the morning* (Genesis 22:3). Where do we find the morning of Isaac? As it is said, *And the two of them walked together* (Genesis 22:6). Where do we

---

I would like to thank the participants at the Brown conference for their helpful suggestions. I would also like to thank Mr. Abe Hendin for his careful and thoughtful editorial assistance.

[1] See also Steven D. Fraade, "The Early Rabbinic Sage," in *The Sage in Israel and the Ancient Near East*, ed. John G. Gammie and Leo G. Perdue (Winona Lake, Ind.: Eisenbrauns, 1990), pp. 425–36; and *From Tradition to Commentary: Torah and its Interpretation in the Midrash Sifre to Deuteronomy* (Albany: State University of New York Press, 1991), pp. 69–121 and 229–54. Sifrei Deuteronomy's claim that rabbinic institutions and activities are continuous with those of the Bible is not directly relevant to the present study. It is one thing to say that Moses was the first patriarch and that the institution of the patriarchate in the present era is the legitimate successor of a biblical institution. It is another thing to say that a particular patriarch, for example R. Yehudah Hanasi, was equal to Moses, or that rabbis in general are the equals or superiors of prophets in general.

[2] See, for example, Ephraim Urbach, *Hazal: Pirkei Emunot ve-Deot* (1969; repr., Jerusalem: Magnes, 1986), pp. 439–49.

find the morning of Jacob? As it is said, *And Jacob arose early in the morning* (Genesis 28:18). Where do we find the morning of Moses? As it is said, *And Moses arose early in the morning* (Exodus 34:4). Where do we find the morning of Joshua? As it is said, *And Joshua arose early in the morning and they travelled from Shitim* (Joshua 3:1). Where do we find the morning of Samuel? As it is said, *And Samuel arose early in the morning to meet Saul* (1 Samuel 15:12). Where do we find the morning of prophets who will arise in the future? As it is said, *In the morning God will hear my voice. In the morning I will plead before You and will wait* (Psalms 5:4). Where do we find the morning of the world to come? As it is said, *They are renewed every morning. Ample is Your faithfulness* (Lamentations 3:23).[3]

This statement cites several prooftexts about biblical heroes, and then moves on to a discussion of future prophets and the world to come. The statement contains no mention of the rabbis themselves, deeming the present era to be irrelevant or unimportant, a period during which God's relationship with the Jewish people is inferior to His relationship with past and future generations.[4]

This paper surveys the opposite perspective: rabbinic assertions to the effect that rabbis and even non-rabbis are equal or superior to biblical heroes. Such assertions are significant even if made merely for rhetorical purposes, for example if they are exaggerated claims about the deceased during a eulogy. Such assertions reveal much about their rabbinic authors, even if they are not meant to be taken literally. If meant literally, they provide important evidence about changing rabbinic attitudes toward the biblical and/or post-biblical periods. If intended rhetorically, they provide important evidence about changing rabbinic rhetorical techniques.

We will attempt to show that by far the majority of such statements are tannaitic or early amoraic. In contrast to tannaim and early amoraim, mid- to later-generation amoraim rarely make such statements, even about early rabbis, even for rhetorical purposes. This evidence of a chronological shift argues in favor of the usefulness of rabbinic texts as historical evidence. And because this evidence is preserved in several rabbinic compilations, it challenges the theory that rabbinic texts are best approached as discrete documents, each composed by a different authorship with its own unique agenda (the "documentary hypothesis" as applied to rabbinic literature). We will also attempt to show that the two Talmudim are frequent repositories of such statements. This finding challenges the notion that later editors either (1) composed most of the Talmudim, or (2) included only material from earlier centuries which corresponded to their own way of thinking.

---

[3] Mekhilta de-R. Yishmael, Beshalah, Massekhta de-Vayehi, Parashah 5, ed. H. S. Horowitz and I. A. Rabin (1931; repr., Jerusalem: Wahrmann, 1970), p. 107.

[4] See also Mekhilta, Yitro, Massekhta de-ba-Hodesh, Parashah 9, p. 238.

Finally, we will argue that tannaim tend to use criteria other than excellence in Torah study when claiming that biblical and post-biblical figures are equal. Babylonian amoraim, in contrast, use excellence in Torah study almost to the exclusion of everything else, and Palestinian amoraim occupy a middle position between tannaim and Babylonian amoraim. For reasons to be examined below, these distinctions correspond to the rabbinic tendency to depict non-rabbis as rabbis. Tannaim tend not to depict non-rabbis as rabbis, Palestinian amoraim do so more frequently, and Babylonian amoraim do so most of all. This finding too poses a problem for the documentary hypothesis, since statements by rabbis from various times and places exhibit features which cut across documentary boundaries. Rabbinic traditions in this particular instance are usefully classified chronologically and geographically, but not on documentary grounds.[5]

* * *

Turning first to Palestinian compilations, we find that Genesis Rabbah preserves three relevant statements.[6] In Genesis Rabbah 35.2, R. Shimon ben Yohai states[7] that Abraham's merit is effective "from him until me,"

---

[5] A note on sources and citations: The term "Bavli," also known as the Babylonian Talmud, refers to a work compiled by rabbis under Persian domination in what corresponds roughly to modern-day Iraq. The final editing of the Bavli took place in the sixth or seventh centuries CE, but it contains material as early as the first century CE. See Richard Kalmin, *The Redaction of the Babylonian Talmud: Amoraic or Saboraic?* (Cincinnati: Hebrew Union College Press, 1989), pp. 1–11 and 151–59. The term "Yerushalmi," also known as the Palestinian Talmud, refers to a work compiled by rabbis in Israel under Roman domination. Its final editing probably took place in the early fifth century CE. See H. L. Strack and G. Stemberger, *Introduction to the Talmud and Midrash* (1991; repr., Minneapolis: Fortress, 1992), pp. 188–89. Both Talmudim comment on or accompany the Mishnah and other tannaitic statements, i.e., rabbinic statements formulated during the early third century and before.

The term "midrashic compilations" refers to works structured as commentaries on the Bible. The compilations included in this study are Sifrei Deuteronomy, Genesis Rabbah, Pesikta de-Rav Kahana, and Lamentations Rabbah. They were also compiled in Israel under Roman domination, and while there is controversy regarding their editing, the scholarly consensus is that their final editing took place between the third century and the early sixth century CE. See Strack and Stemberger, *Introduction to the Talmud and Midrash*, pp. 277–79; 296–98; 303–5; 309–11; 316–17; and 321–22.

[6] See also Genesis Rabbah, ed. J. Theodor and H. Albeck (1912–1936; repr., with corrections, Jerusalem: Wahrmann, 1965), 3.23, p. 202 (Yehudah ben Pedayah); and 24.32, p. 648 (R. Yirmiyah's question to R. Hiyya bar Rabbah).

[7] Throughout this paper, I employ this phraseology in spite of the fact that ancient rabbinic attributions are notoriously suspect. To be more precise, I should say "A statement is attributed to R. Shimon b. Yohai" or employ some similar phrase

and that Shimon's merit is effective "until the king messiah." That is, Abraham's and Shimon's merit protects Israel from punishment by God. Alternatively, the merit of Shimon ben Yohai will combine with that of Ahiya the Shilonite and will be effective "until the king messiah." Shimon ben Yohai next states,

> The world does not have less than thirty righteous people like Abraham. If there are thirty, my son and I are two of them. If there are twenty, my son and I are two [of them. If there are ten, my son and I are two of them. If there are five, my son and I are two of them. If there are two, my son and I] are them. If there is one, I am he.

Shimon ben Yohai emphasizes his own and his son's righteousness, but does not insist that the thirty righteous people must be rabbis.[8]

In addition, in Genesis Rabbah 49.3, based on the biblical verse, "And Abraham will certainly be . . ." (Genesis 18:18), R. Berekhiah states, "They made it known that the world never has less than thirty righteous people like Abraham."[9] R. Alexandrai explains that "they derive this" from the verb meaning "will be," which in Hebrew has the numerical equivalent of thirty. In other words, every generation has at least thirty people as righteous as Abraham. This text too nowhere states that these righteous people must come from the ranks of the rabbis.[10]

Pesikta de-Rav Kahana, another early Palestinian collection of midrash, preserves three relevant statements, two of which parallel the statements quoted above from Genesis Rabbah 35.2.[11] The third, Pesikta 4.6, quotes R. Aha's claim that "Matters that were not revealed to Moses on Si-

---

indicating doubt about the reliability of the attribution. To indicate our doubts consistently would add unnecessarily to the length and readability of the paper, however, and I therefore choose a simpler form of expression, remaining mindful of its limitations. When the reliability or lack thereof of a particular attribution is a major issue, I specifically mention this fact.

[8] Both of Shimon ben Yohai's statements are quoted by R. Hizkiyah in the name of R. Yirmiyah. See Genesis Rabbah, ed. Theodor-Albeck, pp. 329–30. See also Genesis Rabbah 98.9, p. 1260.

[9] Genesis Rabbah, ed. Theodor-Albeck, pp. 501–2.

[10] See also Genesis Rabbah 100.10, ed. Theodor-Albeck, pp. 1294–95:

> Six pairs of people had identical life spans: Rebekah and Kehat, Levi and Amram, Joseph and Joshua, Samuel and Solomon, Moses and Hillel the Elder, Rabban Yohanan ben Zakkai and R. Akiba. Moses spent forty years in the palace of Pharoah, forty years in Midian, and he served Israel for forty [years. Hillel the Elder came up from Babylonia when he was forty years old, and he served sages for forty years, and he served Israel for forty years. . . ."]

[11] Both are found in Pesikta de-Rav Kahana 11.15, ed. Bernard Mandelbaum (New York: Jewish Theological Seminary, 1962), p. 191. In both cases, Shimon ben Yohai's statement is quoted by R. Hizkiyah in the name of R. Yirmiyah.

nai were revealed to R. Akiba and his colleagues."[12] Great rabbis, the Pesikta claims, know even more than the great biblical hero, Moses.

Sifrei Deuteronomy contains one relevant statement:

> Had it not been for those who arose and preserved Torah in Israel, would not the Torah have been forgotten? Had it not been for Shaphan in his time, Ezra in his time, and R. Akiba in his time, would not the Torah have been forgotten in Israel? . . . The teaching of one such as this is equal to all of the rest together.[13]

Steven Fraade observes that this text "implicitly places R. Akiba's status on a par" with the scribes Shaphan and Ezra.[14]

Lamentations Rabbah 1.50 records a story in which Miriam the daughter of a baker and her seven sons are captured by the Romans. One by one the sons are brought before the emperor and ordered to bow before an idol. Each son refuses, and all are taken out to be executed. Miriam tells her seventh and youngest son to go to Abraham "your father" and say to him, "Don't be proud and say, 'I built an altar and offered up Isaac my son.' Behold, our mother built seven altars and offered up seven sons on one day. [For] you [it was only a] test. [For] me, [it really] happened."[15] The story, of course, does not claim that Miriam was superior to Abraham. Rather, it asserts that her one act of sacrifice was superior to Abraham's binding of Isaac. The deed of this obscure woman, "the daughter of a baker," eclipses that of the great biblical hero.

Finally, the Tosefta contains three such statements.[16] T. Sotah 13.3–4 asserts,

> After the latter prophets died the holy spirit ceased from Israel and even so they [the heavenly powers] communicated to them [human beings] through a [heavenly] voice [*bat kol*]. One time the sages entered the house of Guryo

---

[12] Pesikta de-Rav Kahana, ed. Mandelbaum, p. 72.

[13] Sifrei Deuteronomy, ed. Louis Finklestein (1939; repr., New York: Jewish Theological Seminary, 1969), Piska 48, p. 112. See also Sifrei Deuteronomy, ed. Finklestein, Piska 357, p. 429, which is partially parallel to a selection from Genesis Rabbah 100.10, cited above (n. 10). In the Sifrei's version all that links the various figures mentioned is their longevity.

[14] Fraade, *From Tradition to Commentary*, p. 114.

[15] Lamentations Rabbah, ed. S. Buber (1899; repr., Hildesheim: G. Olms, 1967), pp. 84–85. Regarding the date of Lamentations Rabbah and its relationship to the Bavli, see Strack and Stemberger, *Introduction to the Talmud and Midrash*, p. 310. See also the parallel on B. Gittin 57b.

[16] The references to the Tosefta are taken from the edition of Saul Lieberman (New York: Jewish Theological Seminary, 1955–1988), vols. 1–5 (Berakhot–Bava Batra); and M. S. Zuckermandel (1880; supplement with survey, index, and glossary, Trier, 1882). In addition to the three sources cited below, see also T. Pesahim 4.13–14, ed. Lieberman, vol. 2, pp. 165–66.

in Jericho. They heard a [heavenly] voice say, "There is present here a man worthy of the holy spirit but his generation is not worthy." They set their eyes on Hillel the Elder. And when he died they said, "Oh, the humble man; Oh the pious man, the student of Ezra." Another time they were sitting in Yavne. They heard a heavenly voice say, "There is present here a man worthy of the holy spirit but his generation is not worthy." They set their eyes on Shmuel the Lesser. And when he died they said, "Oh, the humble man; Oh, the pious man, the student of Hillel." And at the time of his death he said, "Shimon and Yishmael for death, and the rest of the associates for the sword, and the rest of the people for plunder, and after this there will be great disasters."[17]

Hillel and Shmuel the Lesser, in other words, would have been prophets had they lived during biblical times. Prophecy has ceased because the generations are no longer worthy, but individual sages are the equals of biblical prophets and one of them in fact prophesies at the time of his death.[18]

According to T. Bava Qamma 8.13,

All of the grape clusters [i.e., great men] who arose for Israel from the death of Moses until the advent of Yosah ben Yoezer a man of Zeredah and Yosef ben Yohanan a man of Jerusalem were without blemish. After the death of Yosah ben Yoezer a man of Zeredah and Yosef ben Yohanan a man of Jerusalem until the advent of R. Yehudah ben Bava they were not without blemish.[19]

Finally, in T. Yadayim 2.16 we read, "Ammon and Moab separate the poor man's tithe during the Sabbatical year," following which R. Yosi ben Durmaskit relates,

I was with the former elders when they went from Yavne to Lud and I went and found R. Eliezer sitting in a baker's shop in Lud. He said, "What new thing was there today in the study house?" I said to him, "We are your students and we drink your water." He said, "Even so what new thing was there?" I told him the laws and the responses of the voting body, and when I came to this matter [i.e., "Ammon and Moab separate the poor man's tithe during the Sabbatical year"], tears flowed from his eyes. He said, "*The wisdom of the Lord belongs to those who fear Him* (Psalms 25:14) and [scripture] says, *Surely the Lord God does nothing without having revealed His wisdom to*

---

[17] Ed. Lieberman, pp. 230–32; a parallel appears on B. Sotah 48b. See also B. Yoma 9b and B. Sanhedrin 11a.

[18] For discussion of the rabbinic belief that the cessation of prophecy distinguishes the biblical from the rabbinic periods, see Ephraim Urbach, "Matai Paskah ha-Nevuah?" *Tarbiz* 17 (1945), pp. 1–11; Frederick E. Greenspahn, "Why Prophecy Ceased," *JBL* 108 (1989), pp. 37–49 (and the references cited there); and Chaim Milikowsky, "Sof ha-Nevuah ve-Sof ha-Mikra be-Einei Seder Olam, Sifrut Hazal ve-ha-Sifrut she-mi-Saviv Lah," *Sidra* 10 (1994), pp. 83–94.

[19] Ed. Lieberman, p. 39.

His servants the prophets (Amos 3:7). Go and tell them, 'Don't worry about your vote. I have a tradition from Rabban Yohanan ben Zakkai which he received from the pairs and the pairs from the prophets and the prophets from Moses, a law from Moses at Sinai, that Ammon and Moab separate the poor man's tithe during the Sabbatical year.'"

The rabbis, in other words, through discussions, deliberations, and ultimately halakhic decisions arrived at by majority vote, decide the law just as it was promulgated by God at Sinai. Biblical prophecy and the halakhic decision-making process achieve the same result.

Rabbinic assertions of equality with or superiority to biblical heroes, therefore, are found eleven times in the four Palestinian compilations surveyed above. Examination of portions of the Talmud Yerushalmi reveals eight such statements.[20] According to Y. Berakhot 1.4 3b, R. Tanhum son of R. Hiyya claims that the words of elders are weightier than those of prophets. The following parable illustrates his claim:

A prophet and an elder, who do they resemble? Two commissioners whom the king sent into a province. Concerning one of them he wrote, "If he doesn't show you my seal and my credentials, don't trust him." And concerning one of them he wrote, "Even if he doesn't show you my seal, trust him without seal and without credentials." Thus it is written with regard to the prophet: *And he shall give a sign of confirmation* (Deuteronomy 13:2). But here [regarding elders], *According to the Torah which they shall teach you* (Deuteronomy 17:11).

Elders, i.e., sages, are superior to prophets, who require signs and wonders to confirm their status as emissaries of God; sages require no such confirmation.

Similarly, Y. Berakhot 9.2 12[13]d cites R. Shimon bar Yohai's statement, "I saw those in the next world and they are few. If there are three, I and my son are among them. If they are two, I and my son are them." The Yerushalmi next cites R. Shimon bar Yohai's assertion that Abraham's merit atones for the sins of others until R. Shimon, and R. Shimon's merit atones until the end of time. Alternatively, Shimon's merit together with that of Ahiya the Shilonite atones "for the entire world." Shimon ben Yohai is thus equal and perhaps superior to the great patriarch, Abraham.[21]

A story in Y. Kilayim 9.3 32b–c claims that R. Hiyya and his sons are buried next to Joseph, which suggests that the rabbinic and biblical heroes

---

[20] We examined tractates Berakhot, Taanit, Sotah, and Sanhedrin, all particularly rich in midrashic material, as well as all statements which mention Moses, Joshua, David, Ahitofel, Hezekiah, Elijah, and Ezra.

[21] The latter statement parallels both Genesis Rabbah 35.2 and Pesikta de-Rav Kahana 11.15 (see above). Both statements by Shimon bar Yohai are quoted by R. Hizkiyah in the name of R. Yirmiyah.

are of equal status since in several contexts a rabbi's burial place is intimately bound up with his status in the eyes of God.[22]

A tannaitic statement in Y. Sotah 9.10 24a claims that "All of the pairs who arose after the death of Moses until Yosi ben Yoezer a man of Zeredah[23] and Yosef ben Yohanan a man of Jerusalem were without defect, until the time of R. Yehudah ben Bava, when they were not without defect."[24] Prior to Yehudah ben Bava, rabbinic leaders were every bit as saintly as biblical heroes were following the death of Moses. The decisive break between the golden era of the past and the less-than-golden era of the present took place during post-biblical times.

According to a tannaitic statement in Y. Sotah 9.13 24b, several sages possess the status of biblical prophets even after the time of Haggai, Malachi, and Zechariah when the holy spirit ceased.[25] Sages enter the house of Gadya[26] in Jericho, where they hear a voice from heaven announce,

"You have among yourselves two who merit the holy spirit and Hillel the Elder is one of them," and they set their eyes on Shmuel the Lesser. Another time the elders entered the upper story in Yavne and a heavenly voice announced to them, "You have among yourselves two who merit the holy spirit and Shmuel the Lesser is one of them," and they set their eyes on R. Eliezer ben Hyrcanus. And they were happy that their opinion agreed with the opinion of God.[27]

According to Y. Sotah 9.16 24c,[28] R. Yehoshua ben Levi relates that when Rabban Yohanan ben Zakkai died, he instructed those gathered around him to "ready a throne[29] for Hezekiah king of Judah." This statement views Hezekiah as an extremely important person, perhaps of messianic signifi-

---

[22] See also the parallel in Y. Ketubbot 12.3 35a–b; and see B. Moed Qatan 25a and B. Sanhedrin 47a.

[23] This is the same person mentioned in T. Bava Qamma 8.13 as Yosah; Yosi and Yosah are variant spellings of the same name.

[24] See the commentary of Korban ha-Edah. The present discussion assumes that T. Bava Qamma 8.13 preserves the correct version of the tannaitic source in the Yerushalmi. The version in B. Temurah 15b preserves the substance, if not the language, of the toseftan beraita as well.

[25] See also T. Sotah 13.3–4, discussed above.

[26] In the parallel to this story in T. Sotah 13.3–4, the sages enter the house of "Guryo." This variant has no effect on my discussion.

[27] This source lacks a technical term indicating tannaitic provenance, but it is entirely in Hebrew and is closely paralleled in T. Sotah 13.3–4, ed. Lieberman, pp. 230–31. The Yerushalmi in general is much sparser in technical terminology than is the Bavli.

[28] See also the parallel in Y. Avodah Zarah 3.1 42c.

[29] In translating the word *kise* in this context as "throne" I follow Gerd A. Wewers, *Übersetzung des Talmud Yerushalmi: Avoda Zara: Götzendienst* (Tübingen: Mohr, 1980), p. 93; and Jacob Neusner, *The Talmud of the Land of Israel, A Preliminary*

cance, and a second statement in the immediate context, most likely the continuation of Yehoshua ben Levi's statement, posits the same status for a rabbinic figure, Yohanan ben Zakkai.[30]

Finally, R. Mena claims in Y. Avodah Zarah 2.1 40c,

> The world cannot exist with fewer than thirty righteous people like our father Abraham. . . . At times most are in Babylonia and a minority are in the land of Israel; at times most are in the land of Israel and a minority are in Babylonia. It bodes well for the world when most are in the land [of Israel].[31]

It bears noting that the Yerushalmi's corpus of statements is more impressive than that of the Palestinian compilations surveyed previously. We might expect a sustained midrashic work such as Genesis Rabbah, for example, to contain much more relevant material than the Yerushalmi, which is relatively sparse in midrash.[32] Instead, it contains less. In fact, examination of the four Palestinian compilations *in their entirety* yielded the eleven cases described above, whereas examination of only parts of the Yerushalmi,[33] a smaller corpus of material, yielded fully eight cases.

The Bavli's corpus of statements is substantially larger than that of the Yerushalmi, despite the fact that we examined less Babylonian than Palestinian talmudic material. To be specific, examination of portions of the

---

Translation and Explanation: Abodah Zarah (Chicago: University of Chicago Press, 1982), p. 114.

[30] Yehoshua ben Levi's statement is quoted by R. Yaakov bar Idi. According to Y. Avodah Zarah 3.1 42c the passage concludes: "Some say the throne his master saw, he also saw," and according to Y. Sotah 9.16 24c the continuation reads "Some say the one his master saw he saw." The fact that this conclusion is transmitted in different versions suggests that it is a later addition to the statement. See Shamma Friedman, "Al Derekh Heker ha-Sugya," in *Perek ha-Ishah Rabbah ba-Bavli* (Jerusalem: Jewish Theological Seminary, 1978), pp. 29–30. The fact that this concluding statement is a description of what Liezer said rather than a direct quote, unlike the earlier part of the passage, also makes it suspect as a later addition. Whoever added it appears to have been bothered by the statement's unusual claim that a rabbi possessed lofty, perhaps messianic, status equal to that of a biblical king.

[31] See the parallels to this statement cited above, p. 122. See also Y. Bikkurim 3.3 65d:

> Shimon bar Va was in Damascus, and though lesser men than he were granted appointments, he was not appointed. Shimon was expert in all aspects of pearls, yet he had no bread to eat. R. Yohanan applied to him the verse, *And even the wise have no bread* (Ecclesiastes 9:11). [R. Yohanan] said [about Shimon bar Va], "Whoever does not recognize the deeds of Abraham, let him recognize the deeds of the ancestors of this one (i.e., Shimon bar Va)."[32]

[32] See Richard Kalmin, *The Sage in Jewish Society in Late Antiquity* (London: Routledge, 1999), pp. 112–13.

[33] See n. 20, above.

Bavli revealed twenty relevant statements.[34] The significance of these findings will be examined below.

On B. Sukkah 20a, Resh Lakish asserts, "At first, when Israel forgot the Torah, Ezra ascended from Babylonia and established it. It was again forgotten and Hillel ascended from Babylonia and established it. It was again forgotten and R. Hiyya and his sons ascended and established it." Hillel, R. Hiyya, and Hiyya's sons rescue the Torah from oblivion in Israel, and their importance in Jewish history is comparable to that of the biblical hero, Ezra.

Similarly, a tannaitic statement on B. Sukkah 28a asserts that "Hillel the Elder had eighty students, thirty of whom were worthy of having the Divine Presence rest on them like Moses our master."[35] Along these same lines, a tannaitic statement on B. Taanit 20a asserts that there were three for whom the sun shone:[36] Moses, Joshua, and Nakdimon ben Guryon. The reference to Moses is obscure,[37] while the reference to Joshua is to Joshua 10:12–13, which describes his successful command to the sun to stand still. The reference to Nakdimon ben Guryon is probably to an incident recorded on B. Taanit 19b–20a, which describes the sun reappearing after having apparently set, rescuing the righteous Nakdimon from an enormous debt he incurred on behalf of the community. The text groups together biblical and post-biblical characters, granting no privileged status to the greatest biblical heroes.

A possibly tannaitic statement[38] on B. Megillah 11a, commenting on Leviticus 26:44, further exemplifies this phenomenon:

[*Yet, even then, when they are in the land of their enemies, I will not reject them or spurn them so as to destroy them, anulling My covenant with them* ... (Leviticus 26:44)].[39] *I did not spurn them*, in the days of the Babylonians, for I estab-

---

[34] We examined statements in the Bavli about Moses, Ezra, Esther, and Elijah, as well as tractates Yoma and Gittin. Two of these statements, B. Sotah 48b and B. Gittin 57b, are parallel to passages already addressed (as noted in previous notes), and they are therefore not reproduced in full in our discussion below.

[35] See also the parallel on B. Bava Batra 134a. See also B. Sukkah 45b (and *Diqduqei Soferim*, n. *khaf*), paralleled on B. Sanhedrin 98b (see *Diqduqei Soferim*, nn. *tzadi* and *reish*) (Abaye and R. Shimon ben Yohai).

[36] See Henry Malter, *Massekhet Taanit* (New York: The American Academy for Jewish Research, 1930), p. 78, notes on line 20.

[37] B. Taanit 20a records several amoraic attempts to explain it.

[38] Regarding the tannaitic status (or lack thereof) of statements introduced by the term *be-matnita tanna*, see Hanokh Albeck, *Mavo la-Talmudim* (Tel Aviv: Devir, 1969), pp. 44–45.

[39] The translation of this verse follows that of the New Jewish Publication Society Translation, found in *Tanakh—The Holy Scriptures* (Philadelphia/New York: The Jewish Publication Society, 1988).

lished for them Daniel, Hananyah, Mishael, and Azariah. *And I did not reject them,* in the days of the Greeks, for I established for them Shimon the Righteous, and the Hasmonean and his sons, and Matatyah the high priest. *To destroy them,* in the days of Haman, for I established for them Mordechai and Esther. *To annul my covenant with them,* in the days of the Persians, for I established for them the dynasty of Rabbi [Yehudah Hanasi] and the generations of sages.

Patriarchal and rabbinic leadership saves Israel from foreign domination just as her leaders did during biblical times.

On B. Megillah 21a, a tannaitic statement asserts, "From the time of Moses until Rabban Gamliel they learned Torah only while standing. After Rabban Gamliel died, sickness descended to the world and they learned Torah sitting down." This tradition posits a continuum from biblical times until the early rabbinic period. A break with the past occurs only after the death of Rabban Gamliel.[40]

On B. Bava Batra 9b R. Elazar asserts,

One who gives charity in secret is greater than Moses our master, for it is written regarding Moses our master, *For I was afraid of the anger and the rage* (Deuteronomy 9:19), while it is written regarding one who gives charity, *A gift in secret subdues anger, [a present in private, fierce rage]* (Proverbs 21:14).

Secret charity protects people from God's "anger and fury," divine attributes which Moses fears. This statement attempts forcefully to drive home the importance of giving charity in secret and should not be understood as a serious comparison between Moses and an anonymous donor. Nevertheless, the willingness of R. Elazar to phrase his hyperbole in precisely this manner, to employ this particular rhetorical flourish, is significant.

A story on B. Gittin 57a, cited by second- and third-generation Babylonian amoraim,[41] relates that a man and a woman betrothed to one another are taken captive by idolaters to Kefar Sekhania in Egypt.

She said to him, "Please don't touch me because I have no ketubah from you." And he didn't touch her until the day he died. And when he died, she said to them, "Eulogize this one who argued against his [sexual] urge more than did Joseph. For regarding Joseph it was only one hour, but this one, it was every day. And regarding Joseph it was not in a single bed, but this one, it was in a single bed. And regarding Joseph, she was not his wife, but this one, it was his wife."

---

[40] According to an Aramaic expansion of a tannaitic statement on B. Ketubbot 103b, Rabbi Yehudah Hanasi explains his deathbed instructions to his disciples to resume learning after thirty days of mourning for him: "I am not preferable to Moses our master," for whom the Israelites observed a thirty-day period of mourning on the plains of Moab (Deuteronomy 34:8). Yehudah Hanasi is not preferable to Moses, he claims. Might this imply that he and Moses are equals?

[41] Rav Manyumi bar Hilkiyah, Rav Hilkiyah bar Tuviah, or Rav Huna bar Hiyya.

On B. Gittin 59a either Rabbah son of Rava or R. Hillel son of R. Vals asserts, "From the days of Moses until Rabbi [Yehudah Hanasi] we do not find Torah [learning] and [worldly] greatness in one individual."[42] This statement draws no firm distinction between biblical and rabbinic heroes and suggests that Yehudah Hanasi is Moses's equal, though they may be equated merely for rhetorical effect.[43]

On B. Bava Metzia 85b, Elijah explains his absence from Rabbi Yehudah Hanasi's study session: "I raised up Abraham and washed his hands; he prayed and I laid him down, and so for Isaac and so for Jacob." Why not save time by raising all three patriarchs together, wonders Yehudah Hanasi. Elijah explains that if all three prayed at the same time they would bring the messiah prematurely. "And is there anyone like them in this world?" asks Yehudah Hanasi, and Elijah answers, "There are R. Hiyya and his sons." The prayer of great rabbis is as potent as that of the three biblical patriarchs.

On B. Bava Batra 12a–b, R. Avdimi from Haifa says, "From the day that the Temple was destroyed prophecy was taken from the prophets and given to the sages.... Said Amemar, 'And a sage is preferable to a prophet.'" Three statements by Babylonian amoraim follow and support the opinion of Avdimi:[44]

> Said Abaye, "Know [that Avdimi is correct], for a great man [i.e., a scholar] makes a statement and the same statement is reported in the name of another great man...." Said Rava, "Know [that Avdimi is correct], because a great man makes a statement and the same statement is reported in the name of R. Akiba bar Yosef...." Said Rav Ashi, "Know [that Avdimi is correct], for a great man makes a statement and the same statement is reported as a halakhah of Moses from Sinai."[45]

Along these same lines, a Palestinian amoraic statement on B. Sanhedrin 20a asserts the superiority of the generation of R. Yehudah son of R. Ilai over several generations of biblical heroes:

> Said R. Shmuel bar Nahman in the name of R. Yonatan, "What is [the mean-

---

[42] See also the parallel on B. Sanhedrin 36a.

[43] Rav Aha son of Rava next claims, "From the days of Rabbi [Yehudah Hanasi] until Rav Ashi we do not find Torah [learning] and [worldly] greatness in one place."

[44] It is a chronological impossibility for Abaye and Rava to base their comments on a statement by Amemar, as the arrangement of opinions would lead us to believe. It therefore seems likely that they originated in response to Avdimi.

[45] Compare B. Berakhot 55a (R. Yonatan, quoted by R. Shmuel bar Nahmani), where we read that Bezalel received his name of account of his "wisdom," i.e., his character as a sage. Bezalel points out to Moses that people first make a house and only afterward do they bring in the furniture. "You told me to make the ark, the furnishings, and the tabernacle. The furnishings that I make, where will I put them? Perhaps God actually said to you, 'Make a tabernacle, an ark, and furnishings?'" Moses answers, "Perhaps you were in the shadow of God (*be-Zel El*) and you know."

ing of] that which is written, *Grace is deceitful and beauty is vain, [but she who fears the Lord will be praised]* (Proverbs 31:30)? . . . Another interpretation: *Grace is deceitful*—this [refers to] the generation of Moses and Joshua; *and beauty is vain*—this [refers to] the generation of Hezekiah; *but she who fears the Lord will be praised*—this [refers to] the generation of R. Yehudah son of R. Ilai."

On B. Menahot 29b, Rav relates the story of Moses observing a study session led by R. Akiba. Moses is saddened by his inability to follow Akiba's discourse, but his spirits revive when Akiba describes his opinion as a "halakhah of Moses from Sinai." Moses asks why God delivered the Torah to Israel through Moses rather than Akiba, who seems to be the wiser and more learned man. God refuses to justify His decision, commanding Moses to be silent, just as He refuses to explain Akiba's horrible death, his "reward" for a lifetime of Torah study. Rav's story struggles with the relationship between rabbinic and biblical heroes. It expresses the tension between (1) the rabbis' view of Moses as their scholarly inferior, and (2) their belief that without Moses there would be no rabbis and that Moses's relationship with God was much closer than their own. God revealed the Torah through Moses rather than Akiba, a mystery which only God understands. The rabbis' consciousness of their own unparalleled greatness conflicts with their sense of inferiority to a giant of Israel's past, and no resolution is possible from a merely human perspective.

Finally, on B. Temurah 15b Shmuel states, "All of the grape-clusters [i.e., great men] who arose for Israel from the days of Moses until the death of Yosef ben Yoezer learned Torah like Moses. Afterward, they did not learn Torah like Moses our master."[46] On the same page, a somewhat different tannaitic tradition[47] states, "All of the grape-clusters who arose for Israel from the days of Moses until the death of Yosef ben Yoezer a man of Zeredah had no blemish. Afterward, they were blemished." According to these statements the important distinction is not between the biblical and the rabbinic periods, but between very early and later in the rabbinic period.[48]

* * *

Reviewing the evidence, we find several interesting patterns. First, tannaim tend not to emphasize Torah study in comparing and juxtaposing biblical to post-biblical heroes. Babylonian amoraim, in contrast, use Torah study as the sole basis of comparison. Palestinian amoraim represent a middle position between these two extremes.

---

[46] Shmuel's statement is quoted by Rav Yehudah.
[47] Parallel to T. Bava Qamma 8.13, quoted on p. 124, above.
[48] More precisely, what the rabbis considered to be very early in the rabbinic period.

It should be emphasized that I am comparing Palestinian to Babylonian *traditions* rather than Palestinian to Babylonian *compilations*. I consider traditions to be Palestinian if they are attributed to or involve Palestinian rabbis, and Babylonian if they are attributed to or involve Babylonian rabbis. For my present purposes, it makes little difference whether the sources are found in Palestinian or Babylonian compilations (but see below). Obviously there are exceptions, since I take seriously the phenomenon of pseudepigraphy. Some sources attributed to Palestinians in the Bavli, for example, are very likely authored by Babylonians and attributed to Palestinians for a variety of reasons. Even allowing for these cases, the very fact that the statements and stories exhibit clearly distinguishable patterns when we take seriously their claims regarding geographical provenance is itself confirmation of our methodology.

One might argue that in the ensuing discussion I should treat separately (1) statements attributed to Rabbi X and (2) stories involving Rabbi X. Against this argument, however, it is important to note that statements and stories follow the same chronological and geographical patterns. Such separate examination would add to the length of our paper but would not substantively alter our conclusions.

As far as tannaitic sources are concerned, it will be recalled that B. Sukkah 28a asserts that thirty of Hillel's students resemble Moses in their worthiness to receive the Divine Presence. The source offers no indication that they merit this distinction solely by virtue of their greatness as Torah scholars. Rather, the text includes a lengthy list of powers and capabilities which even the least among the thirty possess. Torah study is prominent in the list, but so are numerous other attributes and attainments which have nothing to do with Torah study as it is characterized throughout rabbinic literature.

Similarly, the tannaitic statement on B. Taanit 20a claims that the sun stood still for Moses, Joshua, and Nakdimon ben Guryon. There is no hint that this miracle has anything to do with Torah scholarship. On the contrary, a story on B. Taanit 19b–20a describes what Nakdimon did to earn this great miracle: At the risk of tremendous financial loss he acquired water for the Jewish community during a time of drought. He convinced a wealthy man to share his water with the community, promising to pay the man a huge sum of money if he fails to return the water within a designated period. Nakdimon never loses faith that God would supply the water and he passionately prays for rain even when it appears that all hope was lost.

A possibly tannaitic statement on B. Megillah 11a[49] states that biblical

---

[49] The source is introduced by the term *be-matnita tanna*. Regarding the problems involved in dating sources introduced by this term, see n. 38, above. My basic argument is unaffected regardless of what period we claim this source derives from.

and post-biblical personalities were "established" by God to protect Israel from destruction by foreign powers. Shimon the Righteous, "the Hasmonean" and his sons, Matatyah the high priest, Rabbi [Yehudah Hanasi] and "the generations of sages," Daniel, Hananyah, Mishael, Azariah, Mordechai, and Esther all have in common their greatness as communal leaders rather than the greatness of their Torah scholarship.

In addition, a tannaitic statement in T. Sotah 13.3–4[50] asserts that Hillel and Shmuel the Lesser, like biblical prophets, were worthy of receiving the Divine Presence. When the two rabbis died, they were praised for their piety, their humility, and for being the disciples of great teachers. Torah learning, therefore, is only one of three attributes which made them great.

Lamentations Rabbah 1.50[51] tells of a woman whose seven sons are about to be executed by the Roman government. The woman compares herself to Abraham, commanded by God to slaughter his son Isaac; obviously the comparison has nothing to do with Torah study. According to one of two versions of B. Gittin 59a, R. Hillel son of R. Vals asserts that from the time of Moses until R. Yehudah Hanasi learning and worldly greatness did not exist in a single individual.

Tannaitic statements on B. Temurah 15b and in Y. Sotah 9.10 24a praise "all of the grape clusters [i.e., great men]," or all of the "pairs," who from Moses until the death of Yosef (or Yosi) ben Yoezer and Yosi ben Yohanan had no blemish.[52] Afterward, they were blemished. The early sages, therefore, are equated with biblical heroes not because of the greatness of their Torah scholarship but because of their perfection, the precise nature of which is not specified.

Genesis Rabbah 35.2 equates the merit of Abraham and that of R. Shimon ben Yohai, which protects people from punishment by God. A second statement in the same context claims that Abraham and thirty people, or at least Abraham and Shimon ben Yohai, were equally righteous.[53] A similar statement in Y. Berakhot 9.2 12[13]d quotes R. Shimon bar Yohai's claim that he and his son are among the few people with a share in the world to come. Nowhere is Torah learning the basis for Shimon bar Yohai's bold claim.[54] Finally, B. Bava Metzia 85b compares R. Hiyya and his sons to the biblical patriarchs on account of the power of their prayers; Y. Kilayim 9.3 32b–c relates that R. Hiyya and his sons are buried next to Joseph, but the

---

[50] Parallels appear in Y. Sotah 9.13 24b and on B. Sotah 48b.

[51] A parallel appears on B. Gittin 57b.

[52] The printed edition of B. Temurah 15b mentions only Yosef ben Yoezer.

[53] Parallels to both statements are found in Pesikta de-Rav Kahana 11.15, and a parallel to the first statement is found in Y. Berakhot 9.2 12[13]d.

[54] The two statements in the Yerushalmi are quoted by R. Hizkiyah in the name of R. Yirmiyah, as are those in Genesis Rabbah and Pesikta de-Rav Kahana; cf. n. 11, above.

text supplies no hint that their close association after death has anything to do with expertise in Torah study.

In all, thirteen or fourteen tannaitic statements do not emphasize the importance of Torah study in determining the relative greatness of biblical and rabbinic figures. Four or five more tannaitic statements emphasize Torah study along with factors unconnected to scholarship. True, seven of these seventeen to nineteen statements are parallel versions found in different collections, but statements in diverse collections often differ from one another in crucial respects. The fact that the feature of concern to me here is found in all of the parallels bears out my claim that tannaitic sources focus on factors other than Torah study. As we shall see below, this tannaitic material is distinguishable from the amoraic corpus, both Palestinian and Babylonian.

Before turning to the amoraic material, it should be pointed out that Torah study is emphasized to the exclusion of other factors in only three of the tannaitic statements surveyed above. Sifrei Deuteronomy Piska 48 asserts that Shaphan, Ezra, and R. Akiba all "arose and preserved Torah in Israel.... The teaching of one such as this is equal to all of the rest put together." T. Yadayim 2.16 asserts that rabbinic exegesis and prophecy are equally inspired by God; both arrive at the same conclusion. Finally, B. Megillah 21a claims that from the time of Moses until Rabban Gamliel "they learned Torah while standing."

We noted above that Palestinian amoraim occupy a middle position between the tannaitic and Babylonian amoraic extremes. According to B. Sukkah 20a, for example, Resh Lakish claims that Ezra, Hillel, and R. Hiyya and his sons moved from Babylonia to the land of Israel and restored Torah learning there. Resh Lakish's statement is surprisingly pro-Babylonian, however, and I strongly suspect it to be a Babylonian statement falsely attributed to a prominent Palestinian rabbi. Its attribution to Resh Lakish serves to make its pro-Babylonian point all the more forcefully: even Palestinian rabbis agreed that Babylonian Torah is superior.[55] If the statement is Babylonian, it further supports my claim regarding the strong Babylonian emphasis on Torah study (see below). Our point, however, does not depend on viewing this statement as a Babylonian pseudepigraph.

Returning to Palestinian amoraim, on B. Bava Batra 12a R. Avdimi from Haifa claims that after the destruction of the Second Temple, prophecy was removed from prophets and given to sages. Presumably the feature most characteristic of sages, indeed, the feature which earns for them the title "sage"—expertise in Torah—earned for them the gift of prophecy. Else-

---

[55] See Kalmin, *The Sage in Jewish Society*, pp. 15–17, where I make this same point based on additional proof. Another possibly Palestinian amoraic statement is found on B. Megillah 11a; cf. nn. 38 and 49, above.

where, in Pesikta 4.6 R. Aha asserts that matters not revealed to Moses on Sinai were revealed "to R. Akiba and his colleagues." Finally, in Y. Berakhot 1.4 3b R. Tanhum son of R. Hiyya claims that the words of a sage are weightier and more trustworthy than those of a prophet.

In all, three to five statements by Palestinian amoraim use Torah study as the basis of comparison between biblical and rabbinic heroes. By contrast, they emphasize factors *other* than Torah study five or six times. For example, a Palestinian amoraic statement on B. Sanhedrin 20a praises the generation of R. Yehudah son of R. Ilai for being God-fearing, surpassing even the generations of Moses and Joshua, and in Genesis Rabbah 49.3 R. Berekhiah asserts that the world never has fewer than thirty people as righteous as Abraham. In Y. Sotah 9.16 24c R. Yehoshua ben Levi asserts that when R. Yohanan ben Zakkai died, he told those around him to ready a throne for Hezekiah the king of Judah; when R. Eliezer died he said the same about Yohanan ben Zakkai. R. Mena asserts in Y. Avodah Zarah 2.1 40c that the world cannot exist without thirty people as righteous as Abraham. On B. Bava Batra 9b R. Elazar asserts, "One who gives charity in secret is greater than Moses our master." Finally, a possibly amoraic statement on B. Megillah 11a states that biblical and rabbinic personalities have in common their greatness as communal leaders, which enabled them to save Israel from destruction by foreign powers.

We see, therefore, that Palestinian amoraic emphasis on factors other than or in addition to Torah study is substantially less than that of Palestinian tannaim. To be specific, the ratio of tannaitic sources which emphasize factors other than Torah study to those which exclusively mention Torah study is 5.7 or 6.3 to 1, while the ratio in the case of Palestinian amoraim may be as low as 1 to 2 or as high as 1 to 1.

Continuing our analysis of the degree to which rabbis emphasize Torah study to the exclusion of all else, we turn now to Babylonian amoraim. The statement attributed to Resh Lakish on B. Sukkah 20a is very likely a Babylonian statement falsely attributed to a Palestinian amora, as noted above. It attributes to biblical and rabbinic heroes the same pivotal role in rescuing the Torah from oblivion in Israel. In addition, according to one of two versions of B. Gittin 59a Rabbah son of Rava asserts that from the time of Moses until Rabbi Yehudah Hanasi we do not find Torah and wordly greatness in a single individual.[56] On B. Bava Batra 12a–b Amemar claims that "a sage is preferable to a prophet," and Abaye, Rava, and Rav Ashi support the claim that "prophecy was taken from the prophets and given to the sages."[57] According to all three Babylonian amoraim, prophetic in-

---

[56] The other version attributes this statement to a Palestinian amora (see p. 133, above).

[57] See the text on p. 130, above.

spiration, which now belongs to the sages, manifests itself in the form of halakhic expertise. Similarly, on B. Menahot 29b Rav relates the story of Moses visiting the study house of R. Akiba. The issue here is (1) the rabbis' conviction that they were greater Torah scholars than Moses, and (2) the problem of reconciling that conviction with the Bible's sacred character and God's choice of Moses to receive the Torah.

Finally, on B. Temurah 15b Shmuel states that all of the grape clusters (i.e., great men) from Moses until the death of Yosef ben Yoezer learned Torah like Moses; afterward, they no longer learned Torah like Moses. Here too, biblical and rabbinic personalities are linked by their knowledge of Torah. Interestingly, Shmuel's statement closely resembles a tannaitic statement found on the same page and in Y. Sotah 9.10 24a.[58] The statements are virtually identical, with one significant exception: In the tannaitic versions, the biblical and rabbinic heroes are both "without blemish/defect," while in the Babylonian amoraic version they learn Torah in the same fashion. Shmuel very likely restates the tannaitic opinion in Babylonian terms, changing the point of comparison to reflect Babylonian rabbinic preoccupations.

In all, six to seven statements by Babylonian amoraim make knowledge of Torah the basis of comparison between biblical and rabbinic heroes. In only one uncertain case do they base themselves on Torah study and one other criterion. What is the significance of these findings? Why do (1) tannaim tend to use criteria other than Torah scholarship, (2) Babylonian amoraim at the other extreme emphasize Torah to the exclusion of almost everything else, and (3) Palestinian amoraim occupy a middle position?

The well-documented tendency of rabbinic sources to rabbinize non-rabbinic figures helps explain these distinctions. As several scholars have shown, non-rabbis are depicted as rabbis to a very limited extent in tannaitic sources. This tendency increases in Palestinian amoraic sources and reaches its apex in Babylonian sources. I observed in an earlier study that the Tosefta, for example, portrays Jesus as a non-rabbi while the Bavli portrays him as a rabbi.[59] In addition, there are only a few ambiguous hints that the Mishnah considers Honi Hameagel to be a rabbi while in the Bavli the evidence for this portrayal is overwhelming.[60] Baruch Bokser has shown that Haninah ben Dosa's rabbinization begins in Palestinian tal-

---

[58] For the tannaitic statement on B. Temurah 15b, see p. 131, above; for the one on Y. Sotah 9.10 24a, see p. 126.

[59] Richard Kalmin, "Christians and Heretics in Rabbinic Literature of Late Antiquity," *HTR* 87 (1994), pp. 156–60.

[60] See William Scott Green, "Palestinian Holy Men: Charismatic Leadership and Rabbinic Traditions," *ANRW* 2.19/2 (1979), pp. 628–47.

mudic sources and is most profound in the Bavli.[61] Jeffrey Rubenstein likewise argues that sources in the Bavli emphasize the importance of Torah study to a greater extent than do parallel sources in Palestinian compilations. I would argue that the Bavli, in effect, rabbinizes the rabbis themselves.[62] I argued in another study, finally, that tannaim do not depict Ahitofel, King David's adviser (2 Samuel 15:12–18:27), as a rabbi but that post-tannaitic sources do.[63]

As a result, tannaitic claims of equality or near-equality between biblical and post-biblical figures tend to be made other than in the domain of Torah scholarship. The same is true, albeit to a significantly lesser extent, of Palestinian amoraim. Babylonian amoraim, in contrast, more routinely depict biblical figures as rabbis; Torah learning therefore serves as an important basis of comparison between biblical and post-biblical figures.

The fact that Babylonian amoraim tend to avoid contact with the world outside the rabbinic study house may help to explain this distinction. The world for Babylonian amoraim consists of relatively little besides Torah study; when they visualize biblical heroes they single-mindedly depict them as Torah scholars. Palestinian rabbis, on the other hand, (1) are more fully integrated into non-rabbinic society, and (2) hold in high esteem virtues such as righteousness and the performance of good deeds which are available to rabbis and non-rabbis alike.[64] Perhaps both factors better equipped them to imagine a biblical world in which Torah study plays a marginal role, and in which biblical heroes achieve greatness other than through devotion to a quintessentially rabbinic preoccupation.

* * *

We will now examine a second pattern displayed by the sources surveyed above. To be specific, by far the majority of the thirty-nine traditions surveyed above describe Palestinian figures, and all but a small minority are authored by or are stories involving tannaim or early amoraim. Once again we describe differences between sources which derive from various times and places, irrespective of the compilations in which the sources are found. Once again, therefore, our findings will contradict the documentary hypothesis.

---

[61] Baruch M. Bokser, "Wonder-Working and the Rabbinic Tradition: The Case of Hanina ben Dosa," *JSJ* 16 (1985), pp. 42–92.

[62] Jeffrey L. Rubenstein, *Talmudic Stories: Narrative Art, Composition, and Culture* (Baltimore: The Johns Hopkins University Press, 1999), p. 125.

[63] See Kalmin, *The Sage in Jewish Society*, pp. 101–9.

[64] Ibid., pp. 75–77, 110–14.

To review, we found fifteen to seventeen tannaitic statements,[65] and six statements by Palestinian amoraim quoting tannaim.[66] We also found eight to ten statements attributed to Palestinian amoraim.[67] Of the statements attributed to Palestinian amoraim, two[68] are attributed in other contexts to the tannaitic sage, R. Shimon bar Yohai.[69] One is attributed to a first-generation amora,[70] and one or two more to second-generation amoraim.[71] Only four or five statements, therefore, are attributed to later Palestinian amoraim and are without explicit parallels in earlier sources. Of the eight or nine statements attributed to Babylonian amoraim, one is attributed to Rav, another to Shmuel, both first-generation amoraim, and a third is at-

---

[65] Sifrei Deuteronomy Piska 48 (about R. Akiba); T. Sotah 13.3–4 (about Hillel and Shmuel the Lesser); T. Bava Qamma 8.13 (about Yosah ben Yoezer a man of Zeredah and Yosef ben Yohanan a man of Jerusalem); T. Yadayim 2.16 (unnamed Yavnean rabbis); Y. Kilayim 9.3 32b–c (about R. Hiyya and his sons); Y. Sotah 9.10 24a (about Yosi ben Yoezer a man of Zeredah and Yosef ben Yohanan a man of Jerusalem, and all sages prior to R. Yehudah ben Bava) and 9.13 24b (about Hillel and Shmuel the Lesser); Lamentations Rabbah 1.50 (about Miriam the daughter of a baker and her seven sons); B. Sukkah 28a (about Hillel's students); B. Taanit 20a (about Nakdimon ben Guryon; see Aharon Hyman, *Toldot Tannaim ve-Amoraim* [London, 1910], pp. 948–49); B. Megillah 21a (about Rabban Gamliel); B. Sotah 48b (about Hillel and Shmuel the Lesser); B. Gittin 57b (about an unnamed woman and her seven sons); B. Bava Metzia 85b (about R. Hiyya and his sons, who should perhaps be considered transitional rabbis, i.e., rabbis who lived during the one or two generations between the tannaitic and amoraic periods. Such rabbis exhibit some features in common with tannaim and other features in common with amoraim. To avoid burdening the reader with an excessive number of statistics, however, I consider this statement as tannaitic); B. Temurah 15b (about Yosef ben Yoezer); possibly B. Megillah 11a (about R. Yehudah Hanasi, his dynasty, and the "generations of the sages"); and B. Gittin 59a (R. Hillel son of R. Vals about R. Yehudah Hanasi).

[66] Three of the six are variants of one another. Genesis Rabbah 35.2, Pesikta de-Rav Kahana 11.15, and Y. Berakhot 9.2 12[13]d all have R. Hizkiyah twice quote R. Yirmiyah quoting R. Shimon bar Yohai.

[67] Genesis Rabbah 49.3 (R. Berekhiah); Pesikta de-Rav Kahana 4.6 (R. Aha); Y. Berakhot 1.4 3b (R. Tanhum son of R. Hiyya); Y. Sotah 9.16 24c (R. Yehoshua ben Levi); Y. Avodah Zarah 2.1 40c (R. Mena); B. Bava Batra 9b (R. Elazar) and 12a (R. Avdimi from Haifa); and B. Sanhedrin 20a (R. Shmuel bar Nahman quoting R. Yonatan); and possibly B. Sukkah 20a (Resh Lakish) and B. Megillah 11a (about R. Yehudah Hanasi, his dynasty, and the "generations of the sages").

[68] Y. Avodah Zarah 2.1 40c and Genesis Rabbah 49.3.

[69] See Genesis Rabbah 35.2 and Pesikta de-Rav Kahana 11.15.

[70] Y. Sotah 9.16 24c (R. Yehoshua ben Levi).

[71] B. Bava Batra 9b (R. Elazar) and possibly B. Sukkah 20a (Resh Lakish; see my discussion above, p. 134).

tributed to Rav Yehudah, a second-generation amora.[72] Only five or six are attributed to later Babylonian amoraim.[73]

The issue of rabbinic or non-rabbinic equality to biblical heroes, therefore, is predominantly a tannaitic and early amoraic concern. Two questions present themselves: (1) Why do early rabbis emphasize the equality of biblical and post-biblical personalities, but later rabbis tend not to? (2) What does it say about the Talmudim that amoraim and anonymous editors rarely make such statements, and yet the Talmudim, especially the Bavli but to a lesser extent also the Yerushalmi, are the largest repository of such statements? Why do the later rabbis most responsible for transmitting and editing the Talmudim include statements which they themselves do not make?

These questions are applicable, it bears emphasizing, whether we understand most of these statements as serious expressions of the view that rabbis equal biblical heroes, or whether we understand most of them as rhetorical or intentionally hyperbolic. Even according to the latter understanding, we must ask why a rhetorical technique used by tannaim and early amoraim is used much less frequently later on.

It is likely that amoraim after the first or second generation, in contrast to some earlier rabbis, considered it inappropriate for them to be so bold as to express, even for rhetorical purposes, a sense of parity with or superiority to the greats of the biblical past. This finding shows that rabbinic compilations are useful sources for history because they attest to changing rabbinic attitudes toward biblical and/or post-biblical heroes, or at least to changes in the way rabbis were willing to express themselves publicly.[74]

In addition, the chronological distinctions described above are not confined to one rabbinic document. Rather, all of the documents surveyed exhibited the same chronological distinction, although to be sure some contained more evidence than others. This finding argues against a documentary approach to rabbinic sources, an approach which views the various rabbinic works as composed by different authorships, each with its own distinct worldview. According to the documentary approach, we would not expect diverse documents to yield a consistent picture of changing rabbinic attitudes.

The second question raised above bears repeating: What does the present study reveal about the later amoraim and anonymous editors who

---

[72] B. Gittin 57b (Rav Yehudah), B. Menahot 29b (Rav) and B. Temurah 15b (Shmuel).

[73] B. Gittin 57a (second- and third-generation amoraim) and B. Bava Batra 12a–b (Abaye, Rava, Amemar, and Rav Ashi); and possibly B. Gittin 59a (Rabbah son of Rava).

[74] See also Richard Kalmin, *Sages, Stories, Authors, and Editors in Rabbinic Babylonia* (BJS 300; Atlanta: Scholars Press, 1994), for example, pp. 1–15.

transmitted and redacted the Talmud? This study shows that the Talmudim are not primarily the creation of later editors, nor did these editors preserve only traditions inherited from the past which conformed to their own opinions and tastes. The Talmudim are not primarily fifth- through seventh-century pseudepigraphs, nor do they contain primarily what later editors chose not to censor out because of ideological or halakhic opposition. The Talmudim contain much material foreign and even obnoxious to the later editors; previous generations had made it part of the developing Talmud, and as such it could no longer be excised. Some of this material they rendered harmless via "reinterpretation," usually distinguishing carefully between the original statement and the reinterpretation, and much they transmitted without comment.

It might be argued that later editors composed some of this material but attributed it to early rabbis because they feared expressing such sentiments in their own names. In response, however, it should be noted first that even if we accept this theory, the evidence attests to changing rabbinic attitudes—the fact that early rabbis were willing to express such sentiments in their own names but later rabbis were not is clear evidence of a chronological shift, which leads to the conclusion that rabbinic compilations are fertile sources for history. Second, this theory does not adequately account for the fact that Palestinian and Babylonian, as well as tannaitic and amoraic, compilations attest to the same phenomenon, albeit to differing degrees. It is strange that so many diverse editors from widely varying times and places (1) had the same sentiments; (2) had the same misgivings about expressing these sentiments in their own names; and (3) eased their consciences in the same fashion: pseudepigraphically attributing their sentiments to early rabbis. The evidence attests to historical shifts of attitude rather than to the heavy hand of later editors.

The two Talmudim, it will be recalled, were the largest repositories of statements asserting the equality or superiority of post-biblical to biblical heroes. Of the thirty-nine statements surveyed above, twenty-eight were preserved in the two Talmudim and only eleven were found in the four remaining compilations. In addition, the Bavli was by far the largest single repository, accounting for twenty statements even though we examined less material from the Bavli than from either the Yerushalmi or the midrashic compilations. Do these surprising statistics permit any tentative conclusions?

It is likely that the midrashic compilations are sparse in such statements because their focus is primarily biblical commentary. As such, the rabbinic hero is not of primary importance. The rabbi is significant primarily as a commentator and as one who imparts meaning to the biblical text, rather than as a personality of interest in his own right. In addition, the Tosefta is primarily a corpus of law, and the Yerushalmi is more narrowly focused on law and Mishnah commentary than is the Bavli, which is more encyclopedic in scope than any other rabbinic work.[75] More so than Palestinian compilations, the Bavli is a compendium of diverse genres. The rabbinic personality is a major preoccupation of the Bavli, as is shown by its large corpus of sage stories[76] and its relatively large corpus of statements asserting the equality of rabbis to biblical personalities.

At first glance, it seems paradoxical that the early Palestinian material discussed in this paper is found with relative frequency in the Bavli and with relative scarcity in Palestinian compilations. The issue of Palestinian material preserved almost exclusively in the Bavli, however, is encountered in other contexts as well.[77] To cite only two examples, in an earlier study I attempted to show that evidence from the Bavli demonstrates that Palestinian rabbis are preoccupied with the issue of Babylonian claims of genealogical supremacy. This preoccupation is missing from the Yerushalmi.[78] In addition, all but a handful of dialogues between *Minim* (heretics) and rabbis are found in the Bavli, and yet the rabbis involved are almost exclusively Palestinian.[79]

It is preferable to account for diverse phenomena by means of a single explanation rather than via diverse, ad hoc explanations. The narrow focus of the Palestinian compilations led to their exclusion of much Palestinian material, material which was acceptable to the Bavli's transmitters and editors because of the Bavli's encyclopedic character.

---

[75] Jacob Neusner, *Judaism, The Classical Statement: The Evidence of the Bavli* (Chicago: The University of Chicago Press, 1986), for example, pp. 211–40.

[76] See Menahem Hirshman, "Al ha-Midrash ki-Yezirah: Yozrav ve-Zurotav," in *Mada'ei ha-Yahadut* 32 (1992), pp. 87–89.

[77] In addition to the examples cited below, see also Kalmin, *Sages, Stories, Authors, and Editors*, pp. 97–104.

[78] See Richard Kalmin, "Genealogy and Polemics in Rabbinic Literature of Late Antiquity," *HUCA* 67 (1996), pp. 90–93.

[79] Richard Kalmin, "Christians and Heretics in Rabbinic Literature of Late Antiquity," *HTR* 87 (1994), pp. 165–67.

Yerushalmi and Genesis Rabbah

Chapter 6

Texts and History:
The Dynamic Relationship between Talmud Yerushalmi and Genesis Rabbah

Hans-Jürgen Becker
University of Göttingen

A fundamental problem in contemporary research on ancient rabbinic literature is the relationship of the transmitted texts to history. Present scholarship is characterized by extensive skepticism regarding the historical value of rabbinic sources. Textual references to occurrences or personalities that were critical to earlier attempts at writing rabbinic history are today fundamentally called into question, due to an increased awareness that the respective traditions were neither formulated nor transmitted with the intention of providing historiographical information in the modern sense. For example, the names of the tradents in the chain cited in M. Avot 1.1 prove to be fictionalizations of history by later rabbis in the interest of rabbinic self-legitimation. In Avot de-Rabbi Natan, the chain serves as a framework for the arrangement of additional aggadic materials and is thus being employed in the rabbis' genealogizing of their tradition. This reason alone is sufficient basis for the assertion that such materials cannot generally be considered to give reliable information on the life and times of the respective sages: rabbinic involvement with genealogy does not meet our interest in history.

In more general terms, the reason for this conflict lies in the fact that rabbinic literature forms an essentially self-referential system. It presents itself as a literary and ideological totality, even though its boundaries may be difficult to discern. Phrased in semiotic terms, meaning is here produced through the relations of linguistic signs to one another and not through their reference to extra-linguistic phenomena. In relation to what we call history, the texts create their own, rather static, reality. Developments, courses of events, the entire dimension of time thereby loses the fluidity usually associated with historical processes: quasi-historical situations of conversation or discussion are depicted stereotypically for the purpose of mnemonic text organization or as frameworks for the more or less formalized exposition of halakhah. The static composition of rabbinic texts conflicts with the dynamic character of historical processes, so that every attempt to secure from these sources something for historiography invariably gives the impression of observing a single frame from a long movie strip.

In place of the dynamic of historical connection, which is practically no longer recognizable in the rabbinic texts, a dynamic of linguistic connection makes its presence felt. As in the Internet or cyberspace, by way of analogy, one moves here from the solid ground of the historically ascertainable into the realm of fluctuating texts and traditions of multiple interrelations. In contrast to an historiographical text, such as Josephus's writings, where reality unfolds on at least two levels, namely the linguistic reality and the reproduced factual reality, in rabbinic literature reality for the most part must be considered both primarily and secondarily linguistic. The rabbis simply did not intend to reproduce factual reality. This is evident in the relationship not only to history, but also to the phenomena and things of the everyday world: they acquire a peculiar reality of their own, insofar as they are embedded in a comprehensive system of reference. This self-governed system is the never-ending, continuously developing text, called Torah.

Of course, only its own transhistorical hermeneutic is adequate to its interpretation—a hermeneutic that does not derive its categories directly from a supposed knowledge of historical processes and relations. The absence of an "historically factual level" automatically problematizes any attempt to use rabbinic literature for historiography. Indeed, rabbinic literature offers a classic example of that which in poststructuralist terms might be called a "prison of textuality." Because of the pure textuality of this tradition, the relationship of rabbinic literature to history must first be reduced to the relationship of the texts to their own histories. In this connection, "history" means nothing more than the development of the texts in relation to each other. And because the texts inevitably possess a linguistic character, a refinement of the methods of linguistic analysis is first and foremost required.

Nevertheless, we should not, on the basis of a deconstructionist dogma, deny rabbinic literature the possibility of relating to anything other than its own reality. To be sure, the texts do not express what we would like to know in any kind of immediate way. According to my view, however, every rabbinic tradition presupposes historical relations and references; that means a context which is not textual. This context is implied in the text, but is integrated in such a way that it can no longer be analytically discerned, neither regarded by itself, nor applied back to the tradition. One method of analysis can make the historical implications obvious, and that is comparative, synoptic analysis. Working philologically, synoptic analysis traces the histories of texts and traditions. It is a historical-critical method, for even though text and tradition histories are not considered the same as "history itself," the paradigm of history with its dynamic reference to time is still the same. Giving information on the history of text-transmission, synoptic analysis might, at the same time, produce information on the transmitting circles and their histories.

In order to obtain such information, one should first of all refrain from attempting to establish the greater historicity or authenticity of one version over another. The synoptic method, as I apply it, sidesteps the consideration of any single text as a bearer of historical information. A single rabbinic text cannot, in and of itself, mediate historical information. It can only do so within the context of its own history, as a part of the dynamic process of its transmission. Therefore, and this is the second significant presupposition of synoptic studies, texts are to be treated as texts and not as bearers of factual information. Even if the texts pretend to be bearers of fact, they nevertheless communicate to us no raw data. The primary facts are rather the texts themselves, and it is as such that they must be analyzed.

But what is this fact, "the rabbinic text"? Simply stated, it is the materialization of a rabbinic tradition at a specific point in time in a specific text-witness. Rabbinic traditions exist only as texts, and as texts only within the more extensive corpus of "rabbinic literature." Rabbinic literature is the sum of the macroforms (e.g. Mishnah, Tosefta, Bavli, Yerushalmi, etc.) which are literarily designated as rabbinic, and within whose framework the rabbinic tradition itself materialized. Of primary significance are the manuscripts and editions, from which the "documents" or "works" are then secondarily derived as abstract concepts. If these definitions are appropriate, the "documents" cannot be considered the primary framework of tradition-history research because they themselves are constructs. Similarly, the categories of "primary text" and "final redaction" are, in view of the rabbinic "works," called into question. It is not simply that the "primary text" and "final redaction" of the collective works are difficult to trace. Rather, on account of the fluidity of handwritten textual transmission, they are questionable concepts. Even in the exceptional cases where successful attempts are made to reach the original textual form of some phrase or passage through textual criticism, one cannot circumvent this fundamental problem.

For this reason, form-critical analysis, as it has been associated with the name of J. Neusner over the last decades, is not capable of contributing anything to the illumination of tradition history. With the description, classification, and quantification of formal units and sub-units in the various works of rabbinic literature, Neusner tries to provide the formulation of historical questions with an adequate point of reference, which, in his view, is the respective literary document. The characterization of the document is therefore the goal of Neusner's form-analytical work. According to Neusner, the formal composition of one work in comparison to that of another permits conclusions with respect to its redaction. Thus, in his "Taxonomy" of the Talmud Yerushalmi,[1] he compares the structure of the Yerushalmi with that of the Mishnah and arrives at the conclusion that—in contrast to the Mishnah—the redaction of the Yerushalmi took place both independent from and subsequent to the formulation of its literary units. Two unexpressed presuppositions inform this approach: (1) there is *one* text of the Yerushalmi, and (2) there is *one* redaction. The text is Neusner's own English translation; I do not know which is the underlying edition of the original, though it is presumably the edition published in Krotoshin. In the case of the Tosefta-parallels, Neusner frequently also uses the text of "the" Tosefta; again, it is unclear which edition is being used. On the basis of this "polished" translation, which Neusner himself refers to as "preliminary" and which sometimes also entails the rearrangement of passages according to Neusner's discretion, all of Neusner's observations support themselves. His approach to the work of the Yerushalmi's redactors is shaped by the model of authorship, a model which then guarantees the integrity and autonomy of the "document." Certainly, in stark contrast to the Mishnah, the originality of the Yerushalmi's redactors manifests itself exclusively in their compilation of materials that were handed down. Still, Neusner's view of the amoraic documents, including the Yerushalmi, does not escape the influence of his Mishnah studies, particularly with respect to his strong emphasis on their "peculiarity" and "autonomy." The sources from which the redactors received their material are for Neusner insignificant; he is only concerned with the profile of the single, entire work. But since he draws generalized conclusions concerning the work of redaction in its entirety, he exceeds the boundaries of that which his form-critical, statistical, and taxonomical method can achieve. The method cannot produce subtly differentiated conclusions concerning the redaction processes in the Yerushalmi because it in no way poses a question concerning the text and tradition history in general, or the redactional revision of any single tradition in particular.

Redactors, however, work not only *with* traditions, but also *within* traditions; that is, they not only compile, but also edit. Therefore, possible redaction-critical statements which are formed on the basis of form-

---

[1] J. Neusner, *Introduction, Taxonomy* (vol. 35 of *The Talmud of the Land of Israel: A Preliminary Translation and Explanation*; Chicago: University of Chicago Press, 1983).

analytical investigations must be supplemented, verified, or perhaps even called into question through source-critical analysis. To this extent, the isolated consideration of a single macroform is not sufficient. Parallel traditions found within other macroforms must be considered and compared. In short, synoptic texts must be read synoptically. This fundamental assignment of rabbinic research, however, is rejected by Neusner from the very beginning. The reason for rejecting this task becomes apparent in his programmatic essay, "Studying Synoptic Texts Synoptically: The Case of Leviticus Rabbah."[2] His primary argument against synoptic studies depicts parallel traditions which reappear in different rabbinic works as a quantitatively negligible and qualitatively unintegral component of the works. But even if we were to accept this judgement, it would not deny the relevance of parallel texts for source and redaction criticism. Their relevance is also not negated by the fact, so strongly emphasized by Neusner, that they cannot be traced back to one single source with its own redaction profile. With regard to the collective amoraic works, no one to be sure would support such a "Q" theory. The actual aim of Neusner's polemics comes to expression in a mere parenthesis: The issue of "Q" is "the claim that rabbinic documents ... constitute components of an essentially synoptic system (or, in Judaic theological language, of a 'tradition' or the 'one whole Torah')" (142). As so often in his reviews, Neusner here opposes both the uncritical utilization of isolated rabbinic texts of various literary origins, as well as the pseudo-historical interpretations of such texts, as part of a theologically, and not historically, defined term of reference. Neusner rightly rejects such an approach. However, he throws the baby out with the bathwater when he simultaneously opposes the literary-critical analysis of parallel versions. In no way does the "synoptic" method assume a synoptic system; rather, it merely presupposes the existence of synoptic passages which are to be found in rather large quantities in rabbinic literature. The synoptic method also does not inevitably ignore the documents in which the parallels exist. To the contrary, it includes the question of a redactional revision of the tradition within the context of the respective collective works. Whether and how a particular text was adapted to a given context through redactional intervention can best be clarified by way of comparison with parallel versions integrated into the context of other macroforms. Fundamentally, the plurality of rabbinic tradition is not only to be sought in the comparison of edited documents as completed entities, as Neusner has suggested, but also on the level of their individual units. It is precisely the observation that the traditions cannot be traced back to a single source which must therefore be the occasion for further source-critical studies.

---

[2] J. Neusner, "Studying Synoptic Texts Synoptically: The Case of Leviticus Rabbah," *PAAJR* 53 (1986): 111–145.

These studies could even support Neusner's concern from another perspective: namely, in the case that divergent redactional intentions can be established not only with regard to the compilation of entire works but already on the level of the different sources which were employed to form such compilations. Contradictions within the rabbinic tradition, as well as the different interests of various transmitting groups, might be disentangled with greater clarity by means of reconstruction and comparison of these sources, rather than through comparison of the structures of the later compositions.

Applying these theoretical reflections to the significant test case of the intertextual relationship of Genesis Rabbah and Talmud Yerushalmi, we must consider, above all, the incomplete and open character of the macroforms. Genesis Rabbah and Yerushalmi are in principle incomplete because, as commentaries on another text, they can be arbitrarily extended; their orientation is external. These macroforms are also in principle open because most of the texts that are ordered in such a way can be integrated into a different literary context, regardless of their "original" formal framework. The boundaries of the texts then must be regarded as flowing and not at all rigid. Both phenomena, the incompleteness and the openness, are not merely theoretical possibilities, but are in fact demonstrable factors of the text- and tradition-history of Genesis Rabbah and the Yerushalmi. Their incomplete character shows itself already on the level of the text history, partially attested to by the manuscripts and printed editions. The differences in degree between the various so-called text "recensions" of Genesis Rabbah in MS Vatican 60 and MS Vatican 30, or in the case of the Yerushalmi, between the glossed and unglossed Leiden manuscript Or. 4720, cannot be explained one-sidedly as partial losses of text material; rather, they are the result of extensive expansions at various stages of the text's transmission. This tendency manifests itself at a rather late stage when the Yerushalmi macroform was extended with Bavli-traditions as witnessed in the London Sirillo manuscript Or. 2822, as well as when the Genesis Rabbah macroform was extended with additions from the Yerushalmi and midrash (for instance, from Tanhuma), as witnessed in the earliest printed editions.

Furthermore, it is impossible to overlook the many points of contact between the two collective works; they attest to the openness of their textures. The numerous parallel traditions demand the construction of models which would be able to explain the reciprocal dependencies and influences. It can be said with certainty that the tradition histories of both collective works were closely interwoven. In fact, they developed in such close proximity to one another that MS Vatican 30, one of the oldest and most important of the Genesis Rabbah textual witnesses, explicitly indicates in three places that text material "from the Yerushalmi" should be inserted. B. M. Bokser has shown that in one of these cases the manuscript refers to a Yerushalmi text whose redaction differs from the redactions of all Yerushalmi manuscripts and editions known to us. From this, one may conclude that the document "Yerushalmi" was still in a period of growth when, according to common opinion, it should already have undergone its final redaction long ago.

Generally, though, the parallels in style and content between Genesis Rabbah and the Yerushalmi are much more conspicuous in the oldest manuscripts than in the later editions. This indicates a much closer connection between the literary geneses of both collective works than has been accepted to this point. Moreover, authors in the Middle Ages contemporary with the writers of MS Vatican 30 often quote indiscriminately from the various "works" of the Palestinian tradition (including Genesis Rabbah!), referring to them as "Yerushalmi." To say the least, this indicates a lack of awareness on the part of these authors of the delimitations between the Palestinian works, which takes one by surprise considering the dating of the final redactions of these works in contemporary research.

Theories of the transmission history of Genesis Rabbah and Yerushalmi will come closer to reality the more the dynamic character of the relationship between tradition and redaction is emphasized. The redaction of Genesis Rabbah and the Yerushalmi cannot be understood as one single event, but only as a network of redactional processes applied in the creation of both collective works as well as the remaining Palestinian midrashim (above all, Leviticus Rabbah, Lamentations Rabbah, and Pesiqta de-Rav Kahana). It is not only in theory that these processes were as incomplete and open as the corresponding macroforms, but they actually prove to have been so until a very late stage in the transmission history. On the basis of such a working hypothesis, the results of literary- and redaction-critical research explain themselves more naturally than on the basis of the old, seldom questioned model of the text-transmission of rabbinic "documents." In order to be able to reconstruct the tradition-history of rabbinic texts, we must in fact submit in part to their own hermeneutic, inasmuch as we consider them within the context of the comprehensive reference system of "rabbinic literature" or "Torah," and not, according to an authorial model, exclusively as parts of specific works.

On this methodological basis, I have synoptically analyzed a series of exemplary texts from Genesis Rabbah and Talmud Yerushalmi: more precisely, I have compared them with one another using literary- and redaction-critical perspectives.[3] These texts are the so-called "Creation Aggadot" in

---

[3] See, in great detail, my book, *Die großen rabbinischen Sammelwerke Palästinas: zur literarischen Genese von Talmud Yerushalmi und Midrash Bereshit Rabba* (Tübingen: Mohr Siebeck, 1999).

Y. Hagigah 2.1 and Genesis Rabbah 1–12, halakhic texts, the Genesis Rabbah parallels to the Bavot tractates of the Yerushalmi (Bava Qamma, Bava Metzia, Bava Batra), and a story whose literary-critical history has been much disputed, the aggada of the death of R. Shemu'el bar Rav Yitzhaq. Primary emphasis was given to the source-critical aspect: each text was considered particularly in light of the literary genesis of the macroform in which it is found (that is, with a retrospective look at its tradition-history). The concept of "tradition-*history*" should not, however, lead to the postulate of a linear development of the redactional processes. Such a perspective is unnecessarily narrow; there is no reason to assume that the redaction process was linear and internally consistent. Indeed, the questions which I have posed to the texts include a wider spectrum than those of the document-centered approaches: Can the traces of redaction be differentiated through the synoptic analysis of a given text? If so, then on which literary level is this redaction to be located? Was previously edited material employed in the composition of the collective works? Were traditions of one collective work carried over into the other? Can it be shown that individual parallel texts in the Yerushalmi *gemara* and Genesis Rabbah were originally composed as commentaries on particular Mishnah passages or Bible verses? Does comparison of the traditions used by the redactors indicate only one or perhaps several sources? Is it possible to say anything about these sources?

In this way, I arrived at results which differ from those that have, until now, been supported in the history of research. The results concern particularly the questions of primacy and dependency between Genesis Rabbah and the Yerushalmi. Dependency cannot be established on the basis of synoptic analysis; neither redactor used the other as a source. The redaction processes developed independently of one another, though certainly in parallel, insofar as they assimilated source texts which were, in part, closely associated with one another. These sources are no longer available to us as they existed in their prior contexts. Whether they were employed earlier or later in one or the other works can no longer be determined because a comparison of the different versions used by the respective redactors does not permit, or at best only partially permits, the conclusion that they derive from one another.

The problem of relative chronology thus exists for these sources, as well as for the collective works. This is a fundamental problem because the "dating" of the documents in relation to one another assumes, theoretically, a definitive point in time when one work was completed and could be used by the others. Such a moment is unascertainable, however, because the documents did not undergo a comprehensive, "once and for all" final treatment. Instead, they (or, mostly, only parts of them) materialized as texts through the independent work of many scribes and editors over a long period of time. Accordingly, the earliest text witnesses known to us (usually manuscripts and editions from the Middle Ages) are different in scope, deviate considerably from one another, and, above all, do not fit into a linear redaction process. For this reason, it appears arbitrary to place the Yerushalmi or Genesis Rabbah as entire edited works at, say, the end of the fourth century. Such a dating is not securable on the basis of form- or redaction-critical analysis, but only on the basis of the texts' contents (i.e., through the names of rabbis, or the allusion to historical events or personalities).

The contents of the texts, however, upon which the generally accepted dating supports itself, remain questionable criteria and are burdened by uncertain factors so long as the impression which they give cannot be verified through literary-critical observations. Again, Neusner's classifying statistical method is in no position to achieve such a verification. This becomes especially obvious in the case of the Bavot tractates. On the basis of his own method, Neusner *can* ascertain that Bava Metzia formally distinguishes itself from the remaining tractates which he examined, as well as the manner in which it does so. Yet Neusner cannot place this tractate historically on the basis of his observations. To explain the differences existing between the Bavot and the rest of the Yerushalmi, he invokes Lieberman's "Caesarea" thesis, yet without critically considering the reasons with which Lieberman justified his theory.[4] Actually, a Caesarean redaction cannot be proven either on the basis of form- or redaction-critical methods.

My own synoptic analysis of the Bavot parallels in Genesis Rabbah has shown that a special literary relationship of Genesis Rabbah to the Bavot does not exist. Redaction-critical research provides no basis by which to date a supposed final redaction of these tractates in relation to the final redaction of the rest of the Yerushalmi. At best, one may hypothesize that the compilation of amoraic traditions based on the Mishnah of the Bavot commenced prior to the compilation of amoraic traditions based on the other Mishnah tractates. But just as the documents Yerushalmi and Genesis Rabbah were not suddenly completed at the end of the fourth century, so the Bavot tractates were not suddenly completed in the middle of the fourth century. Both datings, which Neusner uncritically accepts from Lieberman and other, unnamed authors, do not take into consideration the dynamic of the redaction processes that formed the Yerushalmi, and Neusner's own method is unable to compensate for this dynamic. Consequently, Neusner should have followed the pattern of Arnold Goldberg's form-critical studies of rabbinic literature and foregone dating attempts, thereby dispensing

---

[4] *Taxonomy*, 13, 17, 40, and frequently.

with the illusion of an historical analysis of the Yerushalmi as a document produced in the second half of the fourth century.[5]

Every dating of Genesis Rabbah and the Yerushalmi implies a completion of their redaction and a beginning of the work of copyists. The differentiation between copyists and redactors in the case of rabbinic works is, however, simply not helpful. Moreover, upon more careful consideration we realize that the transition from redaction to copying proves itself to be quite fluid: the copyists are frequently also redactors, and the redactors are always simultaneously copyists. As late as the sixteenth century, the first Yerushalmi commentator, Sh. Sirillo, complains that he cannot trace a single "orderly" manuscript of the Yerushalmi. Consequently, he feels compelled to produce his own Yerushalmi text on the basis of fragments, collections, and quotations. The Sirillo manuscripts attest to his own redacting of, and simultaneously commenting on, this text over a rather extended time period. Totally inadequate is the frequently suggested sequence of events according to which it was first the redactors and then later only copyists who respectively transmitted the documents. We should rather say that revised and copied texts were later re-revised and re-copied.

In this way, the literary genesis of the collective works extends itself well into the manuscripts and editions which are available to us today. The first Venice edition of the Yerushalmi is the result of an intensive redaction by the primary glossator of the Leiden manuscript. Through extensive additions, deletions, rearrangements, and alterations, this glossator-redactor worked on a manuscript which (according to the colophon by its scribe Yehi'el b. Yequti'el) was itself a revision of its draft-copy. What is today available to us as the *textus receptus* of the Yerushalmi is a product of the Middle Ages (Venice, first edition, beginning of the sixteenth century) with a great number of further textual alterations from the seventeenth and nineteenth centuries (the editions of Cracow and Krotoshin, respectively). The Genesis Rabbah text of Theodor and Albeck (1929), which is today widely used for research, is based upon the London manuscript of Genesis Rabbah and Leviticus Rabbah (probably twelfth century). This text was emended ("corrected") by the editors based on manuscripts and was sup-

---

[5] Only after the completion of this paper did Neusner's book *Why There Never Was a "Talmud of Caesarea": Saul Lieberman's Mistakes* (Atlanta: Scholars Press, 1994) come to my attention. This is an especially saddening example of its author's immoderate polemics against most of his former teachers and colleagues. Lieberman's Caesarea thesis, accepted and never questioned in Neusner's *Taxonomy*, here turns out to be "the result of mistakes in scholarship of an elementary character, best dismissed as the work of an immature and on the whole rather limited student" (22) with "formidable incapacities of intellect" (20), etc. I don't wish to deal with this book. Incidentally, it in no way makes progress on the problem of the relationship between texts and history.

plemented according to MS Vatican 30. The end-product is a Genesis Rabbah text which never before existed. Albeck, the redactor, clearly expressed his intention to present the final, conclusive version of Genesis Rabbah.[6] Relevant evidence of the tradition history of Genesis Rabbah and Yerushalmi includes datable manuscripts and archeological findings. Such evidence does not attest to "the work" Genesis Rabbah or Yerushalmi, however, but only to specific textual shapes of (mostly only parts of) these works, shapes whose redactional characteristics sometimes deviate considerably from each other. They therefore do not assist with the establishment of a literary-critical dating of the works, but rather attest to their instability.

In closing, I would like to summarize a few of my findings insofar as they pertain to the *way and manner* of the literary genesis of Genesis Rabbah and Yerushalmi. As previously mentioned, these works drew in part from closely related sources. A wealth of details in my synoptic comparison illustrates the literary treatment of these sources and proves that the analyzed texts were written constructions: in the context of the collective works, they were written texts from the very beginning. Certainly, the written character of the traditions employed in their construction is difficult to prove in view of the long and complicated history of these traditions. Nevertheless, it is in many places more than likely that the parallels in Genesis Rabbah and Yerushalmi were, in fact, produced on the basis of written sources. This working hypothesis fits the data in all the text comparisons that I have made. In no place was there any necessity to posit the existence of oral transmission.

Of what type were the sources which were used? First, it must be emphasized that the vast majority of the texts I examined were not originally tied to passages of Mishnah or Scripture. In only a few cases does my analysis permit the conclusion that the redactors of Genesis Rabbah and Yerushalmi drew material from more extensive, pre-edited sources. Thus, in the case of a series of aggadot concerning the "work of creation," the partly fragmented traditions fit together and form various thematically-oriented collections regarding esoteric speculation; in one of them, the individual traditions are tied to the letters of the alphabet. In the case of other written sources, their pre-talmudic and pre-midrashic contexts are less recognizable, because only a few isolated texts have been transmitted. Here, one is confined primarily to conjecture. My investigation of the parallel halakhic texts suggests the following as original contexts: (1) a collection of decisions for the practice of law; (2) a compendium concerning the theme of

---

[6] "הבראשית רבה העקרי כמו שהוא בהוצאה שלנו" (J. Theodor and H. Albeck, eds., *Midrash Bereshit Rabbah* [1929; 2d printing with additional corrections by H. Albeck; Jerusalem: Wahrmann, 1965], 3:67).

"slaves"; (3) a compilation of various traditions on the number 10; and (4) a tractate consisting of explanations of the Passover liturgy. Texts from the Bavot tractates suggest, as possible sources, a cycle of stories concerning the relation of Jews and gentiles and a collection of beraitot from the early amoraic period. Most of these genres are still extant: alphabet-midrashim and mystical collections outside of rabbinic literature, the "extra-canonical tractates" of the Bavli related to specific halakhic themes, small collections of thematically organized stories, and traditions which are grouped together within the Talmud and Midrash according to specific numbers contained in them. In addition to such collections, Genesis Rabbah and Yerushalmi drew from exegetical texts on Genesis and from early commentaries on the Mishnah which, above all, intended to resolve uncertainties within the tradition as well as the lack of clarity of certain halakhot.

How did the redactors treat these sources? They more or less skillfully adapted the texts which they selected to their new contexts. That is why the most conspicuous alterations often appear on the seams of the traditions. The redactors adapted the contents of their sources to those passages in the Mishnah and the Scriptures upon which they commented. In doing so, they frequently altered their texts substantially. The redactors, furthermore, harmonized halakhic statements and removed inconsistencies. Finally, they performed stylistic alterations, abridgements and expansions. The quality and intensity of the editing varies from text to text within both Genesis Rabbah and Yerushalmi; in this regard, differences between the redactions do not lend themselves to generalization.

Do Genesis Rabbah and Yerushalmi consist only of compiled sources, or is there also "original material"? The texts which I have investigated depict only part of the parallel versions and, by and large, only a small part of the entire works; nevertheless, one may draw some general conclusions. Most of the traditions adapted in parallel versions by both Genesis Rabbah and Talmud Yerushalmi prove to have originally not been tied to Mishnah or Scripture. Similar traditions also exist independently in only one or the other of these works. In each case, the origin of the text in more comprehensive sources (since lost in the course of editing) is suggested. The Yerushalmi underlines this assumption with its large number of close parallels to the Tosefta, a source which was transmitted as an independent work with its own redactional process both before and after Yerushalmi redactors drew from it.

However, even those texts among the Genesis Rabbah–Yerushalmi parallels which were bound to the Mishnah or to Scripture from the very beginning were not originally written for either the Talmud or the Midrash in their later forms. They are not original texts of the later collective works, but, strictly speaking, also belong to their sources as foundational components. Even if these texts anticipate the "commentary"-structure of the later works, the latter differ essentially from their forerunners which always maintained a close relationship to the underlying mishnaic and scriptural texts upon which they commented. To a large extent, it is merely the macrostructure which justifies the description of Genesis Rabbah and Yerushalmi as "commentary," and not the forms and contents of a very different provenance which the redactors placed into them. Because of the authority of Scripture and Mishnah, but above all because of the capacity for integration which no other form of arrangement could provide, the genres of *commentary* were able to function as "melting pots" for texts from other contexts. To what extent the remaining texts in Genesis Rabbah and Yerushalmi (i.e., apart from the parallels between them), which were *originally* written as commentaries, have their primary literary place within the collective works must be investigated in each individual case. Certainly it is to be assumed that in the later stages of the literary genesis of Genesis Rabbah and Yerushalmi a large number of such texts originated directly for these works.

What is the significance for the tradition history of rabbinic literature of this development of Talmud and Midrash into comprehensive macrostructures? With respect to form and content, the "inner" variety of Talmud and Midrash takes the place of the antecedent "external" variety of genres. The varied character of the different sources of Talmud and Midrash is, so to speak, turned inward: out of diverse genres with varying contents emerge the collective works whose formal unity is guaranteed only by its macrostructure (i.e., the external frames of reference, Mishnah and Scripture). The earlier formal variety is qualified through the unity of the macroform. The previously specific and formal unity of each source is sacrificed in favor of the inner diversity of the new macroform. In Babylonia, this development is still more far-reaching because of the extensive integration of even the Midrash into the Talmud. The integration of sources, however, has its boundaries. The formation of the collective works simultaneously offers the redactors the opportunity of selection, and with it, the opportunity to exclude undesirable elements, such as traditions which were regarded as heretical. The process of integration presupposes the intention of replacing the sources with the new structure, and thus of making the sources unnecessary. The unadapted traditions of the sources are thereby rejected.

The concept which comes to expression in the literary genesis of the collective works is thus, in one respect, the integration and the authorization of the integrated texts through the form of commentary, and in another respect, the reduction and diminishing of the authority of the unintegrated texts. Significantly, it is perfectly possible that the literary processes corresponding to this concept could accurately reflect analogous social processes. This is the point where the dynamics of history become apparent through the dynamics of text-transmission. The literary selection process is still to be suspected when comparing the Hekhalot literature with the esoteric traditions included within rabbinic literature. Obviously we are dealing here with different bodies of texts which represent different transmitting groups: the one (the rabbinic) excludes the other as heretically suspicious and thereby defines itself as the norm-setting authority in the delimitation of Jewish tradition. This is only one particularly conspicuous example of the analogy between tradition-history and social processes. Other groups, particularly the priests with their independent traditions, were not excluded, but rather incorporated. That which occurs with the individual components of the tradition has parallels with that which historically occurs with the bearers of these components. Perhaps here we have arrived at a way out of the "prison of textuality," for the dynamic textual processes which characterize the development of rabbinic literature suggest an equally dynamic *Sitz im Leben* in a spiritually and socially radical change: namely, in the ultimately successful movement of the rabbis towards becoming the representatives of authoritative Judaism.

Finally, in view of the dynamic of the tradition, one may question whether the literary genesis of Genesis Rabbah and Yerushalmi is a tradition-historical continuum without beginning or end. Certainly this continuum is a process, but there are two significant moments in this development which one may stress: a) the beginning of the relating of traditions to Mishnah or Scripture which previously had no such connections, and b) the (relative) fixing of the texts through the first printed editions, which had a considerably larger impact than the individual manuscripts. Thus, the decisive points in the literary genesis are to be found in the very places where things were fixed and never thereafter changed: one of these things is the determination of the commentary structure as the ordering principle for diverse traditions; the other is the (rather accidental) fixing and circulation of a particular text through printing technology. These fixed points, however, must also be relativized: the ordering principle need not have been a conscious decision, made at a specific point in time, and the first editions could in no way establish the text-form of the collective works once and for all. Thus, even these stages in the development of Genesis Rabbah and Yerushalmi do not mark a definite "beginning" or "end" of the tradition histories of these works, and are therefore incapable of displacing the popular (but nevertheless inappropriate) concepts of "original text" and "final redaction." They should not be looked upon as temporal limits of the dynamic of text transmission, but rather should be interpreted as a part of this dynamic.

INDICES

Index of Scholars

Albeck, Hanokh, 15, 17, 20, 21, 28, 32, 33, 37, 45, 49, 95, 96, 121, 128, 154–155
Bacher, W., 36
Becker, Hans-Jürgen, xii, xiii, 151
Ben Yehuda, E., 54
Benovitz, M., 36
Berlin, M., 66
Bokser, Baruch M., 136–137, 151
Cohen, Shaye J. D., vii, viii
Diamond, E. B., 44
Elman, Yaakov, 14, 100
Epstein, J. N., 6, 7, 17, 21, 33, 37, 38, 39, 40, 44, 45, 46–49, 50, 51, 83
Fraade, Steven D., 119, 123
Frankel, Z., 38
Friedman, Shamma, x, xi, xiii, 13, 17, 37, 38, 39, 40, 41, 44, 49, 50, 51, 52, 55, 56, 57, 63, 77, 109, 113, 127
Geiger, A., 38
Ginzberg, L., 53
Goldberg, Abraham, 13, 15, 17
Goldberg, Arnold, 153
Goldenberg, Robert, ix, x, xi, xiii, 6
Goldstein, J., 55
Goodblatt, David, 43, 63
Green, William Scott, 136
Greenspahn, Frederick E., 124
Halivni, David Weiss, 67, 68, 75, 76, 77, 92, 93, 95, 97, 100, 101, 110, 112
Hananel, R., 54, 55, 105
Harris, J., 36
Hauptman, Judith, x, xiii, 13, 14, 31

Hayes, Christine, xi, xii, xiii, 62, 98, 115
Heschel, A. J., 36
Higger, M., 47
Hirshman, Menahem, 141
Hoffmann, D., 39
Houtman, Alberdina, viii
Jacobs, L., 43, 47
Josephus, 21, 146
Kahana, M., 38
Kalmin, Richard, xi, xii, xiii, 62, 63, 77, 90, 121, 127, 134, 136, 137, 139, 141
Lapin, Chaim, 22
Lewy, I., 37
Lieberman, Saul, 13, 20, 27, 28, 30, 32, 40, 42, 44, 56, 57, 123, 153, 154
Maimonides, 18, 19, 32
Malter, Henry, 43, 128
Melamed, E. Z., 36
Milikowsky, Chaim, 44, 124
Neusner, Jacob, vii, viii, ix, xi, xiii, 3–8, 10, 61–62, 64, 126, 141, 147–150, 153, 154
Porton, Gary G., 6
Qorban Edah, 32
Rabbenu Tam (Jacob ben Meir of Ramerupt), 38
Rabbinovicz, R. (*Diqduqei Soferim*), 22, 23, 45, 83, 104, 105, 128
Rabin, I. A., 35
Rashi, 20, 30, 31, 33, 45, 53, 55, 84, 91, 97, 105
Reichmann, Ronen, viii
Rosenthal, A., 37

Index of Scholars

Rosenthal, Eliezer Shimshon, 39, 40
Rubenstein, Jeffrey L., 137
Safrai, Shmuel, 67, 70, 71, 74, 75–77, 97, 112
Schäfer, Peter, 13
Schwartz, B., 36
Segal, Eliezer, 9
Shimshon (Samson) b. Abraham of Sens, R., viii, 38
Sirillo, Sh., 154
Siskin, Clifford, 9
Smith, Morton, vii, viii
Steinfeld, A., 55
Stemberger, G., 121, 123
Strack, H. L., 121, 123
Tabory, J., 42, 53
Tosafot, 38, 105, 109
Urbach, Ephraim, viii, 119, 124
Weiss, A., 43
Weiss, I. H., 43
Wewers, Gerd A., 126
Yehi'el b. Yequti'el, 154
Zevin, Sh., 66
Zuckermandel, M. S., 17

Index of Rabbinic Texts

Mishnah (M.)
  Avot — 5
    1.1 — 145
  Bava Batra
    2.3 — 93
  Bava Metzia
    4.11 — 93
  Bava Qamma
    6.6 — 55
  Berakhot
    1.1 — 55
  Betzah
    2.2 — 25, 32
    2.3a — 24–33
    2.7 — 27
    2.8 — 27
  Eduyyot
    8.2 — 93, 108
    8.7 — 67, 71–72, 74, 75, 109
  Gittin
    4–5 — 21
  Hagigah
    1.2 — 79–80
    1.8 — 99
  Hallah
    1.6 — 76
  Hullin
    2.8 — 41
  Ketubbot
    13.7 — 43
  Kilayim
    2.2 — 93
  Megillah
    1 — 7

    4.9 — 95
  Middot
    2.5 — 19–24
  Nazir
    7.3 — 93, 97
  Orlah
    3.7 — 88
    3.8 — 89
  Peah
    2.6 — 67, 68–69, 70, 74, 75, 93, 95, 96, 108, 109, 111, 112
  Pesahim
    1.1 — 55
    2.5 — 48
    3.1 — 47
    3.4 — 49
  Sanhedrin
    11.3 — 95
  Shabbat
    1.3 — 93
    1.6 — 88
    10.4 — 88, 93, 97
  Sheviit (Shev)
    1.4–6 — 94
    1.6 — 84
  Sotah
    5 — 7
  Sukkah
    4–5 — 21
    4.9 — 18
    5.1–2 — 18–24
    5.2 — 18, 22, 23
    5.4 — 20

(Mishnah, continued)
  Terumot
    2.1 — 93
  Yadayim
    2.7 — 72
    4 — 7
    4.3 — 67, 69–70, 72, 74, 93, 102, 104, 108, 109, 111
  Yoma
    2.2 — 38

Tosefta (T.)
  Bava Qamma
    6.28 — 55
    8.13 — 124, 126, 131
  Berakhot
    4.15 — 49
  Betzah
    2.9 — 26–33
    2.15 — 27
  Demai
    5.24 — 49
  Gittin
    5.12 — 43
    7.1 — 42
  Hagigah
    2.9 — 44
  Hallah
    1.6 — 48, 72, 88
  Hullin
    2.18 — 41
  Niddah
    1.5 — 42
  Peah
    3.2 — 72, 73, 76, 88
  Pesahim
    3.11 — 42
    4.13–14 — 123
    10.10 — 42
  Shabbat
    16.11 — 26
  Sheviit
    1.1 — 85
  Sotah
    13.3–4 — 123–124, 126, 133

  Sukkah
    3.2 — 73, 74, 75, 78, 79, 85, 93, 110, 111
    4.1 — 19–24
    4.5 — 18
  Yadayim
    2.7 — 67, 69, 74, 93, 104, 109, 111
    2.16 — 124–125, 134
    4.3 — 74
  Yoma
    1.12 — 38

Yerushalmi (Y.)
  Avodah Zarah
    2.1 40c — 127, 135
    3.1 42c — 126, 127
  Berakhot
    1.4 3b — 125, 135
    5.1 8d — 77, 95
    9.2 12 13 d — 125, 133
  Betzah
    2.3 61b — 31–32
  Bikkurim
    3.3 65d — 127
  Eruvin
    1.6 19b — 44
  Gittin
    9.1 50a — 42
  Hagigah
    1.2 76b — 77, 80, 82–84, 95, 108, 110
    1.8 76d — 87, 96, 109, 111, 112
    2.1 — 152
  Ketubbot
    8.11 32a — 103, 107, 111
    12.3 35a–b — 126
  Kilayim
    2.2 27d — 77, 94
    9.3 32b–c — 125–126, 133–134
  Megillah
    1.7 70d — 96, 111
    1.11 71d — 67, 77, 80, 87, 88, 95, 108
    4.1 74d — 96, 109, 112
    4.9 75c — 77, 95, 108

(Yerushalmi, continued)
Nazir
  2.4 52a — 43
  7.3 56c — 77, 80, 81, 94, 110
Nedarim
  3.2 37d — 36
Orlah
  3.1 62d — 52
  3.8 63b — 77, 79, 80, 81, 88, 95, 97, 110
Peah
  1.1 15b — 55, 102–103, 107, 111
  2.6 17a — 87, 95–96, 107, 109, 111, 112
Pesahim
  2.1 8c — 52
  10.3 47d — 42
Shabbat
  1.6 3b — 77, 87–88, 93
  1.7 3d — 103, 106–107, 111
  10.4 12c — 77, 87–88, 94
Sheviit (Shev)
  1.1 33a — 85
  1.7 33b — 67, 77, 78, 80, 81, 84–86, 94–95, 103, 104, 105, 107, 110, 111
Sotah
  9.10 24a — 126, 133, 136
  9.13 24b — 126, 133
  9.16 24c — 126, 127, 135
Sukkah
  4.1 54b — 67, 77, 78, 80, 81, 84, 85, 86, 94, 103, 110, 111
  4.2 54b — 105
  5.2 55b — 20, 24
Terumot
  2.1 41b — 77, 94

Bavli (B.)
Avodah Zarah
  36b — 77, 91, 97, 112
  42b — 41
  52b — 107
Avot de-Rabbi Natan — 145
Bava Batra
  9b — 107, 129, 135
  12a–b — 130, 134, 135
  12b — 77, 98
  21a — 107
  134a — 128
Bava Metzia
  34a — 44
  60a — 97
  85b — 108, 130, 133
Bava Qamma
  9a–b — 55
  9b — 55
  16a — 46
  64b — 36
Bekhorot
  46a — 36
Berakhot
  13b–14a — 47
  55a — 130
Betzah
  18b — 29–32
Eruvin
  4a — 77, 81–82, 83–84, 91, 108
  45a — 23
  97a — 77, 108, 109
Gittin
  54a — 43
  57a — 129
  57b — 123, 128, 133
  59a — 130, 133, 135
  83a — 42
  83b — 53
Hagigah
  2b — 46
  7b — 46
Hullin
  40a — 41
  42a — 113
  82a — 107
  103b — 107
  107b — 107
  141a–b — 45–46
Keritot
  6b — 113
Ketubbot
  22a — 107
  50a — 107
  103b — 108, 129

(Bavli, Ketubbot, continued)
   110a — 23
Makkot
   11a — 77, 86, 91, 110
   32b — 113
Megillah
   11a — 128–129, 132–133, 134, 135
   19b — 77, 88, 108
   21a — 129, 134
   21b — 112
   24b — 77, 108
Menahot
   7a — 107
   10a — 36
   29b — 77, 79, 98–100, 101, 131, 136, 139
   32a–b — 77, 91, 110
   35a–b — 77, 108, 110
   89a — 67, 77, 79, 101
   99a — 107
Moed Qatan
   3a — 67
   3b — 77, 81, 86, 92, 104, 107
   25a — 126
Nazir — 8
   56b — 77, 97, 107, 112
Nedarim — 8
   37b — 77, 97, 108
   41a — 107
   70a–b — 53
Niddah
   7b — 42–43
   43b — 44
   45a — 77, 109–110, 112
   72b — 67, 77, 79, 91, 101
Pesahim
   21b — 52
   28a–29a — 52
   28b — 50–53
   32b — 52
   38b — 48, 88, 113
   43a — 47
   48b — 49
   49a — 42
   66a — 107, 108
   69a — 107
   70b — 47
   106b — 107
   107b — 50
   110b — 77, 109
   116a — 42
Qiddushin
   38b–39a — 77, 79, 89, 97
   57a — 107
   71b — 107
Rosh ha-Shanah
   27a — 36
   32a — 112
Sanhedrin
   11a — 124
   20a — 130–131, 135
   36a — 130
   47a — 126
   82a — 107
   96a — 107
   98b — 128
   99a — 113
Shabbat
   14b — 107
   15a–b — 106–107
   21b — 53–55
   23a — 54
   28b — 77, 81
   62a — 77, 108, 109
   70a — 113
   79b — 77, 108, 110
   92b — 97
Shevuot (Shevu)
   19a — 36
   28b — 108
Sotah
   48b — 124, 128, 133
Sukkah
   5b — 77, 82, 90–91, 108
   20a — 107–108, 128, 134, 135
   28a — 128, 132
   34a — 77, 81, 91, 104
   44a — 77, 85, 86, 91, 104–106, 112
   45b — 128
   51b — 22–24
   52a — 20
   52a — 24

(Bavli, continued)
  Taanit
    3a — 77, 81, 91, 104
    19b–20a — 128, 132
    20a — 128, 132
  Temurah
    15b — 126, 131, 133, 136
    16a — 108
  Yoma
    9b — 124
    80a — 67, 77, 81, 83, 104, 108, 112
  Zevahim
    59a — 107
    70b — 107
    110b — 77, 104

Midrash
  Deuteronomy Rabbah
    11.1 — 43
  Ecclesiastes Rabbah
    6.1 — 44
  Genesis Rabbah
    1–12 — 152
    3.23 — 121
    19.8 — 43
    22.8 — 43
    24.32 — 121
    35.2 — 121–122, 125, 133
    49.3 — 122, 135
    98.9 — 122
    100.10 — 122, 123
  Lamentations Rabbah
    1.50 — 123, 133
  Mekhilta de-R. Yishmael
    Beshalah, Vayehi 5 — 119–120
    Bo 16 — 50–53
    Hahodesh 7 — 35–36
    Yitro, ba-Hodesh 9 — 120
  Mekhilta de-Rashbi — 46
  Midrash Tehillim
    1.16 — 44
  Pesikta de-Rav Kahana
    4.6 — 122–123, 135
    11.15 — 122, 125, 133
  Sifra
    Tsav 11.6 — 67
  Sifrei Deuteronomy
    48 — 123, 134
    269 — 42
    357 — 123
  Sifrei Numbers
    2 — 36
  Yalkut Shimoni
    Beshalah 245 — 55

Brown Judaic Studies

140001	*Approaches to Ancient Judaism I*	William S. Green
140002	*The Traditions of Eleazar Ben Azariah*	Tzvee Zahavy
140003	*Persons and Institutions in Early Rabbinic Judaism*	William S. Green
140004	*Claude Goldsmid Montefiore on the Ancient Rabbis*	Joshua B. Stein
140005	*The Ecumenical Perspective and the Modernization of Jewish Religion*	S. Daniel Breslauer
140006	*The Sabbath-Law of Rabbi Meir*	Robert Goldenberg
140007	*Rabbi Tarfon*	Joel Gereboff
140008	*Rabban Gamaliel II*	Shamai Kanter
140009	*Approaches to Ancient Judaism II*	William S. Green
140010	*Method and Meaning in Ancient Judaism I*	Jacob Neusner
140011	*Approaches to Ancient Judaism III*	William S. Green
140012	*Turning Point: Zionism and Reform Judaism*	Howard R. Greenstein
140013	*Buber on God and the Perfect Man*	Pamela Vermes
140014	*Scholastic Rabbinism*	Anthony J. Saldarini
140015	*Method and Meaning in Ancient Judaism II*	Jacob Neusner
140016	*Method and Meaning in Ancient Judaism III*	Jacob Neusner
140017	*Post Mishnaic Judaism in Transition*	Baruch M. Bokser
140018	*A History of the Mishnaic Law of Agriculture: Tractate Maaser Sheni*	Peter J. Haas
140019	*Mishnah's Theology of Tithing*	Martin S. Jaffee
140020	*The Priestly Gift in Mishnah: A Study of Tractate Terumot*	Alan. J. Peck
140021	*History of Judaism: The Next Ten Years*	Baruch M. Bokser
140022	*Ancient Synagogues*	Joseph Gutmann
140023	*Warrant for Genocide*	Norman Cohn
140024	*The Creation of the World According to Gersonides*	Jacob J. Staub
140025	*Two Treatises of Philo of Alexandria: A Commentary on* De Gigantibus *and* Quod Deus Sit Immutabilis	Winston/Dillon
140026	*A History of the Mishnaic Law of Agriculture: Kilayim*	Irving Mandelbaum
140027	*Approaches to Ancient Judaism IV*	William S. Green
140028	*Judaism in the American Humanities I*	Jacob Neusner
140029	*Handbook of Synagogue Architecture*	Marilyn Chiat
140030	*The Book of Mirrors*	Daniel C. Matt
140031	*Ideas in Fiction: The Works of Hayim Hazaz*	Warren Bargad
140032	*Approaches to Ancient Judaism V*	William S. Green
140033	*Sectarian Law in the Dead Sea Scrolls: Courts, Testimony and the Penal Code*	Lawrence H. Schiffman
140034	*A History of the United Jewish Appeal: 1939-1982*	Marc L. Raphael
140035	*The Academic Study of Judaism*	Jacob Neusner
140036	*Woman Leaders in the Ancient Synagogue*	Bernadette Brooten
140037	*Formative Judaism I: Religious, Historical, and Literary Studies*	Jacob Neusner
140038	*Ben Sira's View of Women: A Literary Analysis*	Warren C. Trenchard
140039	*Barukh Kurzweil and Modern Hebrew Literature*	James S. Diamond
140040	*Israeli Childhood Stories of the Sixties: Yizhar, Aloni, Shahar, Kahana-Carmon*	Gideon Telpaz
140041	*Formative Judaism II: Religious, Historical, and Literary Studies*	Jacob Neusner
140042	*Judaism in the American Humanities II: Jewish Learning and the New Humanities*	Jacob Neusner

140043	Support for the Poor in the Mishnaic Law of Agriculture: Tractate Peah	Roger Brooks
140044	The Sanctity of the Seventh Year: A Study of Mishnah Tractate Shebiit	Louis E. Newman
140045	Character and Context: Studies in the Fiction of Abramovitsh, Brenner, and Agnon	Jeffrey Fleck
140046	Formative Judaism III: Religious, Historical, and Literary Studies	Jacob Neusner
140047	Pharaoh's Counsellors: Job, Jethro, and Balaam in Rabbinic and Patristic Tradition	Judith Baskin
140048	The Scrolls and Christian Origins: Studies in the Jewish Background of the New Testament	Matthew Black
140049	Approaches to Modern Judaism I	Marc Lee Raphael
140050	Mysterious Encounters at Mamre and Jabbok	William T. Miller
140051	The Mishnah Before 70	Jacob Neusner
140052	Sparda by the Bitter Sea: Imperial Interaction in Western Anatolia	Jack Martin Balcer
140053	Hermann Cohen: The Challenge of a Religion of Reason	William Kluback
140054	Approaches to Judaism in Medieval Times I	David R. Blumenthal
140055	In the Margins of the Yerushalmi: Glosses on the English Translation	Jacob Neusner
140056	Approaches to Modern Judaism II	Marc Lee Raphael
140057	Approaches to Judaism in Medieval Times II	David R. Blumenthal
140058	Midrash as Literature: The Primacy of Documentary Discourse	Jacob Neusner
140059	The Commerce of the Sacred: Mediation of the Divine Among Jews in the Graeco-Roman Diaspora	Jack N. Lightstone
140060	Major Trends in Formative Judaism I: Society and Symbol in Political Crisis	Jacob Neusner
140061	Major Trends in Formative Judaism II: Texts, Contents, and Contexts	Jacob Neusner
140062	A History of the Jews in Babylonia I: The Parthian Period	Jacob Neusner
140063	The Talmud of Babylonia: An American Translation XXXII: Tractate Arakhin	Jacob Neusner
140064	Ancient Judaism: Debates and Disputes	Jacob Neusner
140065	Prayers Alleged to Be Jewish: An Examination of the Constitutiones Apostolorum	David Fiensy
140066	The Legal Methodology of Hai Gaon	Tsvi Groner
140067	From Mishnah to Scripture: The Problem of the Unattributed Saying	Jacob Neusner
140068	Halakhah in a Theological Dimension	David Novak
140069	From Philo to Origen: Middle Platonism in Transition	Robert M. Berchman
140070	In Search of Talmudic Biography: The Problem of the Attributed Saying	Jacob Neusner
140071	The Death of the Old and the Birth of the New: The Framework of the Book of Numbers and the Pentateuch	Dennis T. Olson
140072	The Talmud of Babylonia: An American Translation XVII: Tractate Sotah	Jacob Neusner
140073	Understanding Seeking Faith: Essays on the Case of Judaism II: Literature, Religion and the Social Study of Judiasm	Jacob Neusner
140074	The Talmud of Babylonia: An American Translation VI: Tractate Sukkah	Jacob Neusner
140075	Fear Not Warrior: A Study of 'al tira' Pericopes in the Hebrew Scriptures	Edgar W. Conrad

140076	Formative Judaism IV: Religious, Historical, and Literary Studies	Jacob Neusner
140077	Biblical Patterns in Modern Literature	Hirsch/Aschkenasy
140078	The Talmud of Babylonia: An American Translation I: Tractate Berakhot	Jacob Neusner
140079	Mishnah's Division of Agriculture: A History and Theology of Seder Zeraim	Alan J. Avery-Peck
140080	From Tradition to Imitation: The Plan and Program of Pesiqta Rabbati and Pesiqta deRab Kahana	Jacob Neusner
140081	The Talmud of Babylonia: An American Translation XXIII.A: Tractate Sanhedrin, Chapters 1-3	Jacob Neusner
140082	Jewish Presence in T. S. Eliot and Franz Kafka	Melvin Wilk
140083	School, Court, Public Administration: Judaism and its Institutions in Talmudic Babylonia	Jacob Neusner
140084	The Talmud of Babylonia: An American Translation XXIII.B: Tractate Sanhedrin, Chapters 4-8	Jacob Neusner
140085	The Bavli and Its Sources: The Question of Tradition in the Case of Tractate Sukkah	Jacob Neusner
140086	From Description to Conviction: Essays on the History and Theology of Judaism	Jacob Neusner
140087	The Talmud of Babylonia: An American Translation XXIII.C: Tractate Sanhedrin, Chapters 9-11	Jacob Neusner
140088	Mishnaic Law of Blessings and Prayers: Tractate Berakhot	Tzvee Zahavy
140089	The Peripatetic Saying: The Problem of the Thrice-Told Tale in Talmudic Literature	Jacob Neusner
140090	The Talmud of Babylonia: An American Translation XXVI: Tractate Horayot	Martin S. Jaffee
140091	Formative Judaism V: Religious, Historical, and Literary Studies	Jacob Neusner
140092	Essays on Biblical Method and Translation	Edward Greenstein
140093	The Integrity of Leviticus Rabbah	Jacob Neusner
140094	Behind the Essenes: History and Ideology of the Dead Sea Scrolls	Philip R. Davies
140095	Approaches to Judaism in Medieval Times III	David R. Blumenthal
140096	The Memorized Torah: The Mnemonic System of the Mishnah	Jacob Neusner
140097	Knowledge and Illumination	Hossein Ziai
140098	Sifre to Deuteronomy: An Analytical Translation I: Pisqaot 1-143. Debarim, Waethanan, Eqeb	Jacob Neusner
140099	Major Trends in Formative Judaism III: The Three Stages in the Formation of Judaism	Jacob Neusner
140101	Sifre to Deuteronomy: An Analytical Translation II: Pisqaot 144-357. Shofetim, Ki Tese, Ki Tabo, Nesabim, Ha'azinu, Zot Habberakhah	Jacob Neusner
140102	Sifra: The Rabbinic Commentary on Leviticus	Neusner/Brooks
140103	The Human Will in Judaism	Howard Eilberg-Schwartz
140104	Genesis Rabbah I: Genesis 1:1 to 8:14	Jacob Neusner
140105	Genesis Rabbah II: Genesis 8:15 to 28:9	Jacob Neusner
140106	Genesis Rabbah III: Genesis 28:10 to 50:26	Jacob Neusner
140107	First Principles of Systemic Analysis	Jacob Neusner
140108	Genesis and Judaism	Jacob Neusner
140109	The Talmud of Babylonia: An American Translation XXXV: Tractates Meilah and Tamid	Peter J. Haas
140110	Studies in Islamic and Judaic Traditions I	Brinner/Ricks

140111	Comparative Midrash: The Plan and Program of Genesis Rabbah and Leviticus Rabbah	Jacob Neusner
140112	The Tosefta: Its Structure and its Sources	Jacob Neusner
140113	Reading and Believing	Jacob Neusner
140114	The Fathers According to Rabbi Nathan	Jacob Neusner
140115	Etymology in Early Jewish Interpretation: The Hebrew Names in Philo	Lester L. Grabbe
140116	Understanding Seeking Faith: Essays on the Case of Judaism I: Debates on Method, Reports of Results	Jacob Neusner
140117	The Talmud of Babylonia: An American Translation VII: Tractate Besah	Alan J. Avery-Peck
140118	Sifre to Numbers: An American Translation and Explanation I: Sifre to Numbers 1-58	Jacob Neusner
140119	Sifre to Numbers: An American Translation and Explanation II: Sifre to Numbers 59-115	Jacob Neusner
140120	Cohen and Troeltsch: Ethical Monotheistic Religion and Theory of Culture	Wendell S. Dietrich
140121	Goodenough on the History of Religion and on Judaism	Neusner/Frerichs
140122	Pesiqta deRab Kahana I: Pisqaot 1-14	Jacob Neusner
140123	Pesiqta deRab Kahana II: Pisqaot 15-28 and Introduction to Pesiqta deRab Kahana	Jacob Neusner
140124	Sifre to Deuteronomy: Introduction	Jacob Neusner
140126	A Conceptual Commentary on Midrash Leviticus Rabbah: Value Concepts in Jewish Thought	Max Kadushin
140127	The Other Judaisms of Late Antiquity	Alan F. Segal
140128	Josephus as a Historical Source in Patristic Literature through Eusebius	Michael Hardwick
140129	Judaism: The Evidence of the Mishnah	Jacob Neusner
140131	Philo, John and Paul: New Perspectives on Judaism and Early Christianity	Peder Borgen
140132	Babylonian Witchcraft Literature	Tzvi Abusch
140133	The Making of the Mind of Judaism: The Formative Age	Jacob Neusner
140135	Why No Gospels in Talmudic Judaism?	Jacob Neusner
140136	Torah: From Scroll to Symbol Part III: Doctrine	Jacob Neusner
140137	The Systemic Analysis of Judaism	Jacob Neusner
140138	Sifra: An Analytical Translation I	Jacob Neusner
140139	Sifra: An Analytical Translation II	Jacob Neusner
140140	Sifra: An Analytical Translation III	Jacob Neusner
140141	Midrash in Context: Exegesis in Formative Judaism	Jacob Neusner
140142	Sifra: An Analytical Translation IV	Jacob Neusner
140143	Oxen, Women or Citizens? Slaves in the System of Mishnah	Paul V. Flesher
140144	The Book of the Pomegranate	Elliot R. Wolfson
140145	Wrong Ways and Right Ways in the Study of Formative Judaism	Jacob Neusner
140146	Sifra in Perspective: The Documentary Comparison of the Midrashim of Ancient Judaism	Jacob Neusner
140147	Uniting the Dual Torah: Sifra and the Problem of the Mishnah	Jacob Neusner
140148	Mekhilta According to Rabbi Ishmael: An Analytical Translation I	Jacob Neusner
140149	The Doctrine of the Divine Name: An Introduction to Classical Kabbalistic Theology	Stephen G. Wald
140150	Water into Wine and the Beheading of John the Baptist	Roger Aus
140151	The Formation of the Jewish Intellect	Jacob Neusner
140152	Mekhilta According to Rabbi Ishmael: An Introduction to Judaism's First Scriptural Encyclopaedia	Jacob Neusner

140153	Understanding Seeking Faith: Essays on the Case of Judaism III: Society, History, and Political and Philosophical Uses of Judaism	Jacob Neusner
140154	Mekhilta According to Rabbi Ishmael: An Analytical Translation II	Jacob Neusner
140155	Goyim: Gentiles and Israelites in Mishnah-Tosefta	Gary P. Porton
140156	A Religion of Pots and Pans?	Jacob Neusner
140157	Claude Montefiore and Christianity	Maurice Gerald Bowler
140158	The Philosophical Mishnah III: The Tractates' Agenda: From Nazir to Zebahim	Jacob Neusner
140159	From Ancient Israel to Modern Judaism I: Intellect in Quest of Understanding	Neusner/Frerichs/Sarna
140160	The Social Study of Judaism I	Jacob Neusner
140161	Philo's Jewish Identity	Alan Mendelson
140162	The Social Study of Judaism II	Jacob Neusner
140163	The Philosophical Mishnah I: The Initial Probe	Jacob Neusner
140164	The Philosophical Mishnah II: The Tractates' Agenda: From Abodah Zarah Through Moed Qatan	Jacob Neusner
140166	Women's Earliest Records	Barbara S. Lesko
140167	The Legacy of Hermann Cohen	William Kluback
140168	Method and Meaning in Ancient Judaism	Jacob Neusner
140169	The Role of the Messenger and Message in the Ancient Near East	John T. Greene
140171	Abraham Heschel's Idea of Revelation	Lawerence Perlman
140172	The Philosophical Mishnah IV: The Repertoire	Jacob Neusner
140173	From Ancient Israel to Modern Judaism II: Intellect in Quest of Understanding	Neusner/Frerichs/Sarna
140174	From Ancient Israel to Modern Judaism III: Intellect in Quest of Understanding	Neusner/Frerichs/Sarna
140175	From Ancient Israel to Modern Judaism IV: Intellect in Quest of Understanding	Neusner/Frerichs/Sarna
140176	Translating the Classics of Judaism: In Theory and In Practice	Jacob Neusner
140177	Profiles of a Rabbi: Synoptic Opportunities in Reading About Jesus	Bruce Chilton
140178	Studies in Islamic and Judaic Traditions II	Brinner/Ricks
140179	Medium and Message in Judaism: First Series	Jacob Neusner
140180	Making the Classics of Judaism: The Three Stages of Literary Formation	Jacob Neusner
140181	The Law of Jealousy: Anthropology of Sotah	Adriana Destro
140182	Esther Rabbah I: An Analytical Translation	Jacob Neusner
140183	Ruth Rabbah: An Analytical Translation	Jacob Neusner
140184	Formative Judaism: Religious, Historical and Literary Studies	Jacob Neusner
140185	The Studia Philonica Annual 1989	David T. Runia
140186	The Setting of the Sermon on the Mount	W.D. Davies
140187	The Midrash Compilations of the Sixth and Seventh Centuries I	Jacob Neusner
140188	The Midrash Compilations of the Sixth and Seventh Centuries II	Jacob Neusner
140189	The Midrash Compilations of the Sixth and Seventh Centuries III	Jacob Neusner
140190	The Midrash Compilations of the Sixth and Seventh Centuries IV	Jacob Neusner
140191	The Religious World of Contemporary Judaism: Observations and Convictions	Jacob Neusner
140192	Approaches to Ancient Judaism VI	Neusner/Frerichs
140193	Lamentations Rabbah: An Analytical Translation	Jacob Neusner
140194	Early Christian Texts on Jews and Judaism	Robert S. MacLennan
140196	Torah and the Chronicler's History Work	Judson R. Shaver

140197	Song of Songs Rabbah: An Analytical Translation I	Jacob Neusner
140198	Song of Songs Rabbah: An Analytical Translation II	Jacob Neusner
140199	From Literature to Theology in Formative Judaism	Jacob Neusner
140202	Maimonides on Perfection	Menachem Kellner
140203	The Martyr's Conviction	Eugene Weiner/Anita Weiner
140204	Judaism, Christianity, and Zoroastrianism in Talmudic Babylonia	Jacob Neusner
140205	Tzedakah: Can Jewish Philanthropy Buy Jewish Survival?	Jacob Neusner
140206	New Perspectives on Ancient Judaism I	Neusner/Borgen/Frerichs/Horsley
140207	Scriptures of the Oral Torah	Jacob Neusner
140208	Christian Faith and the Bible of Judaism	Jacob Neusner
140209	Philo's Perception of Women	Dorothy Sly
140210	Case Citation in the Babylonian Talmud: The Evidence Tractate Neziqin	Eliezer Segal
140211	The Biblical Herem: A Window on Israel's Religious Experience	Philip D. Stern
140212	Goodenough on the Beginnings of Christianity	A.T. Kraabel
140213	The Talmud of Babylonia: An American Translation XXI.A: Tractate Bava Mesia Chapters 1-2	Jacob Neusner
140214	The Talmud of Babylonia: An American Translation XXI.B: Tractate Bava Mesia Chapters 3-4	Jacob Neusner
140215	The Talmud of Babylonia: An American Translation XXI.C: Tractate Bava Mesia Chapters 5-6	Jacob Neusner
140216	The Talmud of Babylonia: An American Translation XXI.D: Tractate Bava Mesia Chapters 7-10	Jacob Neusner
140217	Semites, Iranians, Greeks and Romans: Studies in their Interactions	Jonathan A. Goldstein
140218	The Talmud of Babylonia: An American Translation XXXIII: Temurah	Jacob Neusner
140219	The Talmud of Babylonia: An American Translation XXXI.A: Tractate Bekhorot Chapters 1-4	Jacob Neusner
140220	The Talmud of Babylonia: An American Translation XXXI.B: Tractate Bekhorot Chapters 5-9	Jacob Neusner
140221	The Talmud of Babylonia: An American Translation XXXVI.A: Tractate Niddah Chapters 1-3	Jacob Neusner
140222	The Talmud of Babylonia: An American Translation XXXVI.B: Tractate Niddah Chapters 4-10	Jacob Neusner
140223	The Talmud of Babylonia: An American Translation XXXIV: Tractate Keritot	Jacob Neusner
140224	Paul, the Temple, and the Presence of God	David A. Renwick
140225	The Book of the People	William W. Hallo
140226	The Studia Philonica Annual 1990	David Runia
140227	The Talmud of Babylonia: An American Translation XXV.A: Tractate Abodah Zarah Chapters 1-2	Jacob Neusner
140228	The Talmud of Babylonia: An American Translation XXV.B: Tractate Abodah Zarah Chapters 3-5	Jacob Neusner
140230	The Studia Philonica Annual 1991	David Runia
140231	The Talmud of Babylonia: An American Translation XXVIII.A: Tractate Zebahim Chapters 1-3	Jacob Neusner
140232	Both Literal and Allegorical: Studies in Philo of Alexandria's Questions and Answers on Genesis and Exodus	David M. Hay
140233	The Talmud of Babylonia: An American Translation XXVIII.B: Tractate Zebahim Chapters 4-8	Jacob Neusner

140234	*The Talmud of Babylonia: An American Translation XXVIII.C: Tractate Zebahim Chapters 9-14*	Jacob Neusner
140235	*The Talmud of Babylonia: An American Translation XXIX.A: Tractate Menahot Chapters 1-3*	Jacob Neusner
140236	*The Talmud of Babylonia: An American Translation XXIX.B: Tractate Menahot Chapters 4-7*	Jacob Neusner
140237	*The Talmud of Babylonia: An American Translation XXIX.C: Tractate Menahot Chapters 8-13*	Jacob Neusner
140238	*The Talmud of Babylonia: An American Translation XXIX: Tractate Makkot*	Jacob Neusner
140239	*The Talmud of Babylonia: An American Translation XXII.A: Tractate Baba Batra Chapters 1 and 2*	Jacob Neusner
140240	*The Talmud of Babylonia: An American Translation XXII.B: Tractate Baba Batra Chapter 3*	Jacob Neusner
140241	*The Talmud of Babylonia: An American Translation XXII.C: Tractate Baba Batra Chapters 4-6*	Jacob Neusner
140242	*The Talmud of Babylonia: An American Translation XXVII.A: Tractate Shebuot Chapters 1-3*	Jacob Neusner
140243	*The Talmud of Babylonia: An American Translation XXVII.B: Tractate Shebuot Chapters 4-8*	Jacob Neusner
140244	*Balaam and His Interpreters: A Hermeneutical History of the Balaam Traditions*	John T. Greene
140245	*Courageous Universality: The Work of Schmuel Hugo Bergman*	William Kluback
140246	*The Mechanics of Change: Essays in the Social History of German Jewry*	Steven M. Lowenstein
140247	*The Talmud of Babylonia: An American Translation XX.A: Tractate Baba Qamma Chapters 1-3*	Jacob Neusner
140248	*The Talmud of Babylonia: An American Translation XX.B: Tractate Baba Qamma Chapters 4-7*	Jacob Neusner
140249	*The Talmud of Babylonia: An American Translation XX.C: Tractate Baba Qamma Chapters 8-10*	Jacob Neusner
140250	*The Talmud of Babylonia: An American Translation XIII.A: Tractate Yebamot Chapters 1-3*	Jacob Neusner
140251	*The Talmud of Babylonia: An American Translation XIII.B: Tractate Yebamot Chapters 4-6*	Jacob Neusner
140252	*The Talmud of Babylonia: An American Translation XI: Tractate Moed Qatan*	Jacob Neusner
140253	*The Talmud of Babylonia: An American Translation XXX.A: Tractate Hullin Chapters 1 and 2*	Tzvee Zahavy
140254	*The Talmud of Babylonia: An American Translation XXX.B: Tractate Hullin Chapters 3-6*	Tzvee Zahavy
140255	*The Talmud of Babylonia: An American Translation XXX.C: Tractate Hullin Chapters 7-12*	Tzvee Zahavy
140256	*The Talmud of Babylonia: An American Translation XIII.C: Tractate Yebamot Chapters 7-9*	Jacob Neusner
140257	*The Talmud of Babylonia: An American Translation XIV.A: Tractate Ketubot Chapters 1-3*	Jacob Neusner
140258	*The Talmud of Babylonia: An American Translation XIV.B: Tractate Ketubot Chapters 4-7*	Jacob Neusner
140259	*Jewish Thought Adrift: Max Wiener (1882-1950)*	Robert S. Schine
140260	*The Talmud of Babylonia: An American Translation XIV.C: Tractate Ketubot Chapters 8-13*	Jacob Neusner

140261	The Talmud of Babylonia: An American Translation XIII.D: Tractate Yebamot Chapters 10-16	Jacob Neusner
140262	The Talmud of Babylonia: An American Translation XV. A: Tractate Nedarim Chapters 1-4	Jacob Neusner
140263	The Talmud of Babylonia: An American Translation XV.B: Tractate Nedarim Chapters 5-11	Jacob Neusner
140264	Studia Philonica Annual 1992	David T. Runia
140265	The Talmud of Babylonia: An American Translation XVIII.A: Tractate Gittin Chapters 1-3	Jacob Neusner
140266	The Talmud of Babylonia: An American Translation XVIII.B: Tractate Gittin Chapters 4 and 5	Jacob Neusner
140267	The Talmud of Babylonia: An American Translation XIX.A: Tractate Qiddushin Chapter 1	Jacob Neusner
140268	The Talmud of Babylonia: An American Translation XIX.B: Tractate Qiddushin Chapters 2-4	Jacob Neusner
140269	The Talmud of Babylonia: An American Translation XVIII.C: Tractate Gittin Chapters 6-9	Jacob Neusner
140270	The Talmud of Babylonia: An American Translation II.A: Tractate Shabbat Chapters 1 and 2	Jacob Neusner
140271	The Theology of Nahmanides Systematically Presented	David Novak
140272	The Talmud of Babylonia: An American Translation II.B: Tractate Shabbat Chapters 3-6	Jacob Neusner
140273	The Talmud of Babylonia: An American Translation II.C: Tractate Shabbat Chapters 7-10	Jacob Neusner
140274	The Talmud of Babylonia: An American Translation II.D: Tractate Shabbat Chapters 11-17	Jacob Neusner
140275	The Talmud of Babylonia: An American Translation II.E: Tractate Shabbat Chapters 18-24	Jacob Neusner
140276	The Talmud of Babylonia: An American Translation III.A: Tractate Erubin Chapters 1 and 2	Jacob Neusner
140277	The Talmud of Babylonia: An American Translation III.B: Tractate Erubin Chapters 3 and 4	Jacob Neusner
140278	The Talmud of Babylonia: An American Translation III.C: Tractate Erubin Chapters 5 and 6	Jacob Neusner
140279	The Talmud of Babylonia: An American Translation III.D: Tractate Erubin Chapters 7-10	Jacob Neusner
140280	The Talmud of Babylonia: An American Translation XII: Tractate Hagigah	Jacob Neusner
140281	The Talmud of Babylonia: An American Translation IV.A: Tractate Pesahim Chapter I	Jacob Neusner
140282	The Talmud of Babylonia: An American Translation IV.B: Tractate Pesahim Chapters 2 and 3	Jacob Neusner
140283	The Talmud of Babylonia: An American Translation IV.C: Tractate Pesahim Chapters 4-6	Jacob Neusner
140284	The Talmud of Babylonia: An American Translation IV.D: Tractate Pesahim Chapters 7 and 8	Jacob Neusner
140285	The Talmud of Babylonia: An American Translation IV.E: Tractate Pesahim Chapters 9 and 10	Jacob Neusner
140286	From Christianity to Gnosis and From Gnosis to Christianity	Jean Magne
140287	Studia Philonica Annual 1993	David T. Runia
140288	Diasporas in Antiquity	Shaye J. D. Cohen, Ernest S. Frerichs
140289	The Jewish Family in Antiquity	Shaye J. D. Cohen
140290	The Place of Judaism in Philo's Thought	Ellen Birnbaum

140291	*The Babylonian Esther Midrash, Vol. 1*	Eliezer Segal
140292	*The Babylonian Esther Midrash, Vol. 2*	Eliezer Segal
140293	*The Babylonian Esther Midrash, Vol. 3*	Eliezer Segal
140294	*The Talmud of Babylonia: An American Translation V. A: Tractate Yoma Chapters 1 and 2*	Jacob Neusner
140295	*The Talmud of Babylonia: An American Translation V. B: Tractate Yoma Chapters 3–5*	Jacob Neusner
140296	*The Talmud of Babylonia: An American Translation V. C: Tractate Yoma Chapters 6–8*	Jacob Neusner
140297	*The Talmud of Babylonia: An American Translation XXII.D: Tractate Baba Batra Chapters Seven and Eight*	Jacob Neusner
140298	*The Talmud of Babylonia: An American Translation XXII.E: Tractate Baba Batra Chapters Nine and Ten*	Jacob Neusner
140299	*The Studia Philonica Annual, 1994*	David T. Runia
140300	*Sages, Stories, Authors, and Editors in Rabbinic Judaism*	Richard Kalmin
140301	*From Balaam to Jonah: Anti-prophetic Satire in the Hebrew Bible*	David Marcus
140302	*The History of Sukkot in the Second Temple and Rabbinic Periods*	Jeffrey L. Rubenstein
140303	*Tasting the Dish: Rabbinic Rhetorics of Sexuality*	Michael L. Satlow
140304	*The School of Moses: Studies in Philo and Hellenistic Religion*	John Peter Kenney
140305	*The Studia Philonica Annual, 1995*	David T. Runia
140306	*The Talmud of Babylonia, An American Translation IX, Tractate Rosh Hashanah*	Alan J. Avery-Peck
140307	*Early Rabbinic Civil Law and the Social History of Roman Galilee: A Study of Mishnah Tractate Baba Mesia*	Hayim Lapin
140308	*The* Libes Briv *of Isaac Wetzlar*	Morris M. Faierstein
140309	*The Studia Philonica Annual, 1996*	David T. Runia
140310	*Rashbam's Commentary on Exodus: An Annotated Translation*	Martin I. Lockshin
140311	*The Elijah Legends and Jehu's Coup*	Marsha C. White
140312	*The Studia Philonica Annual, 1997; Wisdom and Logos: Studies in Jewish Thought in Honor of David Winston*	David T. Runia and Gregory E. Sterling
140313	*The Echoes of Many Texts: Reflections on Jewish and Christian Traditions, Essays in Honor of Lou H. Silberman*	William G. Dever and J. Edward Wright
140314	*The Sign of the Serpent*	Marc Bregman
140315	*Kol Nidre: Studies in the Development of Rabbinic Votive Institutions*	Moshe Benovitz
140316	*Ben Sira's Teaching on Friendship*	Jeremy Corley
140317	*Some Jewish Women in Antiquity*	Meir Bar-Ilan
140318	*Rereading Talmud: Gender, Law and the Poetics of* Sugyot	Aryeh Cohen
140319	*The Studia Philonica Annual, 1998*	David T. Runia
140320	*Hesed ve-Emet: Studies in Honor of Ernest S. Frerichs*	Jodi Magness and Seymour Gitin
140321	*Women and Womanhood in the Talmud*	Shulamit Valler
140322	*Rhetorical Argumentation in Philo of Alexandria*	Manuel Alexandre, Jr.
140323	*The Studia Philonica Annual, 1999*	David T. Runia and Gregory E. Sterling
140324	*The Idea of Atonement in the Philosophy of Hermann Cohen*	Michael Zank
140325	*"A Wise and Discerning Mind": Essays in Honor of Burke O. Long*	Saul M. Olyan, Robert C. Culley

140326 *The Synoptic Problem in Rabbinic Literature*   Shaye J. D. Cohen

Brown Studies on Jews and Their Societies

145001	*American Jewish Fertility*	Calvin Goldscheider
145002	*The Impact of Religious Schooling: The Effects of Jewish Education Upon Religious Involvement*	Harold S. Himmelfarb
145003	*The American Jewish Community*	Calvin Goldscheider
145004	*The Naturalized Jews of the Grand Duchy of Posen in 1834 and 1835*	Edward David Luft
145005	*Suburban Communities: The Jewishness of American Reform Jews*	Gerald L. Showstack
145007	*Ethnic Survival in America*	David Schoem
145008	*American Jews in the 21st Century: A Leadership Challenge*	Earl Raab

Brown Studies in Religion

147001	*Religious Writings and Religious Systems I*	Jacob Neusner, et al.
147002	*Religious Writings and Religious Systems II*	Jacob Neusner, et al.
147003	*Religion and the Social Sciences*	Robert Segal

BM
497.8
.S96
2000